MW00338960

DAWN'S LIGHT WOMAN & NICOLAS FRANCHOMME

Dawn's Light Woman & Nicolas Franchomme

Marriage and Law in the Illinois Country

Carl J. Ekberg and Sharon K. Person

Southern Illinois University Press
Carbondale

Southern Illinois University Press
www.siupress.com

Copyright © 2022 by the Board of Trustees,
Southern Illinois University
All rights reserved
Printed in the United States of America

25   24   23   22   4   3   2   1

Cover illustrations: Left, *Sha-Kó-Ka, Mint, a Pretty Girl* (Mandan) by George Catlin, 1832, courtesy Smithsonian American Art Museum, Washington, D.C. Right, *Three Studies of a Standing Soldier*, by Antoine Watteau, ca. 1715. Red chalk. Framing lines in pen and black ink, 151 x 199 mm, inv. no. 7208. (Fondation Custodia, Collection Frits Lugt, Paris.)

Library of Congress Cataloging-in-Publication Data
Names: Ekberg, Carl J., 1938– author. | Person, Sharon K., 1956– author.
Title: Dawn's Light Woman & Nicolas Franchomme: marriage and law in the
Illinois Country / Carl J. Ekberg, and Sharon K. Person.
Other titles: Dawn's Light Woman and Nicolas Franchomme
Description: First edition. | Carbondale: Southern Illinois University Press, [2022] | Series: A Shawnee Book | Includes bibliographical references and index. | Summary: "In the heart of France's North American empire, the village of Kaskaskia was a community of French-Canadian fur traders and Kaskaskia Indians who not only lived together but often intermarried. These Indigenous and French intermarriages were central to colonial Illinois society, and the coupling of Marguerite 8assecam8c8e (Dawn's Light Woman) and Nicolas Franchomme, in particular, was critical to expanding the jurisdiction of French law"—Provided by publisher.
Identifiers: LCCN 2022008978 (print) | LCCN 2022008979 (ebook) |
ISBN 9780809338863 (paperback) | ISBN 9780809338870 (ebook)
Subjects: LCSH: Kaskaskia (Ill.)—History—18th century. | 8assecam8c8e, Marguerite—Marriage. | Kaskaskia Indians—Illinois—History—18th century. | French—Illinois—History—18th century. | Marriage—New France—History—18th century. | Intermarriage—New France—History. | Kaskaskia Indians—Legal status, laws, etc.—New France. | Frontier and pioneer life—Illinois—Kaskaskia. | Franchomme, Nicolas, 1703–1728—Marriage.
Classification: LCC F549.K3 E33 2022 (print) | LCC F549.K3 (ebook) |
DDC 977.3/92—dc23/eng/20220311
LC record available at https://lccn.loc.gov/2022008978
LC ebook record available at https://lccn.loc.gov/2022008979

Printed on recycled paper

SIU
Southern Illinois University System

CONTENTS

Illustrations

Maps

Natalia Maree Belting was the most imaginative and audacious of her fellow graduate students in the Department of History at the University of Illinois in the late 1930s. While others were engaged with grand issues of national and international moment—the Great Depression, Hitler's threat to Europe, Japan's expansionism in the Pacific, the perils facing the British Empire—she went doggedly small and local. Belting burrowed into the records of the French village of Kaskaskia that had been lost to the vagaries of the Mississippi River. This was not a flashy topic, but Belting was energetic and innovative with technology. In 1939, she sojourned at the Randolph County Courthouse in Chester, Illinois, and filmed Kaskaskia's civil records for the period between 1720 and 1763, teaching herself how to read the old French manuscripts and how to film documents. Printed materials and photostats at the Illinois Historical Survey on the University of Illinois campus also gave Belting access to many of the sacramental records of Kaskaskia's Parish of the Immaculate Conception, as well as to colonial documents from the government of King Louis XV.

After the interruptions of World War II, Belting's PhD dissertation was published by the University of Illinois Press in 1948 as *Kaskaskia Under the French Regime*. Thanks to Southern Illinois University Press, this splendid small volume (Shawnee reprint edition, 2003) still lives and breathes, and still captivates readers with its wonderful vignettes of early Illinois village life and its lucid, graceful prose. And Belting's appendix, "Notes on the Census of 1752," provides a model for how to use such a document to enrich a historical account. Part II of our book echoes Belting's innovative approach in this regard. Dissertations dealing with "big" issues written by Belting's graduate-school colleagues have all been consigned to gathering dust in some obscure lumber room, while her work endures.

Belting's enticing pages introduce us to a multitude of fabled personalities, whose extraordinary lives could only have unfolded on the remote Mississippi frontier of France's North American empire: Father Gabriel Marest, who led the group of Kaskaskia Indians and French Canadian traders that established Kaskaskia village in 1703; Marie-8canic8e Rouensa, daughter of Kaskaskia chief Rouensa, wife to two French Canadians in succession, matriarch of a Métis mixed-blood family, and eventually laid to rest with full Roman Catholic honors by Jesuit missionaries under her private pew within the parish church; Philippe Renault, flamboyant French mining engineer, who arrived in the Illinois Country with a handful of enslaved Africans, hoping to strike it rich on dreamt-of silver lodes west of the Mississippi River; Jacques Bourdon, French Canadian adventurer, an original settler at Kaskaskia, captain of the militia, and husband, successively, to two important Illinois Indian women.

Since Belting's discovery of Bourdon, every historian of the Illinois Country has felt obliged to deal, in one way or another, with some aspect of his life. We also discuss that remarkable life, but more importantly, *much* more importantly, we also discuss Bourdon's death, with all of its ramifications for the future of the Illinois Country. Bourdon's death brings us face to face with his widow, Marguerite 8assecam8c8e—Dawn's Light Woman—and our book's principal character. Marguerite was also one of Belting's discoveries, although Belting did not comprehend all of the historical riches immanent in that discovery.

Telling the story of Dawn's Light Woman, and of her successive three French husbands, demands deep immersion in, above all, the Illinois Country archives known as the Kaskaskia Manuscripts (hereafter KM), which have been meticulously organized, collated, and indexed by Margaret K. Brown and Lawrie C. Dean. At first glance, these centuries-old manuscripts, replete with legal lingo from Old Regime France, seem dusty and dry at best, and obscure and daunting at worst. But then, unexpectedly, a revelation will leap out—about an orphan child, an enslaved Native American, or a riverboat trip to New Orleans. Women in the Illinois Country—French, French Canadian, Métisses, or Native American—do not appear regularly in these civil records prior to their married lives, for marriage announced the arrival of maturity and the acquisition of legal status. Nonetheless, entries in baptismal registers sometimes contain girls' names, for they did, even as unmarried teenagers, serve as godmothers to newborn infants. Indeed, it is in that role that Dawn's Light Woman first enters the historical record. This entrance, easy to overlook, had wide ranging ramifications and is the underpinning of this book.

Important questions remain unanswered about Dawn's Light Woman's inner life and about the scope of her knowledge of the world beyond the village of Kaskaskia. And, as with the other Native American women who appear in our study, no sources exist about her childhood in the Kaskaskia tribe, as the tribe migrated down the Illinois and Mississippi river valleys. We have squeezed the extant manuscripts until they, in exhaustion, have gasped, but we have consistently shunned the temptation to engage in speculation beyond the range of our original sources. However, frustrating this may be, it is something with which we, as scholars, must live.

ACKNOWLEDGMENTS

French customary law permeates and informs our text from beginning to end. U.S. Appellate Court Judge Morris S. Arnold is today the premier legal scholar of colonial Louisiana, as his many deeply researched books attest. Over the course of the years that this book has been in progress, Judge Arnold has guided us through many legal thickets. Two other accomplished lawyers with an interest in colonial history have also scrutinized our handling of legal issues. James Horstman of Dixon, Illinois, and Michael Rea of Winchester, Virginia, have each offered valuable suggestions to help keep our legal discussions coherent, even for lay persons. Although this book is about a village that was fundamentally (though not exclusively) French in language and culture, many Native Americans appear in it. Michael McCafferty and Carl Masthay have lent much help with issues pertaining to Native Americans. Indeed, McCafferty has been deeply involved with many aspects of this book, from deciphering Indian names to catching us out on flaccid arguments. Professor Gilles Havard is a director of research at the Centre National de la Recherche Scientifique in Paris. His knowledge of the broad swath of borderlands encompassing the Pays d'en Haut and Haute Louisiane during the colonial era is unparalleled. Havard read an earlier draft of this book and offered many penetrating observations, particularly about French-Indian relations. Christine Knutson chauffeured us from Paris to Franchomme's home village of Montmeillant, in the Ardennes, where we shared notes with his extended family and traded a Parisian pastry for a dozen fresh eggs. Ekberg's former colleague at Illinois State University, David J. MacDonald, provided us with help on military affairs, a particular interest of his. Hannah Marie Ekberg, a professional translator, has double checked our translations from the French. Finally, Jennifer Egan, acquisitions editor at Southern Illinois University Press, did something that few editors at university presses do these days: She personally immersed herself in our text and offered many insightful suggestions about style, balance, and coherence.

DAWN'S LIGHT WOMAN & NICOLAS FRANCHOMME

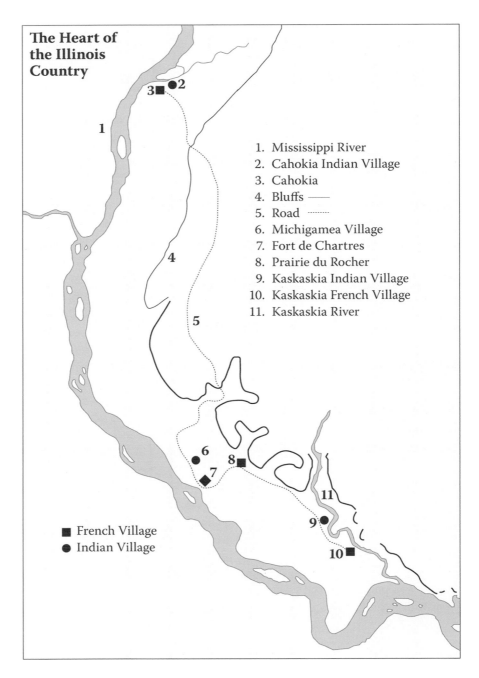

The Heart of the Illinois Country

1. Mississippi River
2. Cahokia Indian Village
3. Cahokia
4. Bluffs ——
5. Road ········
6. Michigamea Village
7. Fort de Chartres
8. Prairie du Rocher
9. Kaskaskia Indian Village
10. Kaskaskia French Village
11. Kaskaskia River

■ French Village
● Indian Village

I.1. Map of the Illinois Country settlements by Lola Wilkening and David MacDonald, based on Thomas Hutchins, "A Plan of the Several Villages of the Illinois Country," from *A Topographical Description of Virginia, Pennsylvania, Maryland and North Carolina* (London: J. Almond, 1778).

Introduction

 A HUNDRED YEARS AGO, Clarence W. Alvord authored *The Illinois Country, 1673–1818*, the first volume in the Centennial History of Illinois series published by the Illinois Centennial Commission.[1] This landmark volume introduced to the public the proposition that a place called Illinois had existed well before statehood, and before the advent of Abraham Lincoln, and that this colonial Illinois was just as important for the history of the Mississippi River valley as colonial Virginia was for the history of the Eastern Seaboard. "Illinois"—variants, Ilinois or Islinois—was the French version of an Algonquian (Ojibwa-Ottawa) word meaning "he/she speaks in a regular way," which was how members of the Illinois Nation referred to one another.[2] The French, beginning in the late seventeenth century, employed "Ilinois" in reference to the Indians of this nation, as well as to the wide swath of real estate (*le Pays des Illinois*) over which they ranged at various times and in various ways.[3]

In any case, Alvord's broad survey dwelt on political events from decade to decade, and was never intended to be a comprehensive history of colonial Illinois. Other studies have appeared since, beginning with Natalia Maree Belting's small and captivating *Kaskaskia Under the French Regime*,[4] which has drawn so many students toward French Illinois studies. These post-Alvord studies have enlarged early Illinois history in various directions—cultural, political, geographical, and even temporal—by demonstrating that early St. Louis was indeed an integral part of the Illinois Country.[5] French scholars have also contributed in significant ways, particularly as seen in the magisterial studies of Gilles Havard.[6] This present study falls within the tradition of these recent volumes; it serves to expand and enrich, both factually and conceptually, Alvord's sweeping and groundbreaking overview of the Illinois Country from a century ago.

Chapter 1 presents a compressed history of the founding and early history of Kaskaskia, which soon after its founding in 1703 became the largest and most important settlement in the region. Missionary priests of the Society of Jesus were essential to early Kaskaskia. In addition to their daunting missionary work, they helped maintain some semblance of a civil society in a community with a diverse population: Kaskaskia Indians, French, French Canadians, Métis, and enslaved people, both Native American and African. Jesuits also

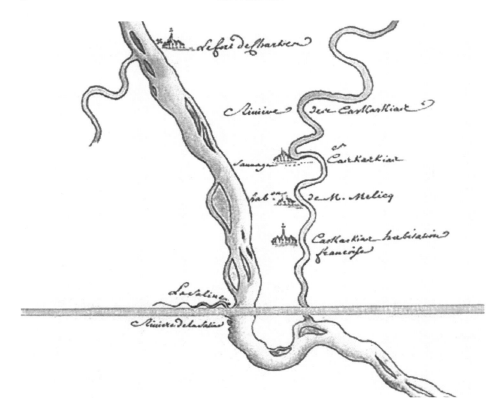

I.2. The Illinois Country by Bernard Diron d'Artaguiette from data collected in 1722. (Notice the two "Cacaskias, one French and the other Indian.) Detail reproduced from: Sarah J. Tucker, ed. *Indian Villages of the Illinois Country* (Springfield, IL: Illinois State Museum, 1942), Plate XVI.

promoted arable—from the Latin *arare,* "to plow"—agriculture in the region, and the rapid spread of wheat and maize cultivation in the open fields lying outside the village revolutionized the region's economy. Kaskaskia village is the geographical focal point of our study, the economic center of gravity of the Illinois Country, and the place where most of our dramatis personae lived. This study is not an ethnohistory of the Illinois Indians, for Kaskaskia during the 1720s, although replete with many Native American wives, was fundamentally—in language, law, religion, and even material culture—a French rural community.

Chapter 2, burrowing deep into contemporary civil and religious manuscripts, delves into three marriages between Illinois Indian women and French men. It explains how these mixed couples were the very pillars upon which early Kaskaskia society rested and

TEXTE

DES COUTUMES

DE LA PREVOSTE',

ET VICOMTE'

DE PARIS,

Avec des Nottes ou Decifions fom-
maires fur chaque article, & les
rapports des articles les uns avec
les autres.

Par Maiſtre CLAUDE DE FERRIERE
Advocat au Parlement.

A PARIS,

Chez J EAN COCHART, au cinquiéme
pillier de la grande Salle du
Palais, au S. Eſprit.

M. DC. LXXX.

Avec Privilege du Roy.

I.3. Claude de Ferrière's 1680 edition of French customary laws, *Texte des Coutumes de Paris* (Paris: Jean Cochart, 1680).

how Native American wives were integrated into Kaskaskia society via traditional French customary laws. French officials brought a published version of these laws (*Texte des Coutumes de la Prévosté et Vicomté de Paris,* or simply *Coutume de Paris*) when they arrived in the Illinois Country in 1719,[7] and these laws were hugely important in putting a stamp of French culture and civilization on the wilderness of the Mississippi frontier. The three Native American-French marriages analyzed in this chapter all unfolded within the legal context of the *Coutume,* which guaranteed wives, including Native American wives, important rights.[8] These mixed marriages provide, the setting for that of Marguerite 8assecam8c8e to Nicolas Peltier de Franchomme, which stands at the very core of this book. A French bureaucrat in New Orleans, who had never lived and breathed the air of the Illinois Country, opined that Frenchmen who married Native American women became insolent, unruly, and more difficult to govern.[9] Although it is intriguing to contemplate this claim, we have found no evidence to support it; certainly, it did not apply to Franchomme.

Chapter 3 deals with the life, the death (more important for this study), and the succession of Jacques Bourdon, first husband of Marguerite 8assecam8c8e. A French Canadian from a bourgeois family—his father was a *notaire* (notary) in Boucherville—Bourdon spent his entire adult life on the Mississippi frontier and was likely present with other French Canadian traders when Kaskaskia village was founded in 1703. Bourdon was the first captain of the parish militia, a position that loudly proclaimed him as a preeminent personage in the community—what is more, when Bourdon died in June 1723, he was accorded the special honor of burial under the floor of the parish church of the Immaculate Conception.[10] Bourdon's successive marriages to two Illinois Indian women (Domitile Ch8ping8eta and Marguerite 8assecam8c8e) helped him to generate a fortune in fur-trade profits. Such fortune-making mixed marriages were not unusual in the Pays d'en Haut (Upper Country), and Gilles Havard has written persuasively about how Native American wives were fundamental to the successful operations of French fur traders in the region.[11] Bourdon's death provoked serious legal issues about the rights of Indian widows to access the very wealth that they had helped to generate.

Chapter 4 describes Pierre Baillargeon's attack, both personal and legal, on Franchomme's wife Marguerite 8assecam8c8e. Baillargeon was the son of Bourdon's first wife, Domitile Ch8ping8eta, by her first husband, Antoine Baillargeon, and Pierre Baillargeon attacked the legitimacy of Marguerite 8assecam8c8e's claim to her deceased husband's estate, arguing that his Illinois Indian mother (*not* Bourdon and *not* Marguerite) had generated all the wealth in the estate. Domitile was Pierre Baillargeon's heroine, and Marguerite his villain; Domitile was the good Indian woman, and Marguerite—greedy and scheming—the bad. Pierre Baillargeon took the outrageous step of suggesting that Marguerite 8assecam8c8e's marriage to Franchomme should be annulled.

Chapter 5 analyzes Franchomme's acerbic response to Pierre Baillargeon's attack on Marguerite, and how Franchomme prevailed by arguing that his wife, although a Native American, was a lawful heir to the Bourdon estate. Franchomme read deeply in the text of the *Coutume de Paris*, and his arguments were solidly based on French customary law. Hanging as a cloud over this particular legal case, and the wrangling between Franchomme and Pierre Baillargeon, was the larger issue of whether Indian widows had the same inheritance rights as French widows.[12] Officers from Fort de Chartres, functioning as an Illinois Provincial Council, adjudicated the case in 1723, and their decision provided two overwhelmingly important results for society in the Illinois Country.[13] First, the *Coutume de Paris* would henceforth be the governing legal authority, indisputably and irrevocably, for domestic affairs in the Illinois Country, as it had been for decades in French Canada.[14] This fundamental aspect of Illinois Country society demands full explication, which until now it has not received. Second, Native American wives in the community were guaranteed the same inheritance rights as French wives. In the words of Jean-François de Fleuriau, *Procureur Général* (Attorney General) of Louisiana: "These [Indian] wives must therefore uniformly enjoy the same privileges as their [French] husbands, having the same status and condition, and living under the same laws to which they are subject."[15]

Chapter 6 provides an up-close, particular depiction of the village of Kaskaskia in the 1720s, illuminating as graphically as French manuscript sources permit *la vie quotidienne* (the daily life) of *habitants* and *habitantes*, enslaved people—both Black and Native American—marine officers and Jesuit priests. This chapter deals with domestic architecture, the material culture of everyday life, the market values of everything from fresh milk to bison ribs to draft animals to enslaved humans. This everything-down-to-the-last-detail accounting of living beings and material things serves to convey the most comprehensive picture possible of the physical setting for our human drama. It also depicts the economic and social intimacy of the French and Illinois Indian settlements, as well as the barter system of goods and services that bound the two communities closely together.

Chapter 7 returns to the absolute centrality of the *Coutume de Paris* for understanding colonial Illinois society, including the lives of the Native American women who were married to French men. When Franchomme and Marguerite were married in 1723, a local *notaire* drafted a civil marriage contract, which included a clause vital to Franchomme's future well-being: a very large donation to him from his wealthy widow-wife. When this document was ravaged by rats (reputed to be large and voracious in the Illinois Country), Franchomme felt compelled to make an impulsive, extraordinary trip downriver to New Orleans to have Louisiana's highest ranking notaire (a servant of the Superior Council) reconstruct, clause by clause, his marriage contract with Marguerite. Original manuscripts housed in the archives of the Louisiana State Museum detail the intricate process that transpired in New Orleans, which confirmed Franchomme's legal relationship as Marguerite's husband and, importantly, vouchsafed his financial interests.

Chapter 8 takes up the *guerre à l'outrance* between French settlers and their Illinois Indian allies on the one side and the Foxes (Renards or Mesquakies) on the other. This war turned the life of Marguerite 8assecam8c8e upside down, and introduces a bloody and pathetic element to our story. The decades-long struggle, which unremitting, intrepid Fox warriors pushed right to Kaskaskia's doorsteps, ran red hot during the 1720s. Franchomme, as a young marine officer, was inevitably drawn into this struggle, and Fox warriors killed him in the summer of 1728. His men buried him in an anonymous grave on the Illinois prairie, his paltry personal possessions were auctioned off, and his widow, Marguerite 8assecam8c8e, was left to find a new French husband. The prolonged Fox-French conflict has attracted much scholarly attention, very largely from the Canadian perspective.[16] This chapter, for the first time, approaches this conflict from inside the Illinois Country villages, and uses original manuscripts to discuss how it was seen from there, and how it affected these villages and their frightened habitants.

Chapter 9 focuses on Illinois Indian wives and widows and their status in French Louisiana society. Indeed, this book is largely about these Native American women. The Illinois Provincial Council decided in 1723 that the Indian widows of French men were accorded, under the rules of the *Coutume de Paris*, the same inheritance rights as French women, for they qualified as *Régnicoles*, citizens of the French kingdom. But an issue arose regarding French patrimonial resources should Indian widows die *sans enfants* (without issue). The Superior Council in New Orleans decided in 1728 that, for the well-being of the colony of Louisiana, these national resources must be protected; that is, not be permitted to devolve on to the non-assimilated Native American relatives of the deceased widows. The words of the Council's decision make it manifestly clear that the councilors were not engaging in any sort of proto-racialist discrimination but rather were determined to serve the larger economic interests of the province of Louisiana and therefore of the Bourbon French state.

Chapter 10 deals with Marguerite's third, and final, marriage, and this one, too, to a French man. Because of her wealth, and her apparent physical attractiveness, Marguerite had the power of choice when it came to choosing a husband, and there was no chance that for either her second or third marriages she would exercise that power in selecting an Illinois Indian man for a husband; Illinois Indian women who married French men improved, with virtual certainty, their condition and status in Kaskaskia.[17] Tracy Leavelle and Linda Jones have emphasized how conversion to Christianity increased the power—social, economic, and sexual, as well as spiritual—of Illinois Indian women.[18] And, as the following study demonstrates, Christianized Native American women who married French men were further empowered by living under the regime of French customary law.

Pierre Blot, Marguerite's third husband, was born and raised on Île d'Oléron in southwestern France, best known for its succulent oysters. Just how he wound up in a distant land where oysters were not to be found remains unknown, but, like Marguerite, Blot brought substantial economic assets, including slaves, into their marriage. They each had a distinct nose for business, and they owned—with fully shared rights of proprietorship—Kaskaskia's first known billiard parlor; it is wondrous to think of Marguerite, in her waning years, as a proper French *petite bourgeoise*, tending bar in her own *établissement*.

The Conclusion to this work addresses issues that were central for defining the Illinois Country during the formative decade of the 1720s. The Kaskaskia of 1725 was most decidedly not the Kaskaskia of 1715. We conclude that two developments—one legal and one economic—were central to transforming the region during that seminal decade. First, the Jacques Bourdon succession case, in which Marguerite 8assecam8c8e prevailed, established the *Coutume de Paris* as the prevailing law in Illinois. Second, the swift spread of plow agriculture, based on wheat and maize cultivation, dramatically transformed the Illinois Country's economy from exclusively fur-trade based to expansively agricultural, while the fur trade continued unabated. This dramatic agricultural transformation during the early 1720s dictated much of the economic future of Illinois, right down to the present day.

We do not believe that, when French men married Native American women, people viewed these unions, which are central to this book, as mixed marriages. That is, neither Native Americans nor French in early Kaskaskia relegated themselves or others to distinct racial categories. Our neologisms "racialism" and "racialization" are simply not useful for examining the principal characters in this book, understanding their thoughts, their motivations, and their actions. Nonetheless, because race has become an increasingly important and fraught topic in French colonial studies,[19] our conclusion briefly addresses this issue from the narrow perspective of the Illinois Country during the 1720s. We conclude that denizens of the region, including Marguerite and Franchomme, possessed fundamentally pre-modern mental structures that precluded viewing race in nineteenth, twentieth, or twenty-first century terms; that is, they were neither racialist nor racist in their conceptions of human society. Marguerite, owner of both enslaved Indians and Africans, did not need to justify that ownership on racial grounds, for slavery was integral to her view of how human society was constructed, and, from her perspective, had been constructed since time out of mind.[20] And concerning intimate relations, Franchomme was not uncomfortable in his courtship of and marriage to Marguerite because of any anxiety in his bosom that he was crossing a racial line or violating any racial taboo.

Finally, Part II is a comprehensively annotated enumeration, household by household, of Illinois Country men, women, and children, free and enslaved, in 1726., This detailed enumeration is based on the first census ever compiled in the American Midwest. Running parenthetical references to discrete individuals in this enumeration appear throughout the book's narrative. Part II is an essential part of the granular depiction of Kaskaskia society during the decade of the 1720s, which is a central goal of this book.

Principal Characters

Jacques Bourdon, captain of the militia in Kaskaskia, 1719–23

Domitile Ch8ping8eta, deceased first wife of Jacques Bourdon

Pierre Baillargeon, son of Domitile Ch8ping8eta and her first husband, Antoine Baillargeon, and adopted son of Jacques Bourdon

Marguerite 8assecam8c8e,[1] married in succession to Jacques Bourdon, Nicolas Franchomme and Pierre Blot

Nicolas Peltier de Franchomme, marine ensign married to Marguerite 8assecam8c8e, 1723

François Noyon, legatee of Jacques Bourdon

Pierre Blot, married to Marguerite 8assecam8c8e, 1730

Important Jesuit Priests at Kaskaskia

Pierre-Gabriel Marest

Jean Mermet

Nicolas-Ignace Beaubois

Jean-Antoine Robert Le Boullenger

René Tartarin

Members of Illinois Provincial Council

Pierre Dugué de Boisbriant

Marc-Antoine de La Loëre des Ursins

Nicolas Chassin

PART I

CHAPTER I

The Illinois Country

EUROPEAN SETTLEMENT OF THE AMERICAN MIDWEST was initiated by French Roman Catholic priests and French Canadian traders in the late seventeenth century. These Europeans arrived in the middle Mississippi River valley in close association with Native Americans of the Illinois Nation. Some years ago, Francis Jennings and James Axtell, two giants in the field of ethnohistory, conducted a spirited debate concerning European "invasions" of North America. Jennings quickly took the offensive and heartily condemned European colonizers for the horrors they inflicted on Native Americans, while Axtell, wary of historians as moralizers, was less judgmental in his assessment of European settlers in America.[1] If French settlement of the Illinois Country constituted an "invasion" of the Mississippi Valley, it was a relatively benign invasion; the gradual transformation of Illinois Indian culture catalyzed by French manners and mores, and the Roman Catholic religion, was generally acquiesced to by the Indians themselves, as they adapted to the presence of French priests and Canadian traders in their midst.[2]

"Settler colonialism," a phrase coined by the Australian scholar Patrick Wolfe, has quickly become an inescapable buzz phrase. Discussion of this issue has been propelled by a recently published "Forum," consisting of eleven essays dedicated to the uses (and misuses) of "settler colonialism" within the context of North American history.[3] The authors all agree that Wolfe's meaning of the phrase was clear and unequivocal: Settler colonialism meant willful elimination of indigenous peoples and illicit seizure of their lands. Although originally applied to post-1800 British colonial dominions, the phrase, as the "Forum" informs us, has recently experienced much wider usage, both in time and space, from seventeenth-century Manhattan to nineteenth-century California. The "Forum's" sole contributor for French North America, Allan Greer, noted that attempts "to reconceive New France's history on a settler-colonial basis have led to lamentable results,"[4] for Wolfe's model of elimination of Natives is out of focus and misleading when applied to French Canada.

The "Forum" included no discussion of the colonial Mississippi River valley, but if "settler colonialism" is a patently useless model for describing or understanding pre-Conquest Canada, it works even less well for the Illinois Country. No French settler in early Kaskaskia wanted to eliminate the Illinois Indians, an absurd notion on the face of it given the symbiotic relationship that existed between these two groups of human beings. A more useful model than Wolfe's for examining early Kaskaskia is the one gracefully articulated in Morris S. Arnold's *The Rumble of a Distant Drum*.[5] Arnold's model is not an airy abstraction, is not based on a priori theorizing, but rather on deep immersion in French and Spanish archives. Arnold's conclusions about Arkansas Post work remarkably well for the early Illinois Country, which was far more like Arkansas than Canada—Quapaw Indians, masters of the hinterlands, engineered during the course of the eighteenth century a noticeably harmonious relationship at the Post with European settlers (mostly French, with a handful of Spanish soldiers), who were hunters, trappers, and small-scale farmers. Indeed, European settlers were more emissaries to the Quapaws than adversaries of the nation that dominated the Arkansas region. This relative harmony, despite inevitable squabbles, was based on trade, mutual dependency, and occasional intimate relations, and it persisted for generations. The same may be said about the Illinois Country, which was in truth Arkansas Post writ large, really large. During the course of the eighteenth century, the Illinois Nation was decimated by disease, alcohol, and warfare, but the impersonal global forces that fueled this decline were most certainly *not* a consequence of volition on the part of the regional French settlers.[6]

· · ·

Father Jacques Marquette and Louis Jolliet were the first recorded Europeans to traverse the continental divide between the Great Lakes Basin and the Mississippi River watershed. In 1675, Marquette founded among the Kaskaskia Indians the Jesuit mission of the Immaculate Conception, on the upper Illinois River.[7] The exploits of Marquette and Jolliet, although of major historical interest, only set the stage for the advent of René-Robert Cavelier, Sieur de La Salle, a man whose dreams about North America's limitless possibilities drove him mercilessly, and ultimately to an early death in east Texas in 1687.[8] During the early 1680s, La Salle and his lieutenant Henri de Tonty encountered the immanent grandeur and the obvious utility of the water corridor provided by the Illinois and Mississippi rivers between the Great Lakes and the Gulf of Mexico.[9] This fecund encounter had enormous and fruitful consequences for Illinois history, for by the turn of the eighteenth century French missionaries, both Jesuits and Seminarians, were descending this corridor and planting mission outposts on both banks of the Mississippi River—Roman Catholic missions that served the various branches of the Illinois Indian confederation (*nation* in standard eighteenth-century French parlance).

Permanent French settlement of the valley began with the emergence of two mission/trading communities (Cahokia in 1699 and Kaskaskia in 1703) on the east bank of the Mississippi, just below the mouth of the Missouri.[10] These French/Indian villages were the nucleus of the Illinois Country—*le Pays des Illinois*—the territory over which ranged the greater Illinois Nation of Indians. This was a loose and ever-changing manner of identifying the region, and during the early eighteenth century Frenchmen viewed the Illinois Country from a variety of perspectives. A royal ordinance of 1722 defined the region expansively to include the valleys of the Arkansas and Wabash rivers, the French settlements on both sides of the Mississippi River, and all the tributaries of this river.[11] This broadest definition of the Illinois Country made it virtually coterminous with Upper Louisiana, that is, all the French-claimed territory south of the Great Lakes and north of the mouth of the Arkansas River, including the lower portions of the Missouri and Ohio river valleys. By the mid-1760s, after the French and Indian War had concluded and new French villages (Ste. Genevieve and St. Louis) had emerged on the west bank of the Mississippi, it became usual to define the Illinois Country more narrowly, as the region dotted by French settlements along both sides of the Mississippi River, running upstream from the mouth of the Kaskaskia River to the mouth of the Missouri.

The village of Kaskaskia, principal setting for our story, was established as the ultimate consequence of the southward migration of the Kaskaskia branch of the Illinois Nation, together with associated Jesuit missionaries and French Canadian traders. This migration commenced in 1691 at the Grand Village of the Illinois, located across the Illinois River and about a mile upstream from Le Rocher (later Starved Rock). On this prominent limestone butte, La Salle's right-hand man Tonty had completed Fort St. Louis in 1683, an outpost that cemented a close relationship between French settlers and Illinois Indians that endured for more than one hundred years.[12] Sauks, Foxes, and most especially Iroquois periodically threatened the viability of the Kaskaskia community on the upper Illinois River, and in 1691 the Kaskaskias moved downriver, settling on the west bank of the Illinois River, at the lower end of today's Lake Peoria. Pimitéoui was the Miami-Illinois appellation applied to this area, and that Indian name stuck for the duration of the French regime in the Illinois Country.[13]

The Kaskaskias remained settled at Pimitéoui for nearly a decade (1691–1700), and during that time their attendant Jesuit missionaries hosted Seminarian priests as the latter descended the waterways of the Pays d'en Haut, preparing to leave the placid valley of the Illinois River and enter the turbulent one of the Mississippi. Pierre-Gabriel Marest was born and raised in Laval, France, in 1662, became a Jesuit novice in Paris, and underwent extensive schooling before being sent to Canada in 1694.[14] After various adventures in the far north, Marest was posted to the Illinois Country in 1698 to serve the Mission of the Immaculate Conception, founded on the Illinois River by Father Jacques Gravier in 1689.[15] On April 29, 1699, Marest reported from téoui that "three gentlemen of the Quebec Seminary, sent by Monseigneur the Bishop to establish Missions on the Mississipi, passed through here. We received them as well as we were able, lodging them in our own house. . . ."[16] These Seminarians were headed downriver on their way to establish their mission headquarters at Cahokia, where they would serve the Cahokias (or Tamaroas), a major component of the Illinois Nation, until the end of the French regime.

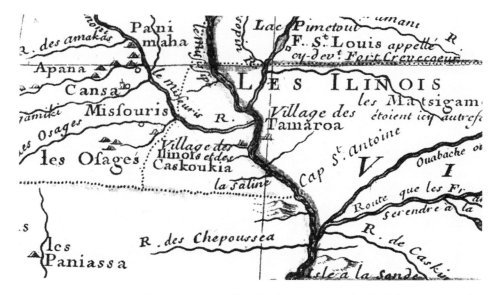

1.1. Notice at the center of the image, the *Village des Ilinois et des Caskoukia.* This represents the Rivière des Pères settlement site, which was occupied 1700–1703. Across the Mississippi, the Village des Tamaroa was the location of the Seminarian mission. *Carte du cours et des environs de la Rivière de Mississipi.* Guillaume Delisle, 1703. Library of Congress.

Marc Bergier arrived at the Seminarian mission at Cahokia (among the Tamaroas) in February 1700, having been appointed Superior by Jean-Baptiste de Saint Vallier, the Bishop of Quebec.[17] On April 13, 1701, Bergier wrote from Cahokia that "the Kats [Kaskaskias] to the number of about thirty cabins have established their new village two leagues below here on the other side of the river."[18] This new settlement appears on Guillaume Delisle's 1703 map (above) as "Village des Ilinois et Cascoukia," and the creek upon whose bank it lay would eventually acquire the name Rivière des Pères (today, River des Peres in south St. Louis), a reference to the Jesuit fathers.[19] Father Marest was a leader, both spiritual and moral, among the Kaskaskias and their associated French traders when they relocated (from Pimitéoui) to this site in 1700, although Marest himself declared that Father Jacques Gravier, who was present with the Kaskaskias at both Pimitéoui and Rivière des Pères, "properly ought to be regarded as the founder of the Illinois Mission."[20]

Rivalry between Jesuits and Seminarians was a staple of French missionary activity in North America, and in the Illinois Country that rivalry was sharp enough to require the intervention of Louis XIV. King by divine right, Louis had no intention of permitting divines from rival orders to disrupt peace in his Mississippi River valley colonies. A royal decision resolved the matter on June 7, 1701: "The Priests of the Foreign Missions [Seminarians] are to remain alone in the place called Tamarois and are to receive fraternally the Reverend Jesuit Fathers when they pass through to go to assist the Illinois and Tamarois in their hunting and fishing quarters, in which quarters the Reverend Jesuit Fathers will be authorized to settle."[21] How much real impact royal decrees had in distant colonies is always in question, but as long as Marest was the guiding Jesuit and Bergier the Seminarian Superior, the two principal missionary orders in the Illinois Country were more cooperative than competitive.

In early 1703, Marest was in charge of the Jesuit mission at the Rivière des Pères, and Bergier was stationed across the Mississippi at the Seminarian mission with the Tamaroa. Bergier was a sharp observer of the region and a prolific epistolary, and as Marest observed Seminarians leapfrogging downriver in 1699, so the Seminarian Bergier observed Jesuits doing the same in 1703. On April 16, he wrote that "Père Maretz is going twenty-five leagues farther down [the Mississippi] with his village, about a day's journey from the Ouabache [in this instance the Ohio River]." Marest's decision to abandon the Rivière des Pères settlement was likely prompted by several factors,[22] perhaps most importantly by threats from Sioux Indians, whose raiding parties swept down, like a bitter April sleet storm, out of the northwest all the way to the mouth of the Missouri River, and beyond.[23] During this period of Sioux threats, Bergier and Marest remained close, as each of these extraordinary men worked with his respective flock to the point of exhaustion. Theirs was a deep comradeship bonded by the blood of Christ. When Bergier lay in his sickbed, Marest administered to him the Viaticum, and later walked miles through rain in order to conduct his comrade's funeral Mass.[24]

On April 25, 1703, Marest inscribed in his parish records "Ad ripam Metchagamia dictam venimus—we arrived on the bank of the Metchagamia."[25] The terseness of Marest's phrase lent gravity to his words and conveyed the priest's manifest relief at discovering, at long last, a safe refuge for his flock on the right bank of the Metchagamia River (later renamed Kaskaskia).[26] These pilgrims, mostly Kaskaskia Indians with a handful of French Canadian traders, had been on the run for more than a decade. The wives and mothers in Marest's vulnerable, precious flock were all Illinois Indian women, for neither French nor French Canadian women were yet residents of the region at that early stage. By 1715, a trickle of White women had joined the settlement, coming from both Canada and the Gulf Coast, and by 1726 there were many more White than Indian wives in Kaskaskia (see Census, below). In any case, it is Indian wives who are the dedicated focus of this book.

· · ·

Kaskaskia, at the beginning, was more a sprawling campsite than a village. As some semblance of a village emerged, it was a helter-skelter affair, with no geometric plan like the one effected in New Orleans beginning in 1718. The Jesuits, led by Father Marest, had significant resources, and soon the Jesuit compound situated hard on the right bank of the lower Metchagamia River assumed a large presence in the settlement. An anonymous description

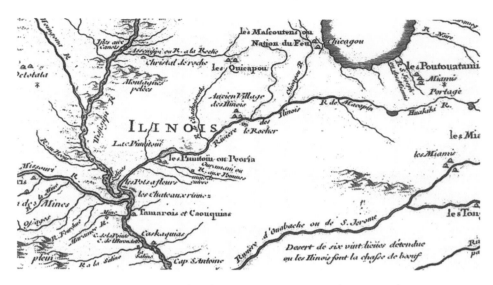

1.2. This was the first map (1718) to depict the Kaskaskia (Caskaquias) Village.
Carte de la Louisiane et du cours du Mississipi [*sic*]: *dressée sur un grand nombre de mémoires entrautres sur ceux de Mr. le Maire.* Guillaume Delisle, 1718, Library of Congress.

sent to Versailles in June 1720 summarized the outsized importance of Jesuits to the Illinois colony: "They have a large house, a good plantation, four plows, a windmill, 16–18 enslaved people [Africans and Native Americans], and 200 head of cattle."[27] Marest may have had a Native American slave or two (Panis) right from the start, but enslaved Africans only arrived in the region later on, ca. 1720. On the 1726 census, the Jesuit establishment owned nine Africans and two Native Americans (Census, no. 62).

In the early years, Jesuits at Kaskaskia often served in civil capacities, drafting wills and marriage contracts; this voluntary work was a matter of public service and convenience in a community where appropriate civil officials (that is, notaires) were often not readily at hand.[28] When Father Beaubois drafted a marriage contract at Kaskaskia in 1721, he explained that he was doing so "in this particular instance in the absence of any other public official."[29] The first two decades of the eighteenth century may justly be considered the golden age of the Jesuit mission in the Illinois Country.[30]

During the first decade of the eighteenth century, the Jesuit *établissement* at Kaskaskia became a shining center of learning, a diamond set in an emerald landscape. Father Jean Mermet was born at Grenoble in 1664, became a Jesuit novice in Avignon in 1683, and studied all over southern France (Carpentras, Roanne, Vesoul) before taking a theology degree at Dole in 1696. Mermet sailed for Canada in 1698 and immediately headed west to work with various Miami-Illinois (Algonquian) villages south of Lake Michigan (also Lac

Illinois).[31] Before arriving at Kaskaskia ca. 1705, Mermet was embedded in a Mascouten village on the Ouabache (Wabash) River, where he witnessed the village's devastation by a deadly disease of unknown origin. Mermet made special note of the fact that Mascouten medicine men—*charlatans,* as he called them—and whom he certainly viewed as competitors, experienced no luck in curbing the course, and the curse, of the disease. Writing from Kaskaskia in 1712, Father Marest claimed that Mermet, despite his fragile health, demonstrated a special talent for winning the respect and friendship of Native Americans, and that he had become "the soul" of the mission.[32] In addition to his spiritual skills, Mermet added serious cerebral weight to the Jesuit establishment at Kaskaskia.

In March 1706, Mermet remarked that "Jacques *dit* le Castor" was an important presence among the French in Kaskaskia.[33] Jacques Largillier *dit* (called) le Castor (the Beaver) is one of lesser known but more important persons to have inhabited the early village. Born in France (probably in Picardy ca. 1644), he joined his uncle at Quebec ca. 1664, when Canada was a very rude place. Largillier did as young men in seventeenth-century Quebec habitually did: he headed for the western waterways, to the Pays d'en Haut. Largillier was a canoe man on the seminal expedition of Louis Jolliet and Father Jacques Marquette down the Mississippi to Arkansas in 1673, and his skill as a fur trader earned him the sobriquet "Le Castor." Unlike many of his fellow French Canadian *voyageurs* and *coureurs de bois,* Largillier apparently found no pleasure in pursuing and debauching Native American women. Rather, his daily contact with Illinois Indians aroused in him an appetite to explore their language; close association with Native Americans had stimulated his brain rather more than his glands. About 1676, he swore a solemn oath of fidelity to the Society of Jesus, thereby becoming a *donné,* a lay person with a given (*donné*) commitment and devotion to the Order. Largillier never took holy orders as a priest, but he turned out to be a perfect fit for the Jesuits, possessing physical stamina, mental acuity, and an eagerness to endure the most challenging hardships of the Mississippi frontier.[34]

With the presence of Largillier and the arrival of Father Mermet, Marest had a dream team assembled in the Jesuit compound at Kaskaskia, a team that was exceptionally well-equipped for completing the Miami-Illinois-French dictionary. This dictionary is the single most important cultural artifact produced by the Illinois French during the colonial era. When Marest, Mermet, and Largillier gathered to work on this splendid product of the human mind, they represented as much intellectual firepower as the committee (which included Franklin and Jefferson) that drafted the Declaration of Independence in 1776; and, given their mastery of Indian languages, in addition to French and Latin, the Frenchmen had vastly superior language skills. All three men contributed to the dictionary, but Michael McCafferty has exquisitely demonstrated that Largillier was the principal scribe.[35] This is a bit surprising, given that both Marest and Mermet had high-octane Jesuit educations, while Le Castor is known principally as a man of the woods and the waters. But we now know that the Illinois Country offers many unexpected vignettes and pleasures.

Work on the dictionary was facilitated by the omnipresence of Kaskaskia Indians. To check on a word or a phrase, one had only to leave the calm of the *étude* (study) within the Jesuit compound and enter the dusty hubbub of village life, where cordial conversations between black-robed priests and Kaskaskians, men, women, and children, were everyday scenes. The published dictionary, laboriously edited and collated by Carl Masthay, is chock-a-block with insights and delights; to open it is to enter an Indian-French transcultural world that is not otherwise accessible to us. Randomly flipping through the pages of the hefty volume, one is smitten by entry after entry: "**pakitingiki**—*fleur blanc jaune au dedans*" (white flower with yellow inside); "**peccapikic8rata**—*nez bien fait*" (well-proportioned nose); "**kimitchi8a**—*femme grosse d'adultère*" (woman pregnant from adultery); "**mimiram8a m8nns8**—*chevreuil traverse la rivière à la nage*" (deer swims across a stream); "**nimiara8it8itche**—*je suis misérable, personne n'a compassion pour moi*" (I'm feeling miserable, but no one shows me any compassion).[36]

Make no mistake: The intelligence, diligence, and love that Marest, Mermet, and Largillier poured into this dictionary constitutes scholarship at its most intense and highest level, equal to that devoted to the King James version of the Bible a century earlier. These three men were all utterly convinced of the superiority of French civilization and of the Roman Catholic religion. But it could not have been entirely lost on these Jesuit scholars that a bilingual dictionary, which by definition consisted of linguistic equivalencies, also implied some cultural equivalencies, and, at the outer extreme, even cultural equalities. Michel de Montaigne's famous essay, "Of Cannibals," cast the subject of cultural relativism into high relief for French intellectuals, and almost certainly Marest and Mermet had read their countryman's work and absorbed some of its lessons.[37]

The linguistic work of Marest, Memet, and Largillier represented a cultural efflorescence in Kaskaskia of remarkable proportions, but it came crashing down with the savage epidemic that swept through Kaskaskia in 1714. The winter of 1714–15 was a lugubrious season for Father Mermet, and in a February 1715 letter to Joseph-Louis Germain,[38] Father Superior of Jesuit missions in Canada, Mermet reported the deaths of Marest (September 15, 1714, age 53) and Largillier (November 1714, age 70); he also described the devastating plague that ended their remarkable lives. Marest's terminal illness began with debilitating fatigue, followed by high fever, and death came within eight days. Mermet tried both bodily (One can only imagine!) and spiritual remedies to ease the pain of the ailing Marest, but only the latter was of any value. "When he could no longer speak," wrote Mermet, "he kissed his cassock as a sign of his gratitude to God for permitting him to live and to die within the Society of Jesus." After Marest died, Kaskaskia Indians came and covered his body with *peaux passées* (worked leather goods) and small presents to signify their grief at the loss of their good father. Mermet conducted Marest's funeral Mass in a vertical-log church with ragged *a cappella* accompaniment by the local French population ("ils chantèrent la messe de mort").[39] This population, identified simply as "les français" by Mermet, included villagers like Jacques Bourdon and François Noyon.[40] A young Marguerite 8assecam8c8e (baptized as a Roman Catholic) would also have attended the Mass, and she likely would have been awed by the rustic solemnity of the occasion, although she would not have understood the ancient Latin words resonating through the American oak trusses of the chapel. This was an altogether fitting farewell for a French Jesuit missionary who had spent much of his adult life in the forests and on the rivers of the Pays d'en Haut. Father Ignace de Beaubois, who arrived at Kaskaskia in 1720, had Marest's bones exhumed from the village burial plot and reinterred under the floor of the parish church in 1727.[41]

Mermet was emotionally crushed by the epidemic, and he grieved that at the height of the epidemic four or five villagers were dying every day in the Kaskaskia settlement, and that the total loss was a staggering 200–300 souls. The vast majority of the dead were Native Americans who lived in crowded quarters and who may have had less resistance than French to the disease, whatever it was. The French knew *la petite variole* (smallpox) when they saw it, and Marest himself had described an outbreak in the Illinois Country in 1712.[42] So the 1714 epidemic was evidently not smallpox, although it may have been yellow fever.[43] The range of the *Aedes aegypti* mosquito, which carries the yellow-fever virus, includes southern Illinois, and the epidemic that ravaged New Orleans and Memphis in 1878 did reach as far up the Mississippi as Illinois.[44] A demographic historian, Joseph Zitomersky, claims that between 1701 and 1723 the Illinois Nation (all branches included) lost 55 percent of its population, mostly to various diseases.[45] This devastation of the Native American population may account for the fact that we cannot, try though we may, locate any kinsfolk for the principal character of this book—Marguerite 8assecam8c8e.

Precious few manuscripts survive from Kaskaskia before the year 1720—Mermet's letter is one, and the Miami-Illinois-French dictionary is another. They represent the first phase of Kaskaskia's colonial history, namely the phase of Jesuit primacy. The remainder of this book deals with the second phrase, which began with the arrival of French administrators in 1719 and the ensuant proliferation of written records, both civil and religious. The settlements (both Indian and French) that lay along the right bank of the lower Kaskaskia River were manifestly different in 1725 than they had been ten years earlier. Jesuit fathers remained important, really important, but they would never again exercise the kind of influence at Kaskaskia, and in the Illinois Country at large, that they had during the first two decades of the eighteenth century.

• • •

Neither the Bourbon monarchy nor the Roman Catholic Church planned the original Illinois Country French/Indian villages in top-down fashion. Rather, the communities were chance coalescences of Native Americans, French Canadian traders, and Roman Catholic priests, who, coming together for purposes of mutual protection, economic advantage, and spiritual advocacy, created missionary centers and trading entrepôts. These, over time, became increasingly agriculture settlements, where nuclear villages served as focal points for extensive open-field production of wheat and maize, almost mirror images of villages in rural France.[46] The aging King Louis XIV had no knowledge of these early Mississippi Valley villages, but, if he had had, he would have been proud of what "his" people were accomplishing in "his" realm in faraway Illinois.

Father Marest wrote from Kaskaskia in 1712 that local habitants had experimented with using *bœufs sauvages* (bisons) as draft animals, which would have been a marvelous spectacle to behold—French Canadians trying to install French yokes on American bisons.[47] This comic bit of syncretism, unsurprisingly, was a failure, as the American animals rejected European attempts to domesticate them. Domestic bovine livestock soon arrived in the area (brought down from Canada), and soon habitants were guiding their oxen, drawing heavy, wheeled plows, and carving long furrows in the *terres* (plowlands) that lay outside Kaskaskia.[48] Maize and wheat fields soon transformed the landscape of the rich Mississippi bottom lands. An ornamented pamphlet promoting Illinois wheat circulated in Paris ca. 1723, and it described the birth of wheat cultivation in Illinois.[49] The pamphlet claimed that in 1718 one Zebedée de Breda, a Jesuit *donné* like Jacques Largillier, first experimented with growing wheat in the area. The famous sojourner, Father Pierre-François-Xavier de Charlevoix, passed through the Illinois Country in 1720 and referred to Zebedée as "le Flamand, domestic of the Jesuits, who taught them how to sow wheat."[50] Charlevoix (who returned to France in 1722) was very likely the source of the pamphlet promoting Illinois wheat, which claimed that from one *boisseau* (twelve and one-half liters or one bushel) sown, an extraordinary ninety could be harvested. Although this was surely an exaggeration bred of promotional enthusiasm, Charlevoix was clearly dumbstruck by the richness of the Illinois soil and the abundant harvests it could produce.[51] The new arable agriculture was cooperatively done, with common pastures for livestock, commonly agreed upon planting times, and commonly maintained fencing around the outlying grain fields.

By 1720, rich soil, a temperate climate, and new—to the region—technology had come together synergistically at Kaskaskia, and a process had begun that would change the face of the Midwest forever. While trade in peltries persisted, for the first time in human history, a serious market agriculture arose in the region during the 1720s; this constituted a revolution that affected everything from material culture to slavery, to the rhythms of daily life. In addition to sustaining the villages of the Illinois Country, the new agriculture was soon providing flour to an insatiable market in faraway New Orleans, and during the 1720s, commerce on the Mississippi River grew exponentially.[52]

The new agriculture was distinctly *arable*, and the heavy, unwieldly *charrues* (plows) meant that women, even enslaved women, were little involved in the new style Illinois Country agriculture, except occasionally at harvest time. This was radically different than the traditional gendered division of agricultural labor in Algonquian culture. As Richard White laconically remarked about Algonquian maize cultivation: "There was spring when women would plant and fall when they would harvest."[53] In 1712, Father Marest explained, regarding Illinois Indians, that "hunting and war form the whole occupation of the men; the rest of the work belongs to the women and the girls—it is they who prepare the ground which must be sowed, who do the cooking, who pound the corn."[54] In 1723, the French officer Bernard Diron d'Artaguiette remarked that Illinois women "occupy themselves with housework, in sewing and gathering the Indian corn, in dressing deer and buffalo skins, and the rest of the time they do porcupine quill work."[55] Illinois Indian women certainly continued to hand cultivate, with hoes, their plots of maize, but the fundamental transformation of Illinois grain production, from hoe to plow cultivation, must have had a serious impact on the lifestyle, and also on the *mentalité*, of Illinois Indian women, whose principal occupation as major grain producers was much diminished.

The arable agriculture that Jesuits introduced to Illinois was quintessentially a French style endeavor, which meant that its cultural impact was to make Kaskaskia a bit less Indian and a bit more European. A recent study goes so far as to suggest that the introduction of French-style agriculture to North America had the conscious, willful purpose of destroying Native American cultures. The author remarks that, "although the violence of pruning, clearing, and cultivating might seem trivial alongside documented attempts at genocide such as the eighteenth-century Fox wars, we should nevertheless see these as related manifestations of a broader impulse aimed at subduing indigenous agencies for their effective replacement."[56] In other words, when Jesuit priests introduced plow agriculture to the Illinois Country, they were pursuing a dedicated mission of destruction, and were intent on crushing Native American ways of life. To juxtapose in the same sentence Jesuit advocacy of French-style agriculture with the bloody Fox wars of the 1720s is a wild and risible anti-clerical stretch. The author might well have prudently wielded Occam's razor and acknowledged that when French priests applauded the blessing of abundant harvests in Illinois their minds were fixed more on the providential grain produced by arable agriculture than on cultural conquest.

What was decidedly not European about the new Illinois agriculture was the use of enslaved people as farm laborers. The practice of Indian slavery in Illinois Country villages descended from the long-time, common use of Native American slaves in Canada, where such slavery was officially sanctioned in 1709.[57] Indian slaves were a small, invisible presence in the tatterdemalion assemblage of Native Americans, priests, and traders who settled at Kaskaskia in 1703, yet it was those early enslaved people who assisted Kaskaskia Indian women in their labor-intensive cultivation of maize. The first recorded appearance of Native American slaves at Kaskaskia came when Father Jean-Antoine Le Boullenger baptized two Indian—or, at least, half Indian—children in late 1719.[58] The first, daughter of Paniasic8e— whose name was Wichita, meaning Little-Pawnee Woman[59]—a Native American slave belonging to Paul Boucher, was christened "Marguerite" (after her godmother, Marguerite 8assecam8c8e) on November 22 of that year. The mother had no Christian name, and Le

Boullenger included no father in the baptismal record. Then, in the same mode, the priest baptized on December 18 "Paul," the namesake of Paul Lamy, owner of the infant's mother. The newborn bore precisely the same Native name as Boucher's slave, Paniasic8e; again, the mother had no Christian name, and there is no mention of a father. Le Boullenger's exclusive use of tribal names suggests that these two Native American women—the mothers—had only recently arrived in Kaskaskia.

These two brief baptismal records tell a story, a decidedly unpleasant story, which had commenced far out on the high western plains, and unfolded like this: Sometime in early 1719, a slave trader—Jean-Baptiste Poudret was one such trader—who had been operating out west, showed up in Kaskaskia with several enslaved women for sale, and Paul Boucher and Paul Lamy each purchased one. Both slaves came originally from a branch of the Wichita tribe (hence the name Paniasic8e) and likely had been seized by another tribe (perhaps Padouca, the Plains Apache), and then sold to a French Canadian trader, who finally brought them to market in Kaskaskia.[60] By whom these two Native American women had been impregnated, at about the same time, cannot be determined—conceivably they were pregnant when captured out on the western plains. Much more likely, their Indian captors, the French slave trader, or their new owners in Kaskaskia had raped them—unceremoniously and repeatedly. Rape is the only plausible explanation for the doleful situation of these two Indian women, who were living with past traumas when each endured the additional (though rather different) trauma of childbirth in late 1719. Perhaps in this ordeal they were comforted by Marguerite 8assecam8c8e, godmother to the first's daughter. We witness the pain of these women only remotely, through Le Boullenger's elliptical baptismal records of the children they bore.

Native American slaves residing within the embryonic village of Kaskaskia had accustomed the villagers to the institution of human slavery, but the arrival in the Illinois Country of African slaves from the Gulf Coast took slavery to a new and different level in the region. The first mention of an African slave in Kaskaskia dates from 1720, when Antoine Bosseron dit Léonard (Census, no. 81) purchased "a Negro" from Charles Garel dit St. Martin.[61] There were African slaves at Mobile early on, and it is possible that Illinois traders, who frequented the Gulf Coast, had acquired enslaved Africans and brought them upriver to Kaskaskia.[62] However, as the new entrepôt of New Orleans grew during the 1720s, the number of enslaved Africans arriving in the Illinois Country surged, and by 1726, Bosseron and his wife, a former Wichita slave, whose name was Susanne Paniasic8e, owned seven Black slaves and two Native Americans.

It was no coincidence that Black slaves arrived in Kaskaskia at the same time that French-style plow agriculture was quickly spreading in the region. African slaves were preferred to Native Americans for agricultural labor, and soon they were laboring, shoulder to shoulder, with their owners and neighbors, in the grain fields that lay outside of the village. Decades later, Henry Marie Brackenridge remarked about agriculturists at Ste. Genevieve that "their agricultural labors commence in the month of April, when the inhabitants, with their slaves, are seen going and returning, each morning and evening, with their ploughs, carts, horses and &c."[63] The plowmen's destination was the Grand Champ that lies to this day south of town, between the bluffs and the Mississippi River. Brackenridge's description of the rhythms and routines of agricultural life in the Illinois Country comes from the 1790s, but the *tableau vivant* he presented, of free and slave agricultural labor, descended directly from life at Kaskaskia during the third decade of the eighteenth century.

Slave enumerations on the 1726 Kaskaskia census (see Part II) include 129 Africans and sixty-six Native Americans, the majority of the latter women and children.[64] As arable agriculture became an increasingly important component in the region's economy, African slavery became commensurately more important, and African slaves were consistently worth about twice the value of Native Americans, due to their significance in agriculture.[65] By 1752, Kaskaskia's Black slave population totalled 246 souls, while only 75 Indian slaves were enumerated.[66] This revolution in Illinois's agricultural labor force was in full sway during the brief, five-year marriage of Marguerite and Franchomme, and, as we shall see below, their household included both African and Native American slaves.[67]

· · ·

During the second decade of the eighteenth century, the Scottish financial wizard and adventurer, John Law, assumed control of French royal finances under the regency government of Philippe, duc d'Orléans (great cousin to the young king, Louis XV).[68] In 1717, Law oversaw the incorporation of the Illinois Country into Louisiana and turned control of Louisiana over to the Compagnie de l'Ouest, which in 1719 was rolled over into the consolidated Compagnie des Indes.[69] The Compagnie's metropolitan headquarters was in Paris (on rue des Petits Champs, just north of the Palais Royal), while in Louisiana its provincial office bounced around—Dauphin Island, Mobile, Biloxi—until finally settling down at New Orleans (adjacent to the Place d'Armes in the center of town) in 1722. When Pierre Dugué de Boisbriant—who signed his name simply "Boisbriant"—and his cadre of marine officers arrived to take command of the Illinois Country in the spring of 1719, they came under the auspices of the Compagnie des Indes.[70] The dream of turning Louisiana into a North American El Dorado quickly evaporated, the Compagnie gave up on the colony, and in 1731 Louisiana, the land of Louis XIV as proclaimed by La Salle in 1682, including the Illinois Country, once again became a crown colony.[71] The rise and fall of the Compagnie in Louisiana does not impact our story in any material fashion, although it is worth noting that French marine officers in the Illinois Country during the 1720s, whether they were engaging Fox Indians on the Illinois prairie, or adjudicating a succession litigation in Kaskaskia, functioned officially as servants of the Compagnie.

Boisbriant arrived in the Illinois Country from New Orleans in the spring of 1719 and immediately went about erecting Fort de Chartres and establishing a civil government for the region.[72] Antoine de La Mothe Cadillac's mad-cap excursion to the Illinois Country in 1715 had left nothing of any permanence—no protective fort, no organized militia, no governing structure, and no *greffe* (depository for civil records). His single-minded pursuit of gold and silver mines came to nothing.[73] It was only with the arrival of Boisbriant and his entourage of officials in 1719 that notaires began to draft legal records (marriage contracts, real estate transactions, succession documents, slave sales, and so forth) and file them in the local greffe. And, finally, in 1723 the three Provincial Councilors declared French customary law (*Coutume de Paris*) to be the governing legal authority for domestic affairs in the region.

Commandant Boisbriant separated the mission of Kaskaskia from the French village of Kaskaskia; the first was Indian while the second was populated by a diverse mixture of French Canadians, Illinois Indians, and some metropolitan French, both men and women. The mission, which moved a few miles up the Kaskaskia River from the French village, consisted of what remained of the Kaskaskia element of the Illinois Nation. The move was apparently promoted by the local Jesuits, who, for religious reasons, wished to maintain a separate and integrated flock of Native Americans removed from the threat of debauchery and moral corruption presented by transient fur traders.[74] French missionaries had deplored the moral laxity of *coureurs de bois* since Canada's earliest days, and it was axiomatic in early Louisiana that French Canadian traders' pursuit of Indian women was unrelenting.[75] Our own Father Gabriel Marest asked Louisiana authorities to send soldiers to Kaskaskia to prevent French Canadian *voyageurs* from debauching the "wives and daughters" of resident Native Americans.[76]

A "Mémoire concernant les Illinois," written at New Orleans in 1732, explained that the Kaskaskia Indians themselves cooperated in the relocating of their village, "ceding their residential lands to the Canadians [the French inhabitants of Kaskaskia] about twenty years ago and retiring a league and a half from the French, where they still live, numbering about 200 men."[77] No evidence exists that the separation of the two communities was a traumatic affair for any of the parties involved, or that the Kaskaskias objected to relocating. Segregated is too strong a word and has too many modern-day overtones to use in characterizing the separation of the two villages.[78] Constant communication and interchange, personal and commercial, connected the two communities, day-in and day-out, and the French village counted many Indian wives and scores of Métis children.[79]

By 1726, the compact French villages of the Illinois Country (Kaskaskia, Cahokia, and Chartres) could boast a population of more than 500 souls, roughly one-third of them enslaved humans, Africans and Native Americans (see Census). The Kaskaskia and Michigamea Indian villages formed other nuclei of substantial populations,[80] and adding to these more or less permanent residents, itinerant traders and sojourning Indians added size and diversity to the villages. At the same time, the drawn-out war between Fox Indians and their principal adversaries, Illinois Indians and French colonists, was reaching a new and bitter stage. Into this fluid, dynamic but fragile, racially mixed frontier society stepped Nicolas Peltier de Franchomme,[81] a royal marine ensign, only twenty years old, and a provincial but highly intelligent and literate subject of King Louis XV. Franchomme's brief yet tumultuous life in the Illinois Country thrust him into the very midst of the region's most importunate issues: the rule of law, government, Indian-White relations, and the existential question of whether French village life in the region could withstand the desperate push of Fox Indians, who themselves thought that their very existence as a nation depended on crushing French settlements in what is now the American Midwest. Franchomme's life in Kaskaskia properly began with his marriage to an Illinois Indian woman. Such Indian-French marriages were the essential foundations of society when Franchomme arrived in the Illinois Country in early 1723; the village of Kaskaskia was veritably erected upon them. Chapter 2 will explore the nature and quality of three Indian-French marriages that provide the context for the marriage of Marguerite and Franchomme.

CHAPTER 2

Native American Wives
and French Husbands

MARGUERITE 8ASSECAM8C8E AND NICOLAS FRANCHOMME were married at Kaskaskia in September 1723.[1] This marriage, which commands the center of our narrative, was remarkable but not extraordinary, or even unusual, for it occurred in an Illinois Country environment where Indian-French marriages were utterly routine.[2] Jesuits, who accompanied the Kaskaskia Indians on their 1691–1703 migration from the Grand Village on the upper Illinois River to their final settlement on the lower Kaskaskia River, encouraged Christian marriages between couples who were romantically involved, and most of the early marriages at Kaskaskia were between Indian women and French Canadian men.[3] In 1712, Father Marest noted that "the Illinois are much less barbarous than other Savages; Christianity and intercourse with the French have by degrees civilized them. This is to be noticed in our Village, of which nearly all the inhabitants are Christians; it is this also which has brought many Frenchmen to settle here, and very recently we married three of them to Illinois women."[4] Marest claimed that Illinois women had become thoroughly Frenchified before they married French men, but it is not clear if this was always the case.

Illinois Indian women are ubiquitous as brides, mothers, and godmothers in the early Kaskaskia parish registers, and their captivating Indian names leap off the manuscript pages where Jesuit priests faithfully inscribed them.[5] Indian women whose names appear in sacramental records had of necessity been baptized and bore Christian names along with their original Indian names, as in the case of this book's leading character, Marguerite 8assecam8c8e. Many of these Indian women had participated in the downstream migration that led to the settlement of Kaskaskia in the spring of 1703, all were baptized Roman Catholics, all were close to the Jesuit missionaries, all had, in varying degrees, adopted French cultural norms, and many were married to prominent Frenchmen and French Canadians.[6]

Marie Rouensa-8canic8e's successive marriages to Michel Accault (1694) and Michel Philippe (ca. 1703; Census, no. 77) have become legend, and Marie's justifiable fame continues to burgeon among historians, including those in France; everyone wants a piece of her.[7]

But it is the lives of other Illinois Indian women, less famous than Marie but demonstrably important personnages in early Kaskaskia, that provide a more immediate context for our story and are the focus of this chapter. Catherine 8abanakic8e first appears in Illinois Country records as a godmother in a January 1707 baptism of a Métis child at Kaskaskia.[8] Catherine 8abanakic8e was young to serve as a godmother at this time, likely pre-pubescent, although in assisting at a holy sacrament she was serving in an adult capacity. Catherine 8abanakic8e married Louis Tessier at Kaskaskia ca. 1715, although no civil or sacramental record survives to confirm this. Louis was born at Montreal in 1672 into a large extended family, which had left the temperate climes of western France to settle in frigid Canada in the mid-seventeenth century.[9] Louis, like many young French Canadians, had first experienced the Illinois Country as an *engagé* in the fur trade, when he was twenty years old. Marie-Rose was the couple's first child, born ca. 1716,[10] and she grew to ripe maturity as a Métisse in racially diverse Kaskaskia during the 1720s. Marie-Rose married Pierre St. Ange (Census, no. 90) at Kaskaskia in 1732, and she married well, for Pierre was the eldest son of Robert Grotton St. Ange, commandant at Fort de Chartres at the time.[11] A second Tessier daughter was born there, Symphorosam, baptized in February 1717, and a son Paul two years later, in April 1719.

Louis Tessier died at age forty-nine years at Natchez, in June 1721, as he was ascending the Mississippi River, returning from a trading trip to New Orleans.[12] At the time of his death, Tessier stood at the top of the social-economic hierarchy in Kaskaskia society, having an important religious position as church warden (*marguillier*), as well as possessing substantial worldly assets. His death occasioned the drafting of the most important civil record drafted in the Illinois Country up to that time. The document was intended to resolve issues pertaining to Tessier's estate, and it informs us in remarkable ways about the living and the dead, and their relatedness in early eighteenth-century Illinois. Nicolas-Michel Chassin, a member of Commandant Boisbriant's three-men Provincial Council,[13] rode down to Kaskaskia from Fort de Chartres to serve as legal authority and scribe. Chassin had a heavy responsibility to get things done right, and he bent over backwards to be accurate and complete.[14]

Catherine 8abanakic8e (Chassin spelled it "8banakikoy" in this particular manuscript), Tessier's widow, occupies the very heart of Chassin's document. In Natchez, Tessier had, in a clotted voice, informed his trading partners, who were gathered about his death bed and who subsequently completed their river trip back to Kaskaskia, how he wanted his estate handled; he was moving too swiftly toward eternity to summon up the mental and emotional energy to dictate a final will and testament. Tessier, before he died, could only express the desire that "all of his estate's properties, both real and personal, be remitted into the hands of Catherine 8abanakic8e, his wife." There was an important caveat, however—Catherine 8abanakic8e would need help managing her deceased husband's estate, and Commandant Boisbriant was preparing to appoint a person to take on that responsibility. Chassin's language is unclear about whether Tessier had expressed this wish on his deathbed at Natchez or whether Boisbriant had decided this issue on his own accord at Fort de Chartres, but it is clear that Boisbriant himself would select the person to assist Catherine 8abanakic8e with her husband's estate. Chassin's tone is solicitous of Catherine 8abanakic8e, for not only was she a widow with three young children (ages two, four, and probably six), but she could "neither write nor speak French nor [understand] the customs that are observed among us."

Curiously, Chassin did not use the word itself, but he was in fact discussing the appointment of a *tuteur* for Catherine 8abanakic8e. *Tuteurs* (and *tutrices*) assisted minor orphaned children with managing their finances, were an integral part of French customary law, and appear with great frequency in civil records from the Illinois Country. Tuteurs for managing the affairs of minor children were especially important in a society where many parents died before their children reached maturity. In rare instances, tuteurs were appointed to provide assistance to adults who were deemed incapable of managing their own financial affairs, and Catherine 8abanakic8e, lacking fluency in French, manifestly fell into that category. Under French customary law, tuteurs could be designated in final wills and testaments, but in the absence of any such they could also be appointed by a local magistrate (in consultation with close relatives), and in Catherine 8abanakic8e's case that magistrate was Commandant Boisbriant at Fort de Chartres.[15]

In any case, the appointment of a tuteur for Catherine 8abanakic8e (and her children), as well as the compilation of the Tessier estate inventory, would be conducted under Chassin's supervision, in the presence of an august assembly of Kaskaskia's most important citizens: Le Gardeur Delisle, Bourdon, Danis, Barrois, Philippe, and Lamy (Census, nos. 72, 76, 77). Chassin pointedly expressed that all of this was being done "according to the *Coutume*," which meant that he had at least some passing knowledge of the *Coutume de Paris*, the Customary Law of Paris. This is the first mention of the *Coutume* in any known manuscript originating in colonial Illinois, but from this point onward references to this magnificent compilation of French customary laws multiply exponentially in Kaskaskia's corpus of civil records. As for Nicolas Chassin, we shall see that he was destined to spend more time, much more time, burrowing into the *Coutume's* complex, illuminating, and remarkably egalitarian provisions than he had ever imagined when he headed up the Mississippi for the Illinois Country in the autumn of 1718.

The estimated value of the Tessier estate was huge by contemporary norms: Over 20,000 livres, and it included a large house constructed of mulberry posts, a barn, a stable, and a horse-driven gristmill. Six large horses and two young bulls reveal that oxen had not yet supplanted horses (they eventually would) as the draught animals of choice for pulling the heavy charrues employed in the Illinois Country. An assortment of thirteen enslaved people, most if not all of whom were Africans—few were named, and, curiously, none was evidently Indian—was the most valuable portion of the Tessier estate, worth an aggregate of 6,194 livres. Tessier would have acquired the Africans from the Indies Company in New Orleans, which was the principal supplier of African slaves to Louisiana during the 1720s.[16] The marriage of Catherine 8abanakic8e and Tessier, which had endured for only six or seven years, had produced extraordinary wealth by the standards of that time and place. And Tessier's dying words in Natchez reveal his deep understanding that his Illinois Indian wife, Catherine 8abanakic8e, had been his full partner in accumulating this wealth.

The household furnishings and farm implements in the Tessier inventory are overwhelmingly and distinctly French rather than Indian, unmistakably demonstrating that the transformation of Indian-French villages into French colonial villages was swift and radical. This transition occurred during the first decade of the eighteenth century, and as French material goods flowed into the Illinois villages from Canada and, even more from the Gulf Coast, beginning ca. 1700, the domestic comforts of a French rural lifestyle were appealing to Illinois Indian wives as well as to their French Canadian or French husbands. In addition to household goods, the Tessier estate included a fortune in trade goods, some of which would remain in Kaskaskia and some of which would be carried out via riverain trade routes to various Indian villages. These goods included twenty trade guns, aggregately valued at 676 livres; fabrics from France, Germany, Holland, and India, valued at 918 livres; and, of all things, twenty-two handkerchiefs of Indian cotton worth 132 livres.[17] When Tessier uttered his dying words, "Give everything to my wife," he knew that he was making her a very wealthy woman.

Commandant Boisbriant, as chief provincial magistrate, had apparently appointed Jean-Baptiste Guillemot dit Lalande (Census, no. 90) tuteur for widow Catherine 8abanakic8e *and* her three children, which meant that Lalande managed the resources of the Tessier estate on their behalf.[18] Lalande, like Tessier, had been born and raised in Montreal, and surely the men, although of different generations, had been close friends in Kaskaskia before Tessier's ill-fated trading trip to New Orleans. Catherine 8abanakic8e, widow Tessier, and Lalande, her advisor, were married in December 1721,[19] and quickly produced two sons, Marc-Antoine (born in 1723) and Jean-Baptiste (born in 1725) (Census, no. 90). The first's name did not reflect either of the parents' classical learning but came directly from Marc-Antoine de La Loëre des Ursins,[20] one of the triumvirat of the Illinois Provincial Council, who served as the child's godfather. Catherine 8abanakic8e died sometime in the early 1730s—no burial record has survived—after having lived her entire remarkably rich and fulfilling life in Kaskaskia, a village with a human diversity and vibrancy of color like no other North American community at the time.

· · ·

Dorothée Michiper8a ("She with Big Tresses")[21] had a knack for picking good husbands. She married Charles Danis at Kaskaskia ca. 1715, becoming Charles's third wife. Nothing is known about Charles's first two marriages, although those first wives were surely also Native Americans, and very likely of the Illinois Nation. Charles was born at Montreal in

February 1684, and he headed west at an early age as an engagé in the fur trade.[22] Dorothée was born and baptized somewhere along the Kaskaskias' extended route of migration, which ran from the Grand Village on the upper Illinois River all the way to their final destination on the lower Kaskaskia River. Dorothée and Charles eventually produced three children who survived to maturity—Marianne, Charles-Pierre, and Michel (Census, no. 72). Charles Danis had attained the rank of ensign in the militia company of the parish of the Immaculate Conception at Kaskaskia, before he died in July 1724, age forty-one years, leaving behind his Native American wife and three Métis children. His burial under his *banc* in the parish church reflected in death the high esteem in which he had been held in life.[23]

The estate that Charles Danis and Dorothée Michiper8a had built up in their fourteen years of marriage (1710–24) was considerable, and they inhabited one of the grander residential complexes in Kaskaskia, with a house forty-five pieds wide (huge for that time and place).[24] Nicolas Chassin was dispatched forthwith from Fort de Chartres to deal with the Danis estate, as he had been earlier to handle the Tessier succession. The Illinois Provincial Council was taking a direct interest in the inter-generational transference of family wealth, which these succession cases were all about. Upon arriving in Kaskaskia, Chassin deputized a group of six responsible citizens (*commissaires/arbitres*)[25] to plow through the entire Danis estate, detailing every item, inanimate and animate (including slaves, livestock, and real estate), and then divide them into two equal lots—one for the widow Dorothée Michiper8a and one to be shared among the three children; all of these proceedings were effected in exact accordance with the *Coutume de Paris*. In general, French customary laws were more equalitarian in dealing with successions than the English laws obtained in the thirteen British colonies, where widows had fewer rights and eldest sons were still often privileged heirs.[26] Primogeniture, even within the wealthiest families, was unheard of in the French Illinois Country, the mere suggestion of which was considered aberrant.

The commissioners dug into the Danis estate for two long, hot days—Sunday, July 26, and Tuesday, July 28, 1724, although the proceedings were briefly interrupted on Monday the 27 for the important feast day of the Blessed Virgin Mary. Chassin's scribe recorded the proceedings by drafting a document in two discrete columns, with equivalent items on the left for the widow and on the right for the children, the symmetry of the two columns affirming the equivalencies of the values.[27] As each page was tidily inked in with the possessions that had defined the material parameters of the married lives of Dorothée Michiper8a and Danis, Chassin validated the account with his signature at the bottom.

The commissioners' first work was relatively easy and proceeded smoothly: To each lot went a dozen trade shirts; to each "une chemise de naigre [slave shirt]"—one would dearly like to know the difference between a trade shirt [presumably for the Indian trade] and a slave shirt—to each, seven used axes; to each, four bison robes; to each, two Spanish crucifixes; to each, twenty-five pots of bear's oil. "Spanish" may have connoted distinctive stylistic features, or perhaps it merely indicated that the crucifixes were cast of silver. The many trade shirts in the Danis estate and the large quantity of bear oil clearly reveal that Charles had been heavily invested in the Indian trade. Bear oil was highly esteemed in all Louisiana, and according to Paul Alliot was produced in large quantities by the residents of the Illinois Country. "In their forests they find bears prodigiously fat and large, the oil from which is much sought after by the inhabitants, even by those of New Orleans. Although it is very bitter to the taste, it is preferred to the poor oil of Provence [that is, olive oil]."[28]

The bald material possessions of the Danis estate were easily sorted out and distributed, but the commissioners had to ruminate a bit about apportioning, in an equitable fashion, the human property: To widow Dorothée Michiper8a went two "pièces d'Inde," Black males;[29] to the children, two prime Black people, one male and one female; to the widow, a Native American woman about sixteen or seventeen years old; to the children, a Native American boy of ten or eleven years, plus 200 livres in cash. The two prime African slaves were in fact a couple (though apparently not formally married), Estaca and Leveillé— Leveillé meaning "The Watched-Over One"—and they produced a child in February 1726, who was baptized Germain, namesake of his godfather, Germain Boulé (Census, no. 72). In any case, the division of the estate into the two respective lots continued until 6:00 p.m. on July 28, when the commissioners wrapped it up, signed off on the proceedings, and made official the initial division of the Danis property.

Charles Danis's death had left widow Dorothée Michiper8a wealthy, and she was still a young woman. This meant, in Kaskaskia of the 1720s, that she would not remain a widow for long. She soon attracted the attention of the widower Louis Turpain. Human events in Kaskaskia, most governed in one way or another by the *Coutume de Paris*, were moving fast and furiously during 1724, as deaths impelled important citizens to rethink and rearrange their life strategies. On February 24, Turpain's wife, Marie-Magdeleine Coulon (Census, no. 72), had died at age twenty-two.[30] Jean-Baptiste Placé, notaire and deputy of the Provincial Council, soon arrived at Turpain's large house in the center of Kaskaskia with a twofold task: First, to oversee the selection of tuteurs for Turpain's young daughter, Élisabeth; second, to supervise the inventorying of the Turpain estate. Turpain's avowed intention to remarry demanded a complete inventory of the estate, for Élisabeth, although a mere infant, had as the sole surviving legitimate child a legal claim to one-half of the Turpain estate. The *Coutume* dictated this with unmistakable clarity.[31]

Placé had legal status as a notaire, and he oversaw the selection of Élisabeth's tuteurs, who would help manage her substantial financial assets. According to the *Coutume*, widows and widowers were eligible to serve as tuteurs to their own children, but this did not occur automatically—due process was required. Placé drafted the document, and his precise wording is of interest: "Louis Turpain—in the presence of sieurs Brunet dit Bourbonnois, Turpain the elder (Jean-Baptiste Turpain, Louis Turpain's older brother), Loisel, Potier the

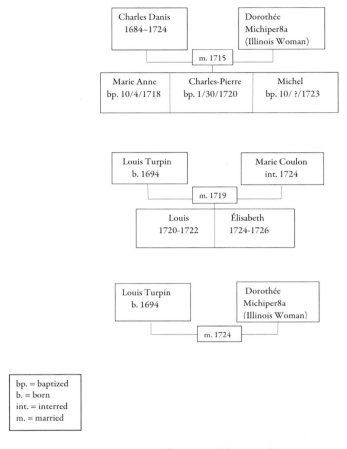

2.1. Pertinent Marriages I

younger, Beauvais, Delauney, and Potier the elder—has been declared tuteur of his minor child, Élisabeth. And they have, among themselves, the assembled friends and relatives, elected sieur Jean-Baptiste Turpain, the child's uncle, as deputy tuteur."[32] The Provincial Council's "magisterial" approval, was technically required to legitimize these tuteurs, but the process of their selection was an exercise in grass roots democracy.[33] This sort of thing occurred on a regular basis in the French villages of the Illinois Country, through which coursed a marked strain of egalitarianism.

Young Élisabeth's tuteurs having been selected, notaire Placé moved on to organizing the inventory, which was a compilation of the entire *communauté* of possessions that Turpain and Coulon had amassed during the five years of their marriage (1719–24).[34] The inventory provides a valuable window into the worldly affairs and lifestyle of the man who became, over three decades, and until his death in 1751, one of the Illinois Country's most important and influential citizens. The outer shell of the couple's residence was constructed of *poteaux-en-terre* (posts-in-the-ground, the most common style of residential construction in the Illinois Country at the time), and the house[35] was situated at the center of Kaskaskia. The structure's terrestrial footprint was thirty-eight by twenty pieds, making it a very commodious residence for that time and that place. The total estate was appraised at 13,530 livres, which, though modest compared to the 1725 estate of the famous Marie Rouensa (45,214 livres), was still very substantial.[36] Moreover, it reveals that a willing man could yoke up a team of oxen to his charrue, tackle the alluvial land stretching, with all of its black richness and promise, out beyond the village of Kaskaskia all the way to the Mississippi River, and make a decent living. These yeoman habitants were the heart and soul of Illinois Country communities, and they constituted the core of the important parish militia companies.

The final inventory left Turpain with half of his estate, 6,765 livres, the other half going to his young daughter, Élisabeth, with Turpain serving as her tuteur. These legal affairs having been resolved, the way was cleared for Turpain, widower, to marry, the very next day, Dorothée Michiper8a, the wealthy widow of Charles Danis. The Jesuit father, Ignace de Beaubois, performed the marriage in Kaskaskia's parish church of the Immaculate Conception. In a nice display of syncretism, the marriage brought together different families and different races, all under the umbrella of a Roman Catholic Church that was managed by ecumenically minded Jesuits; these priests promoted diversity and inclusiveness among their parishioners, not for their own sake but ad majorem Dei gloriam, the greater glory of God. The group of witnesses attending the Dorothée Michiper8a /Turpain union was heavily larded with French marine officers: two from Kaskaskia, Pelletier de Franchomme and Pierre Melique; and three from Chartres, namely, Diron d'Artaguiette, Jean-Georges de Pradel, and Charles Le Gardeur Delisle. These men constituted the bulk of the commissioned French marine officer corps in the Illinois Country, and their graceful signatures ornament the sacramental record of the marriage.[37] In stark contrast to these signatures stood Dorothée Michiper8a's lone X; there is no evidence, either, that any Native American relative was present to lend Dorothée Michiper8a support—moral, spiritual, or even physical. Turpain himself seems to have possessed a certain military bearing, and he would soon be appointed (by the commandant at Fort de Chartres) an officer in the parish militia, eventually rising through the ranks to become captain of the company.

Dorothée Michiper8a had a good eye for selecting husbands from the ranks of Kaskaskia's power elite. On the other hand, Turpain was also choosing well, for surviving records reveal that Dorothée Michiper8a brought more financial assets (including slaves) into the marital communauté than Turpain did. She may have married for status, while he married for wealth; a French Canadian man was shrewdly advancing himself in Illinois Country society by marrying a Native American widow whose first marriage had been a booming financial success. This would be replayed in the case of Nicolas Peltier de Franchomme, who, fittingly, was a witness at Turpain's marriage to Dorothée Michiper8a in September 1724. These processes of marital strategizing tell us a huge amount about the evolution of early Illinois Country society at the highest levels, a society that was anchored by mixed Indian-French marriages.

Many of the legal affairs transpiring in Kaskaskia in the autumn of 1724 revolved around protecting the interests of the three young children of Dorothée Michiper8a and the late Charles Danis. Michel, the youngest (one-year old), was still nursing and was living, fittingly, with his mother Dorothée Michiper8a and her new husband, Turpain, while Michel's somewhat older siblings, Marianne and Charles-Pierre, were living elsewhere, chez Lalande, who had been selected as their tuteur.[38] In the autumn of 1725, Lalande "judged it appropriate" to turn over to Turpain, "their stepfather [*beau père*]," responsibility for the "feeding, support, and education" of the three Danis children.[39] Turpain would be compensated for his efforts with revenues coming from the children's own inherited assets.[40] Turpain obligated himself "to instruct (*instruire*)" the children, or "to have them instructed" in accordance with their status and position for a period of eight years. The verb *instruire* in this context referred to overall raising and upbringing, not necessarily related to any kind of book-learning, or at least that is the way Turpain understood it; for, though literate himself, not one of the three Métis children whom he promised to instruct was ever able to sign her or his name. Dorothée Michiper8a of course provided hands-on instruction in the domestic skills (more French than Native American) that made her one of the most successful women—French, French Canadian, French Creole, Métisses, or Indian—in the entire history of the Illinois Country. Lalande remained tuteur of the three Danis children, and his responsibility was personally to assure that Turpain stood by this guarantee to raise the children properly. The fact that his wife was mother to these children obviously took some of the burden off Turpain's shoulders, for wife and husband worked together as a team in raising the children.

By the summer of 1726, the Turpain-Michiper8a household had been consolidated, both in living quarters and in family unit (Census, no. 72): The couple lived in Dorothée Michiper8a's commodious house with her three children by Charles Danis, and with Turpain's daughter (Élisabeth) by his first wife, Marie-Magdeleine Coulon; Élisabeth's de facto stepmother was Native American, and her household playmates were all Métis. Adding to the size and complexity of the household were two hired hands (engagés), as well as four enslaved people, two Africans and two Native Americans, revealing that Turpain and Dorothée Michiper8a were managing one of the more substantial domestic enterprises in Kaskaskia. The two Africans and one of the Native Americans had all been part of Dorothée Michiper8a's share in the *partage* (division) of the Danis estate that had been effected in July 1724, confirming that Dorothée Michiper8a had brought into her nuptial communauté worldly assets of more value than had her new husband, Turpain.

Turpain and Dorothée Michiper8a made excellent strategic decisions after they united their mortal destinies in marriage at Kaskaskia in the early autumn of 1724. The new nuclear family thus created, thrived, and by the time that the 1732 census of the Illinois Country was compiled, had assumed a major presence in the region.[41] The household was composed of fifteen human beings, including seven enslaved people, four Africans and three Native Americans. Given that Indian slaves were generally used for domestic tasks, Dorothée Michiper8a had a substantial household staff to help out with her growing family, which by now included six children.[42] By 1732, the Turpain/Dorothée Michiper8a family-owned terres (agricultural land) valued at one hundred livres (only the Jesuit establishment at Kaskaskia owned more plowland), and their ten head of bovine livestock was the largest herd in the Illinois Country. Some of these would have been oxen for drawing bulky charrues through the heavy alluvial soils of the Kaskaskia plowlands, while others would have been milk cows. The Turpains had two barns for storing their harvests of wheat and maize (more of the former than the latter), and eight horses, used for powering their gristmill among other things. In short, the Turpains operated a very substantial agricultural establishment, one of the largest grain-producing complexes in all French North America. And some of the wheat flour they milled (mostly with horse-driven mills) made its way down the Mississippi, Louisiana's great fluvial highway, to markets in New Orleans, where there was an insatiable appetite for Illinois agricultural products.[43]

Dorothée Michiper8a died in late 1746 or early 1747.[44] She was one of the more remarkable citizens ever to have graced the colonial Illinois Country—in a league with Marie Rouensa 8canic8e, François Vallé, Marie-Claire Catoire, and Marie-Thérèse Bourgeois Chouteau, and in stature standing head and shoulders above the undeservedly famous Pierre Laclède as an historic personnage. At the time of her death, Dorothée Michiper8a left behind eight surviving children—three by Charles Danis: Marianne, Charles-Pierre (generally known as Pierre), and Michel, and five by Turpain: Marie, Marie-Josephe, Louise-Françoise, Jeanne, and Thérèse, all girls between the ages of six and fourteen. That all of these children, who appear on the 1752 Illinois census as "Mineurs de Louis Turpin,"[45] survived through infancy was utterly astonishing in a society in which the infant mortality rate was above 30 percent.[46] Dorothée, married in succession to two French Canadian men, and bearing multiple children by each, more than any other person was responsible for the burgeoning Métis population that characterized the Illinois Country during the first half of the eighteenth century—and which contributed to a regional sensibility in which skin colors and bloodlines did not preoccupy the daily thoughts of the residents.

· · ·

Marie Apechic8rata's—"She Who Has a Little Nose"—is an odd case.[47] She was a member of the cohort of Illinois Indian women that included Marguerite 8assecam8c8e, Catherine 8abanakic8e, and Dorothée Michiper8a, yet Marie Apechic8rata's name appears only briefly in early Kaskaskia records, in the baptismal records of her children.[48] Her eldest child, Marie-Marguerite, was baptized in April 1720; the infant girl's double Christian name signifying that she was the namesake of both her mother, Marie Apechic8rata, and her godmother, Marguerite 8assecam8c8e, who, at the time, was still married to her first husband, Jacques Bourdon. Despite the rarity of her presence in early local records, Marie Apechic8rata was the only Illinois Indian woman ever to capture the attention of Louisiana's principal governing body, the august Superior Council in New Orleans.

Marie Apechic8rata married a French Canadian, Guillaume Pottier (Census, no. 85), in Kaskaskia ca. 1718. She bore four children between 1719 and 1727, two boys and two girls, although only the boys survived infancy. Pottier, her husband, died at age thirty-five years in 1728, and when his succession was settled in November 1728, his widow Marie and the two boys, Guillaume *fils* and Charles, shared in the *partage* of the estate.[49] Several years earlier, a question arose about Charles Pottier's legitimacy and therefore his right to share in his father's estate—a year or so before his death, his father had drafted a last will and testament (not extant), specifically for the purpose of disinheriting the child, whom his Native American wife, Marie Apechic8rata, was carrying at the time. He did this on the grounds that he was not the unborn child's unnamed father.[50] When the Superior Council in New Orleans finally took up this case, in December 1728, Pottier was already dead and Marie Apechic8rata had already born the child (Charles); a clerk at the Council, however, recorded that "Poirier [that is, Pottier], *habitant* of Illinois, declares that the child with whom his Native American wife Marie Achipicourata [*sic*] is pregnant is not his, and he delegates Sieur [Joseph] de Launay to pursue a charge of bastardy against the child whom his wife will bear."[51]

If the Superior Council had sustained Pottier's charge against his wife, Charles, Marie's last child (probably born in 1727) would have been totally disinherited, for French customary law strictly forbade inheritance by *bâtards*—legitimacy was imperative for the transmission of family name and wealth.[52] But the Councilors flatly rejected the charge of bastardy, concluding that the Pottier marriage had been too messy ("mariage inconstant")[53] for them to make judgments about legitimacy, and that the best solution for the mother and the child—and for the stability of society in French Louisiana—was to declare the child legitimate. The child in question, Charles, was already de facto enjoying his share of Pottier's estate[54]—the Superior Council's decision simply affirmed this sharing, making it legal. Furthermore, the Council required the tuteur of the Pottier children, Joseph de Launay (Census, no. 75), to ensure that Marie Apechic8rata shared in the Pottier estate by receiving an annual pension. This would endure "so long as she remains with the French, whether she remarries or not, but at the moment that she returns to live with the Indians in their manner the said pension will cease to be paid."[55] In other words, to share in her late French husband's estate, Marie had to remain true to a French lifestyle, residing in Kaskaskia as *une véritable française*.[56] But this was, in the Council's words, strictly a matter of residence and culture, not of race or ethnicity.

Marie Apechic8rata did in fact remain as a French *habitante* of Kaskaskia, and she did eventually remarry, bearing with her new husband, Raimond Quesnel, at least one child, Marie-Louise (Census, no. 85). It is not known when Marie Apechic8rata died, but as a Native American woman in the Illinois Country she managed with skill and success an existence within a culturally and racially diverse society, marrying twice, bearing at least five children, and seeing a son (who was perhaps the product of an illicit liaison) legitimized by the highest law court in Louisiana. All of this speaks volumes about Marie Apechic8rata's intellect, energy, and self-possession, but it also says a bit about French colonial Kaskaskia, namely, its diversity, its tolerance (though not on religious issues), and its willingness to accept Native American wives as whole persons, with the same legal rights as French women.

• • •

Illinois Indian women as wives of Frenchmen formed a cadre of female Indian aristocracy within early Kaskaskia society, an elite that set them apart from their Indian male counterparts and in some ways made them superior, economically and socially. This was the world turned upside down, for in the polygamous Illinois tribe women had traditionally occupied distinctly inferior positions.[57] This helps to explain, perhaps, why Illinois Indian women were eager to marry French men. Gilles Havard has thoroughly explicated the reason why Native American women were attracted to French men—they vastly improved their social and economic positions in life.[58] Moreover, these Indian women were baptized Christians, while fewer of their male counterparts were. What Native American men, and for that matter women, thought about this dramatic reversal of positions, as Christianized Illinois women married Frenchmen and elevated their status in early Kaskaskia society, is not known. It must have, however, generated a fair amount of tension, as Indian men watched the most desirable (physically, socially, economically, or all three) Indian women being courted by Frenchmen and routinely becoming their partners in marriage and estate.

The Native American wives of Frenchmen, who are most important to our story, were Domitile Ch8ping8eta—married first to Antoine Baillargeon, then to Jacques Bourdon— and Marguerite 8assecam8c8e—married first to Jacques Bourdon, then to Nicolas Peltier de Franchomme (Census, no. 91), and finally to Pierre Blot (Census, no. 49). As we will see anon, these women occupy the heart of this book. Marguerite first emerges in early Illinois manuscripts as the young wife of Bourdon, and it is to their lives together in Kaskaskia that we must now turn.

CHAPTER 3

Jacques Bourdon in Life and in Death

NORMANDY AND NEIGHBORING BRITTANY provided the largest number of immigrants to French Canada,[1] and Jacques Bourdon *père* arrived in the parish of Boucherville (facing Montreal from across the St. Lawrence River) ca. 1670. Bourdon père was a man of some education and had qualified to serve as *notaire*,[2] an important position in France and throughout French North America. On February 8, 1672, Bourdon père married Marie Ménard in Boucherville, and their third child (of, eventually, fourteen), Jacques Bourdon fils, was baptized on February 18, 1680.[3]

French Canadian youths often preferred the dangers and adventures of fur trading to that of agriculture. The sedentary and arduous life of farming, with the generally thin soils and bitter climate of the St. Lawrence River valley, was not very enticing. Late in the eighteenth century, the French observer Nicolas de Finiels noted that young men in the Illinois Country were toughened by "ascending roaring rivers," adding that a youngster could not avoid taking to the rivers "without facing the scorn of his comrades, which has become a focal point of their rivalry from boyhood onward."[4] Bourdon fils was still a teenager when he left home and headed westward, following the route of the voyageurs up the St. Lawrence River, through the Great Lakes and into the Pays d'en Haut.

Bourdon *fils*—from now on referred to simply as Bourdon—arrived in Kaskaskia early on, shortly after its founding in 1703, when the Indian-French village was a mere embryo of a settlement. Like many other French Canadian voyageurs Jacques was seduced by the rich soil and temperate climate of the Illinois Country, and he chose to forsake his nomadic ways in order to pursue agriculture, in what would soon become the bread basket of French Louisiana.[5] In July 1704, Bourdon stood as godfather at the baptism of Marie Rouensa's son by her second husband, Michel Philippe, and the infant was christened Jacques, namesake of his godfather.[6] Children, both boys and girls, were commonly christened after a godparent in the nascent French Canadian and French Creole society of early eighteenth-century Illinois. Kaskaskia sacramental records reveal that, at that early time, Bourdon was one of the few persons in the community with the ability to sign his name, and he soon established himself as one of the community's preeminent and most respected citizens.[7]

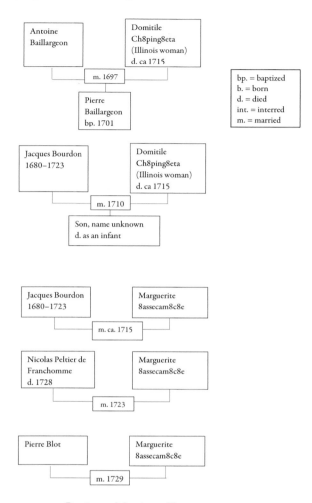

3.1. Pertinent Marriages II

Bourdon's domestic life in Kaskaskia was complicated, but extant manuscripts permit us to unravel a remarkable number of its intricacies.[8] He was married in succession to two Native American women, both from the Illinois Nation. When Domitile Ch8ping8eta—"person with a long visage"[9]—was christened by a Jesuit priest (likely either Jacques Gravier or Gabriel Marest), a Christian name was added to her Native American name. Her Christian name was taken from St. Flavia Domitilla, a first-century Christian martyr, whose fame has now diminished. Domitile Ch8ping8eta's Indian mother and father, unknown to us, had nothing to do with selecting this deeply Christian name, a name only very rarely

3.2. Jacque Bourdon and Marguerite 8assecam8c8e as godparents for Symphorosam, daughter of Louis Tessier and Catherine 8abanakic8e, February 11, 1717. Illinois, Diocese of Belleville, Catholic Parish Records, 1729–1956." Images. *FamilySearch*. http://FamilySearch.org : 14 June 2016. Diocese of Belleville, The Catholic Church of Southern Illinois, Belleville.

selected by French families, either in France or in overseas French colonies. Early Kaskaskia sacramental records reveal that Domitile had married Antoine Baillargeon ca. 1700, bore him a son, Pierre, in 1701, and died before 1717.[10] Their early domestic life transpired at the Rivière des Pères settlement, before they joined in the migration of Illinois Indians, Jesuits priests, and French Canadian traders that culminated with the establishment of Kaskaskia in 1703, a seemingly minor event that carried far-reaching consequences. Source materials for the history of the Illinois Country during the first two decades of the eighteenth century are scarce, but those that exist reveal that Domitile was a major figure in early Kaskaskia. She was already a half-dozen years in the grave when our story begins in 1723, but her presence looms large over the affairs at hand, for her financial legacy, carried forward by her second husband, Jacques Bourdon, suffuses the complicated and contentious legal proceedings that followed his death.

Bourdon's second wife, Marguerite 8assecam8c8e, appears for the first time in written records on April 14, 1715, when she served in Kaskaskia as godmother for the Métisse daughter, Marie, of Augustin La Pointe and Marthe Mer8ki8etam8c8e (Census, no. 59). Bourdon and Marguerite appear together for the first time in a baptismal record of February 11, 1717, when they served respectively as godfather and godmother to Symphorosa, daughter of Louis Tessier and Catherine 8abanakic8e.[11] This baptismal record suggests that Bourdon and Marguerite were, at the time, husband and wife, and likely they had been married shortly before this baptism occurred. Marguerite was a full generation younger than Domitile Ch8ping8eta, Bourdon's first wife, but the two Illinois women had both participated in the extended migration of the Illinois tribe from the Grand Village on the upper Illinois River to the Kaskaskia River site.[12] From what we see of them via extant manuscripts, at a distance of 300 years, the two Native American women had very different personalities: Domitile, assertive, entrepreneurial, and memorable; Marguerite, shy, wily, and seductive, having no trouble attracting successive French husbands.

· · ·

On July 25, 1723, four days before his death, Bourdon dictated a final will and testament that sheds much light on his life, but also on those of many other citizens of Kaskaskia.[13]

The form of Bourdon's will and the process by which it was created were fully in accord with Article CCLXXXIX of the *Coutume*. The document had been dictated by Bourdon himself, and, for lack of a qualified notaire, taken down by Father Nicolas-Ignace Beaubois, who was *curé* of the parish of the Immaculate Conception in Kaskaskia (Census, no. 62).[14] The *Coutume* granted parish curates the right to draft last wills and testaments,[15] and Beaubois drafted civil marriage contracts as well. Bourdon signed his will in the presence of appropriate witnesses, that is, males, at least twenty years of age, none of whom could be beneficiaries in the will.[16] Various provisions in Bourdon's will would eventually be challenged, indeed overturned, but the legal validity of the manner in which it had been drafted was never questioned.

Father Beaubois spelled out Bourdon's situation, physical and mental, in a clear-eyed fashion: Bourdon was a resident of the parish of Notre Dame des Cascakias[17] and captain of the parish militia; he was ill in bed, but his mind and understanding were clear. Bourdon wanted a testament to dispose of the possessions that it had pleased God to give him, for "the hour of death is always uncertain." Bourdon was doing this entirely of his own accord, taking direction from no other person. First, as a good Christian he was consigning himself to God the Father almighty, to Our Savior, and to the Holy Spirit, one God in three manifestations ("*personnes*"); also, to the glorious Virgin Mary, to St. Jacques, his guardian angel and patron saint, and to all the saints, asking them to intercede on his behalf with God for the remission of his sins. He wanted his body interred within the walls of Church of Notre Dame des Cascakias, an honor that could not be denied to a man who was both wealthy and captain of the parish militia.

Bourdon's bequests included 400 livres to the local parish, plus remission of an earlier loan of 115 livres. Two hundred livres would go to the mission of St. François Xavier at the Metchigamia Indian village near Fort de Chartres, and yet another 200 livres to the "Indian mission close to Kaskaskia." Bourdon's bequests make manifest how porous the lines were between French and Native American communities. Bourdon's entire estate was in the French village, and his Native American wife lived in the French village, too, but he had also maintained intimate ties—social and economic and cultural—with the Indian mission community. Indeed, it seems that Bourdon had been about as close to the Indians of this mission as any White man ever was, and that he served as a regular intermediary between village and mission—as, of course, did Jesuit priests who served both communities.

Bourdon's will contains the first appearance of the Saguingora (also Saguingoira, Saguingouara, Sakingoara, Sakinghoara) name in Kaskaskia's civil records, although the name is common in the Kaskaskia sacramental records before that date.[18] On January 6, 1702, while Kaskaskia Indians and French Canadian traders were settled temporarily at the Rivière des Pères, Father Gabriel Marest baptized Marie, daughter of Jean Gauthier dit Saguingora and Marie-Susanne Capei8pei8e.[19] Gauthier, born in Montreal in 1669,[20] had gone west as a fur trader and joined the Kaskaskias sometime during their southward migration in the 1690s. Marest had likely married Saguingora and Marie-Susanne Capei8pei8e shortly before the birth of their daughter, although no marriage record survives. All of Kaskaskia's early families (the best-known being that of Marie Rouensa and Michel Philippe) were headed by Illinois Indian women and French Canadian men. The Saguingora couple, with their growing family (Census, no. 96), must be honored as part of the core group of important families that founded what soon became the undisputed metropole of the Illinois Country.[21] Bourdon was close to Saguingora's family, and, because he had no son of his own, he took their youngest child, Jean-Baptiste, into his household and bequeathed to him in his will 300 livres. Born in 1713,[22] Jean-Baptiste Saguingora's life as a Métis boy in early Kaskaskia intersects with our larger narrative several times and in several ways, and he will appear in it repeatedly.[23]

Pierre Baillargeon—referred to as "Sieur Baillargeon"—was a beneficiary of 600 livres in Bourdon's will. He was a son of Bourdon's first wife, Domitile Ch8ping8eta, by her first husband, Antoine Baillargeon. Antoine Baillargeon first appeared in Illinois Country records when Father Jacques Gravier listed him as godfather in a 1698 baptism at Pimitéoui,[24] also at about the same time he and Domitile Ch8ping8eta were married. Their son, Pierre, was baptized April 17, 1701, at the Rivière des Pères site, and the family was among the original settlers of Kaskaskia in 1703. Upon Antoine Baillargeon's death and Domitile Ch8ping8eta's marriage to Bourdon ca. 1710, Pierre Baillargeon, not yet a teenager, became Bourdon's de facto stepson. Bourdon's dictated words in his will reveal no particular affection for the boy, and it appears that they had never had a warm relationship. Given the size of Bourdon's estate, a mere 600-livre bequest to a stepson was positively galling, as Pierre Baillargeon would eventually point out when he petitioned the Provincial Council to have Bourdon's will quashed.

Bourdon was not generous with Pierre Baillargeon but he was, markedly so, with one Sieur (François) Noyon, "for his good services during my last illness." Such sentiments of gratitude often occupy people on their deathbeds, and Noyon's bequests included both plowland and a small house "close to the stable." Noyon and Bourdon were both natives of Boucherville, and Bourdon's mother had served as Noyon's godmother (Census, no. 95). Noyon will reappear later in our story, for Bourdon named him executor of his estate, and, pointedly, entrusted him to take custody of that portion of the estate being left to Bourdon's parents, who were still alive back in Canada.

Bourdon then requested that the entire remainder of his "goods, plowlands, slaves, cattle, horses, lots, houses, furniture, silver, grains, merchandise, pelts, and outstanding promissory notes be shared equally by his wife, Marguerite 8assecam8c8e, and his father and mother, in such a manner that the house in which he was living would fall to the share of his wife." Bourdon left no surviving children, which meant that *mère* and *père,* back in the St. Lawrence Valley, were in his thoughts. Article CCXVI of the *Coutume de Paris* spelled out the limitations of what a husband could convey in a last will and testament. He could not dispose of personal property held in common with his wife, or real estate acquired

3.3. Pierre Baillargeon baptismal record, April 17, 1701. Illinois, Diocese of Belleville,
Catholic Parish Records, 1729–1956." Images. *FamilySearch*. http://FamilySearch.org :
14 June 2016. Diocese of Belleville, The Catholic Church of Southern Illinois, Belleville.

during their marriage, for such conveyances worked "to the prejudice of his wife." It is not
altogether clear if Bourdon's will protected his wife's interests as fully as required by the
Coutume; probably, it did not. However, Father Beaubois, who drafted the will and who
was by far the most highly educated person present at the will's signing, clearly recognized
Marguerite 8assecam8c8e as Bourdon's principal heir, as would the Provincial Councilors
when the succession was finally resolved in October 1723.

Father Beaubois recorded that he had read and reread the will, clearly and intelligibly,
so that Bourdon fully understood it. But before the witnesses could sign the document,
Bourdon had afterthoughts, not uncommon for folks on their deathbeds. He wanted to
give 1,000 livres in beaver pelts to his brother's son, and a strip of plowland (*terre*) lying "on
the other side of his barn" to Jacques Pottier, his godson (Census, no. 70). Pottier died some
months after Bourdon, in September 1723. Bourdon signed his will, despite his debilitating
mortal illness, with a steady-enough hand, as of course did Father Beaubois. To make things
official, the lead witness was Jean-Baptiste Girardot, "officer in the detachment of marines
and commandant in Kaskaskia." Kaskaskia had had no such officer before 1719, and Girardot's chief task, other than providing a symbolic royal military presence in Kaskaskia, was
to organize the town militia and appoint its officers.

Though the form of Bourdon's last will and testament was perfectly proper and in keeping with the *Coutume*, three of our story's principals—Pierre Baillargeon, Marguerite 8as-
secam8c8e, and Nicolas de Franchomme—had grave questions about the validity of the
specific provisions in the will. No one present at the drafting and signing of Bourdon's
will had any awareness of what was to follow—that this occasion would provoke lengthy,
complicated litigation over Bourdon's estate, leaving a rich paper trail for historians to pursue. And all of this had important consequences for the definitive introduction of French
customary law to the Illinois Country.

. . .

Before Nicolas Peltier de Franchomme's remarkable life in Kaskaskia could properly begin,
that of Jacques Bourdon had to end; Bourdon died four days after dictating his will, at
4:00 a.m., on June 29, 1723, age forty-two. Digging a grave (*fosse*) within the parish church

3.4. Jacques Bourdon's burial record, June 29, 1723. Illinois, Diocese of Belleville, Catholic Parish Records, 1729–1956." Images. *FamilySearch.* http://FamilySearch.org : 14 June 2016. Diocese of Belleville, The Catholic Church of Southern Illinois, Belleville.

under the flagstone floor was no easy matter, and Bourdon had bequeathed one hundred livres for the task, and another thirty-five for the interment itself.[25] The grave diggers were in no rush, and, as in Shakespeare's *Hamlet (*Act V, scene i), were drinking and jesting, about things both mortal and immortal, while they plied their shovels and nipped their eau-de-vie. Grave diggers in early Kaskaskia doubtless had thirst and wit to match those in either Renaissance Denmark or Elizabethan England, for in none of those places was excessive reverence paid to the dead. Father Beaubois officiated at Bourdon's interment at 2:00 p.m. on the day of his death, after "the customary church ceremonies."[26] French colonists laid their dead quickly to rest, reflecting a sensibility that generally adhered to Christ's admonition, "Let the dead bury their own dead" (Luke 9:60), for the living had to move on with the pressing affairs of this world: harvesting crops, cutting firewood, baptizing the new-born.

Deaths in the Illinois Country were usually followed, and quickly, by a comprehensive inventory of the deceased's family's physical possessions. Under the terms of the *Coutume de Paris*, dissolution of the marital communauté required the compilation of an estate inventory, and once the inventory process had begun it had to be officially wrapped up within three months. The surviving spouse was under no compulsion to set this process in motion, but once it had been begun, the law required that it be "done and perfected" within this fixed time period; if not so completed, the communauté simply continued to exist as a legal and financial reality.[27] In the Illinois Country, inventories usually (but not always) followed quickly, within days, or even hours, after the death of a spouse.

On Thursday, July 1, 1723, two days after Bourdon's burial on June 29, local authorities, both civil and religious, invaded his widow's residence—Marc-Antoine de La Loëre des Ursins, first councilor of the Provincial Council, Lieutenant Girardot, military commandant of Kaskaskia, and Beaubois, parish curate, came as a group. In principle, it was up to

Bourdon's widow, Marguerite 8assecam8c8e, to initiate this process, and, in principle, she could have rebuffed the invaders, could have said, "No, wait, I must first tidy up the place for you, distinguished visitors." But it is quite beyond the realm of the possible that Marguerite would have done this. We do not know what courtesies she may have been tendered, if any, but she does not appear in the preamble to the official inventory; the three French officials simply entered "the house of the deceased Jacques Bourdon, captain of the militia, in order to record the inventory." If the assessors did this at the invitation of Marguerite we have no evidence of it. On this occasion, she was an invisible Indian widow, although *tout le monde* knew that she was also exceedingly wealthy.

When Bourdon died in June 1723 his household was likely the wealthiest in Kaskaskia—the initial estate inventory runs nineteen manuscript pages.[28] His worldly possessions certainly mark him as a North American frontiersman, what with the abundance of bison robes, animal pelts, and firearms enumerated in the inventory. But his position as captain of the militia, as well as his abundant plowland and agricultural implements, reveal him at that time as an established and sedentary habitant of Kaskaskia rather than a voyageur coursing the streams of the Mississippi watershed. Moreover, the flavor of the inventory is decidedly French, and most of the material possessions listed might just as well have appeared on a similar notarial document from eighteenth-century Normandy. The inventory does not, for example, reveal that Bourdon's two successive wives were Native American, or that Indian manners, customs, and morals influenced daily life in the household—which they surely did.[29] As Gilles Havard and Cécile Vidal remark succinctly and elegantly about French colonization in the heart of North America, the entire system was "premised entirely on mixtures; for better or worse (in contemporary eyes), the empire could be based only on mixtures—of ideas, of possessions, of flesh, of peoples."[30]

Local officials began their work on the Bourdon estate on July 1, probably right after lunch, for they worked right through the day until 7:00 p.m., having adequate daylight in July at that latitude. They picked up their work at 8:00 a.m. the next morning, July 2, broke for lunch at noon, returned and continued on once again until 7:00 p.m. The same routine was followed on July 3, Saturday, and then Sunday was a day off, dedicated to listening to Beaubois's sermon that morning and perhaps to fishing in the Kaskaskia River that afternoon. Animal remains from archeology done at an early Fort de Chartres site reveal that French colonists in the Illinois Country quickly developed a taste for catfish (*barbue*, that is, whiskered like cats).[31] On the other side of the Mississippi, the Meramec River often appears as Rivière à la Barbue (Catfish River) on eighteenth-century French maps.

The officials plodded on laboriously for five days, working their way through an almost indescribable mass of goods, furniture, real estate, cattle, agricultural products, and enslaved people. The large mass of imported products, especially fabrics and metal objects, in the Bourdon inventory as well as in that of the Tessier succession two years earlier, raises a question: New Orleans had only been established in 1718, so, how could all these European imports have made their way so quickly to the Illinois Country, an onerous upriver trip that usually consumed six to eight months? Some goods, of course, had been laboriously transported down from Canada via the waterways. But another answer lies in an expression that was regularly used in Kaskaskia as a substitute for New Orleans during the 1720s: "*à la mer*" (at the sea).[32] Indeed, during this early period, "la Nouvelle Orléans" appears only rarely in Illinois records. This strongly suggests that material goods were being brought up to the Illinois Country from places like Mobile, Dauphin Island, Biloxi, and Fort Maurepas, well before New Orleans was founded; and, conversely, Illinois products, especially skins and pelts, were being shipped downriver to Gulf Coast establishments. Indeed, in 1705, fifty voyageurs arrived in Mobile from the Illinois Country, and the animal pelts they brought to market on the Gulf Coast would have been exchanged for imported European products to carry back to the Illinois Country.[33] This vibrant exchange economy had become routine by the early eighteenth century.

On July 12, 1723, just two weeks after Bourdon's death, Pierre Baillargeon signed a document in which he formally renounced all claims to anything whatsoever that might fall to him from the succession of his "mother, married in a second nuptial to Sieur Bourdon," with Pierre noting that he was doing this "in order to avoid all lawsuits and disputes with the heirs of [his] stepfather, Sieur Jacques Bourdon."[34] In return for Baillargeon's renunciation the other (unnamed) heirs were willing to remove Baillargeon from the formal succession process by conveying to him "a negro named Robin and his wife, plus one hundred livres in merchandise, which has been bequeathed to me in the will of the said Jacques Bourdon, without prejudice to other bequests which have been made to me." Baillargeon was in a hurry to get things settled and receive his portion of the estate because his wife, Domitile Chacateni8a8a, had just become pregnant with their second child.[35] This renunciation document was drafted and signed by Beaubois, the same Jesuit father who had taken down Bourdon's will, and also signed by Baillargeon himself, as well as by La Loëre des Ursins, Father Jean-Antoine Robert Le Boullenger,[36] a second Jesuit, and by Yves Pinet, the last of whom had also witnessed Bourbon's will. Why des Ursins, who had official notarial powers, left the drafting of this document to Father Beaubois is a bit of a mystery, but the fact that he did so perhaps reduced the legal weight of the document; this soon became an issue of some significance.

· · ·

Work on Bourdon's estate came to an abrupt halt on July 6, 1723. Serious problems had arisen. During their five days of work, in a highly unconventional manner, the officials compiling the inventory had begun to distribute portions of the estate, designating which things would devolve upon which persons named in Bourdon's will. For example, "sixteen slave clothing outfits, half going to the widow [Marguerite] and half to Sieur de Noyon."[37] Noyon received goods both for himself and on behalf of Bourdon's parents back in Canada, for he had been named executor in Bourdon's will. Day after day, as Widow Bourdon's and

3.5. Village of Montmeillant in the Ardennes. Detail of *Cassini Map*, created between 1750 and 1815 by César François Cassini et. al. Library of Congress.

Noyon's piles of goods increased, eyebrows began to arch-up about the way in which the Bourdon succession was being handled, which in turn raised questions about the validity of his will. Folks, including members of the Provincial Council, began to wrestle with legal issues, and everything was put on hold. This wrestling match was all the more confused because of the general ignorance in the Illinois Country of French inheritance and property laws. And then, during the first week in September 1723, the Bourdon succession case was made more complicated, much more complicated, by the marriage of Marguerite 8asse-cam8c8e—Widow Bourdon—to Nicolas Peltier de Franchomme, a royal marine ensign and village newcomer.[38]

• • •

Franchomme was baptized on January 4, 1703, son of Thomas Peltier and Jeanne Douc. His home parish was Montmeillant, situated on the boundary between the Pinot vine-yards of northern Champagne and the pine forests of the southern Ardennes.[39] Indeed, Franchomme later described his father as "general guardian of waters and forests of France, department of Champagne at Montméliant."[40] This meant that his father, and perhaps his mother, may have been literate, and that the family was distinctly bourgeois rather than

3.6. Parish church in Montmeillant, France. Photo Gloria L. Ekberg.

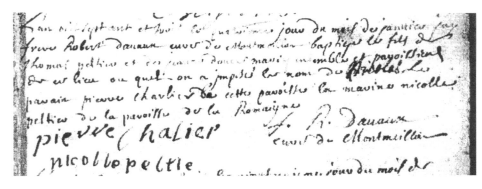

3.7. Baptismal record of Nicolas Peltier de Franchomme, January 4, 1703. Archives départementales des Ardennes, cote edepot/Montmeillant/e2.

3.8. Franchomme's baptismal font, Montmeillant, France. Photo Gloria L. Ekberg.

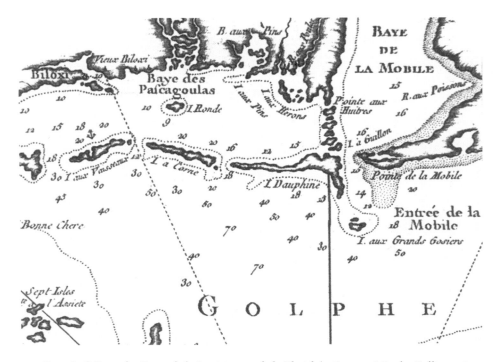

3.9. Detail of *Carte des Costes de la Louisiane et de la Floride* by Jacques-Nicolas Bellin, 1764. Notice *I. Dauphine*, where Franchomme landed in 1720. Library of Congress.

peasant.Bright and remarkably well-educated in a local parish school, and possessed of an adventuresome spirit, Franchomme found village life too confining. At age sixteen, in 1719, he joined the French marines as an ensign and sailed out of La Rochelle, for Louisiana on the *Duc de Noailles*.[41] Franchomme arrived in March 1720 in the harbor on the east end of Isle Dauphine (now Dauphin Island), a barrier island located just beyond the mouth of Mobile Bay. Just having turned seventeen that January, he was mature beyond his years. Stepping onto the sandy shore, Franchomme was greeted by his cousin Jean Jadard dit Beauchamp (baptized at Montmeillant three years before Franchomme), who served for decades at Mobile as a marine officer.[42] Jadard described his cousin's arrival in America: "My cousin, Peltier from Montmeillant, named Franchomme, has arrived here on the ship le *Duc de Noailles*. The best advice I can give him is to go back to France as soon as he can, perhaps even on the ship that brought him here." Louisiana was an impossibly nasty and difficult place, and Jadard was pessimistic about the colony's future, but the French officer had not lost his *esprit gaulois*: "Ninety-six *filles ou femmes* [that is, some virgins and some not] have arrived here, but we have not received foodstuffs sufficient to put us in condition to service them well."[43] One thinks of colonial America as a land of plenty, but French Louisiana was perennially short of foodstuffs, even after regular flour shipments began coming down the Mississippi from the Illinois Country in the 1720s.[44]

Jadard's words of advice to his cousin were dark, hardly encouraging, but the siren call of New World adventure had summoned Franchomme, and he was not turning back. He made his way from Mobile to New Orleans, and ascended the Mississippi River to the Illinois Country.[45] He disembarked onto the left bank of the river, and stepped into a swiftly evolving and tumultuous environment, fraught with existential risk but bursting with potential. Reporting first to Fort de Chartres, Commandant Boisbriant posted Franchomme on to Kaskaskia as an ensign, serving under Lieutenant Jean-Baptiste Girardot (Census, no. 63), village commandant. Coincidentally, Franchomme arrived in Kaskaskia from his native village in the Ardennes shortly before the death of Jacques Bourdon in July 1723.[46] Marguerite, on the other hand, had arrived in Kaskaskia as a child with her migrating nation, about the time the settlement was founded in 1703; by the summer of 1723, she stood out as the young Widow Bourdon. The mutual attraction between the Native American woman and the French man was apparently immediate. Franchomme was a dashing young marine officer, and Marguerite—in so far as these kinds of things can be known, three centuries removed, and with no portraits to aid us—was an attractive woman. Several French commentators remarked that Illinois Indian women had noticeably light skin color, although they did not necessarily valorize that characteristic.[47]

Marguerite was also about to become very wealthy by local standards, as Bourdon's succession was contentiously adjudicated by the Provincial Council. Franchomme's courtship of Marguerite moved swiftly toward culmination during the summer and early autumn of 1723. They were married in Kaskaskia in September, less than three months after the death of Marguerite's first husband. The marriage itself provoked no scandal, for Illinois Country widows often remarried soon after the deaths of their husbands; life on the frontier was more a matter of getting on with the future (which was likely not to be very long) than dwelling on the past.[48] Franchomme was just twenty years old when he married, and Marguerite perhaps a few years older, based on her first marriage to Jacques Bourdon ca. 1715.

The sacramental record of the Franchomme-8assecam8c8e wedding has not survived, but this much about the ceremony may safely be said: Because Father Beaubois was at the time serving as curate of the parish of the Immaculate Conception in Kaskaskia, he would have performed the marriage in the local parish church. Bernard Diron d'Artaguiette commented at about this time that the tithes were substantial in this parish and that the church in Kaskaskia was "certainly the finest in the colony [Louisiana]."[49] Witnesses at the marriage would have included a glittering array of French officials and marine officers: Pierre Dugué de Boisbriant, Diron d'Artaguiette, Pierre Melique—and likely de La Loëre des Ursins, Nicolas Chassin, and Jean-Baptiste Girardot (commandant in Kaskaskia). Whether any of Marguerite's Native American friends (Marie Rouensa, for example) or relatives among the Illinois attended the wedding is unknown and unknowable. In any case, when Franchomme married Marguerite, he committed himself (for he took his promises seriously) to abandoning his French homeland and to spending the remainder of his life in the remote but intoxicating Illinois Country; Marguerite had already given herself over to a French colonial lifestyle (that is, largely French, with substantial riffs of Indianness) when she was baptized a Christian and married Jacques Bourdon.

The original Franchomme-8assecam8c8e civil marriage contract has also not survived, but other legal documents tell us a good deal about its drafting and its salient provisions. Jacques-Nicolas Buffreau de Bellegarde, "a young man who had been commissioned to serve as notaire in the Illinois Country," had drafted a marriage contract for Franchomme and Marguerite in September 1723.[50] The most important (by far) clause in Franchomme's marriage contract was that Marguerite, Bourdon's wealthy widow, granted to the penniless French officer a "donation" of 20,000 livres (a very large sum) in the event that she should die before he did. This did not in fact occur, but no one could have predicted this in September 1723. And when word of this clause in Franchomme's marriage contract made the rounds in Kaskaskia, it provoked an explosive reaction, for the 20,000 livres would of course have to come from widow Marguerite 8assecam8c8e's share of the Bourdon estate. A legal battle over this estate raged throughout the months of September and October 1723. This litigation was of the highest importance, not only for the individuals involved but also for its effects on the legal foundations of the French Illinois Country, foundations that undergirded domestic relations and family property in the region for nearly one hundred years. Pierre Baillargeon, son of Domitile Ch8ping8eta and stepson of Jacques Bourdon, was first to act.

CHAPTER 4

Marguerite 8assecam8c8e Is Attacked

PIERRE BAILLARGEON'S BEST CHANCE to enlarge his inheritance from the Bourdon estate was to discredit Marguerite 8assecam8c8e, Jacques Bourdon's widow. And Marguerite's chance to receive her full inheritance lay in the hands of her advocate, her new husband, Franchomme. Baillargeon soon came to regret that he had signed the renunciation document on July 12 that same year, in which he had forfeited any legal claim on Bourdon's estate in return for a fixed quantity of goods and slaves. Scratching his head, he began to think that as a lawful heir, and with Bourdon having no surviving children, he deserved more, especially in view of the fact that some—perhaps much—of Bourdon's wealth had come from his first wife, Domitile Ch8ping8eta, Baillargeon's mother by Antoine Baillargeon; and just exactly how much wealth would become a matter of contentious dispute. In preparation for a formal petition, Baillargeon solicited depositions from various townspeople in an attempt to demonstrate that the bulk of Bourdon's estate had derived from Domitile Ch8ping8eta, Pierre's exceptional mother. These depositions, all sworn out in Kaskaskia on September 10, 1723, are fascinating historical sources from several perspectives and are central to our story.

First came Jean Brunet dit Bourbonnois, second lieutenant in the Kaskaskia militia (Census, no. 80). He swore that he had ascended the Mississippi "from the sea"—that is, from New Orleans—with Antoine Baillargeon (Pierre Baillargeon's father and Domitile Ch8ping8eta's first husband) with 500 or 600 livres worth of trade goods from France. Brunet and Antoine Baillargeon had deposited the merchandise at the warehouse in the Jesuit compound, a neutral and secure enclave, and the Jesuits had, as promised, delivered the goods to the widow Domitile Ch8ping8eta after Antoine Baillargeon's death, ca. 1710.

Next came Michel Philippe, husband of the now famous Marie Rouensa and first lieutenant in the parish militia at Kaskaskia (Census, no. 77). First, he asserted that most of the large residential property (*terrain*) on which were located the "two houses of the deceased Jacques Bourdon" and all the parcels of plowland (*terres*) of any value belonged either to his first wife (that is, Domitile Ch8ping8eta) or to her close relatives. Second, that Antoine Baillargeon's widow (Domitile Ch8ping8eta) had brought into the marriage a substantial quantity of merchandise. Third, that when she had married Jacques Bourdon, her assets amounted to at least 15,000 or 20,000 francs (that is, livres), including a sizeable number of enslaved people that Bourdon had acquired.

Étienne-Philippe du Long Pré (Census, no. 68) stated that he had arrived in Kaskaskia from Canada eighteen months after the death of Widow Baillargeon—Domitile Ch-8ping8eta, Bourdon's first wife—and that Bourdon, who had not yet married his second wife—Marguerite 8assecam8c8e—was worth 15,000 or 20,000 francs. Furthermore, the said Sieur Bourdon had personally told du Long Pré several times that he had possessed absolutely nothing when he married his first wife, that it was she who had first covered his wretched body with a capot, and that the lion's share of his material possessions had resulted from her industry. Bourdon, in his conversations with du Long Pré, had apparently been painfully self-aware and forthright about his earlier humble circumstances.

Jean du Pré certified that he had observed Domitile Ch8ping8eta as the owner of all manner of material goods when she was Antoine Baillargeon's widow, before she married Bourdon. Du Pré testified that she even lent trade goods to those who importuned her, for she owned a little warehouse, well furnished, and with good merchandise. Although brief, du Pre's deposition is remarkable, for it casts Domitile as one the most successful entrepreneurs in early Kaskaskia. Domitile Ch8ping8eta's may also be the only documented case of a Native American woman occupying such a position of eminence in the history of Upper Louisiana, or indeed of North America.

Pierre Fafard dit Boisjoli (Census, no. 89), the fifth deponent, warrants some discussion, and we must pursue this short diversion within our larger story. Although illiterate, Fafard had been appointed captain of the Kaskaskia militia soon after Bourdon's death in the summer of 1723.[1] So, although an obscure figure to historians of the Illinois Country, Fafard clearly had high status in the community.[2] The Fafards were a Normand family that had been in Canada since the 1630s, and by the late seventeenth century family members were widespread in the St. Lawrence Valley. Master genealogist, René Jetté, claimed that Fafard was the son of François Fafard and Marie Richard, although no baptismal record has survived. François Fafard was an employee (that is, an engagé) in the western fur trade before becoming an interpreter of Indian languages in Detroit.[3] The absence of a baptismal record and Fafard's father's occupations suggest that Fafard may have been the natural son of a Native American woman. In any case, Fafard pushed on farther west than his father ever had and wound up in Kaskaskia, as did many restless and adventuresome French Canadians. His daughter by Thérèse Pat8kic8e was baptized Marie-Anne in Kaskaskia in 1714 as a young child, an indication that Marie-Anne's parents had been living in the wilderness at the time of her birth and had gone to a priest in Kaskaskia to have their daughter baptized when they finally arrived in town in 1714.[4]

Thérèse Pat8kic8e died sometime after the baptism of her daughter, and Fafard married a second Native American woman, Marguerite Anskekae. At the very time, in September 1723, that Pierre Fafard was assisting Baillargeon with his legal problems, Fafard was having serious personal problems of his own with which to cope. The Provincial Council had found, on the basis of written testimony by three witnesses, that Fafard's wife, Marguerite, was guilty of "the crime of adultery." Fafard was given permission to *enfermer* (secure) her for two years—if he could ever catch up with her.[5] That he ever succeeded in accomplishing this is doubtful, for the documentary record on this case goes completely cold immediately after the Council's severe judgment was handed down. Marguerite Anskekae may have simply fled Kaskaskia, perhaps with her audacious lover, and the two of them wound up God only knows where in the vastness of French North America.

In any case, Fafard curtailed his search for his errant Native American wife long enough to give a deposition on behalf of Baillargeon, and he affirmed what the first deponent had already declared. Fafard stated that he himself had ascended the Mississippi with Antoine Baillargeon (three months before Antoine Baillargeon's death), and that when they had returned home to Kaskaskia, Antoine had deposited at least 600 livres worth of trade goods in the Jesuit compound. The fathers were to safeguard the merchandise on behalf of the widow, to whom it was eventually delivered. It seems likely that Antoine Baillargeon had returned from New Orleans to Kaskaskia in poor health, and anxiety-ridden about his impending death he had deemed it best to deposit his merchandise with the responsible and disinterested Jesuit fathers until it could be turned over to his widow, the indomitable Domitile Ch8ping8eta.

With these depositions, Baillargeon was laying the groundwork for his final petition to the Provincial Council. He was absolutely confident about the justice of his case: It was most certainly his mother, Domitile Ch8ping8eta, who had ultimately turned Jacques Bourdon into a very wealthy man. And, given the fact that she and Bourdon had had no surviving children—their one son having died young, perhaps a decade earlier—Pierre Baillargeon had, as his mother's direct heir, a strong claim to a substantial portion of the Bourdon estate, much more than he had been allotted in Bourdon's will or in the financial settlement to which he had naïvely and imprudently agreed on July 12, 1723.

Baillargeon submitted his first petition to the Council on September 11, and his words were visceral and agonized.[6] First he had to deal with the awkward issue of his signature on the July renunciation document, and had to persuade the Provincial Council to render null and void a document initiated by himself. He had signed it, he claimed, despite himself, because he was under great pressure to do so, and because he had thought that he was making a virtue of necessity. Moreover, Baillargeon had only recently received additional information and further clarification concerning the material possessions of his parents (Antoine Baillargeon and Domitile Ch8ping8eta), which had passed on into the hands of Jacques Bourdon, Domitile Ch8ping8eta's second husband, when she died. And lastly, Baillargeon claimed that his signature on a document of such huge importance was not valid since he was still a minor and had not maturely mulled over his own interests, as, he admitted, he should have done. Given that French customary law decreed children to be minors until age

twenty-five,[7] and that Baillargeon was born in 1701, his argument on this point was valid
and would eventually have to be addressed. And, making a final moral and personal point,
Baillargeon alluded to the fact that his own wife—Domitile Chacateni8a8a—had become
demonstrably pregnant in the interim between July 12 and September 11. Pierre was about
to become a father to his second child, and, as head of a burgeoning family, he had urgent
financial issues to consider.[8]

Baillargeon continued his plea: Bourdon's wealth had largely derived, via his marriage
to Domitile Ch8ping8eta, from Baillargeon's parents, and Baillargeon had witnesses to
support this claim. Bourdon's property—both *biens propres* (personal properties) and *biens immeubles* (real estate properties)—were in fact the patrimony of Baillargeon's family,
making Baillargeon the lawful heir. And, in conclusion, Bourdon's widow, Marguerite 8as-
secam8c8e, should receive, in accordance with the "law of the custom" only the amount
of one hundred écus (equal to 500–600 livres). How Baillargeon and his advisor—an
important person to this story, and yet who defies identification—arrived at this figure
is an imponderable. Baillargeon's petition alluded to the *Coutume de Paris* without citing
specific articles, although it is apparent that Baillargeon's advisor had some familiarity with
French customary law. Furthermore, Baillargeon's claim, as the son of Antoine Baillargeon
and Domitile (who were the original sources of Bourdon's wealth) and the stepson of
Jacques Bourdon, had a certain emotive appeal, if not legal weight, especially in view of the
fact that Bourdon and Domitile Ch8ping8eta, Baillargeon's mother, had left no surviving
children.

After the preliminaries, Baillargeon's petition took off on a tear: He wanted Bourdon's
will quashed "in its entirety." Given the fact that the will was a preemptive attempt to settle
the largest estate ever adjudicated in the Illinois Country up to that time, and the fact that
Bourdon as captain of the Kaskaskia militia was a high-status person, this was no light matter. Furthermore, Baillargeon wanted the Provincial Council to suspend the marriage of
Franchomme and Bourdon's widow, Marguerite 8assecam8c8e, at least for the time being,
although Baillargeon adduced no coherent reason for doing so. Baillargeon demanded justice for himself and wanted to take possession of Bourdon's assets, which he would happily
share with the other lawful heirs—that is, Bourdon's parents back in Canada.

The Provincial Council, understanding the importance of the Bourdon-estate affair,
replied immediately to Baillargeon's petition: He should forthwith produce depositions
concerning the wealth of his mother, Domitile Ch8ping8eta, and he should explain how
he had been forced to sign the awkward renunciation document of July 12. Then came a
bit of advice to Pierre from the Councilors, Boisbriant, de La Loëre des Ursins, and Chassin: Step back, cool down, and desist in your opposition to the marriage of Franchomme
and Marguerite 8assecam8c8e; all this gets you nowhere. Baillargeon's demand that this
marriage be suspended was way beyond the bounds of serious discussion. Not only did the
Provincial Council have no authority to undo a holy sacrament, but these Councilors had

also very likely attended Franchomme's wedding themselves, some of them even serving as witnesses at the marriage of a fellow French officer.

Baillargeon took the Council's advice to heart. He went back to his advisor—or perhaps sought out additional legal help—to counsel him and assist in drafting a lengthier and more sober petition, which occupied several weeks.[9] To dress things up a bit in a professional fashion, Baillargeon's new petition used the Latinate "Factum" (statement of facts) as a heading, and he specified clearly that this was a case "against Widow Bourdon, Marguerite Wassacamw (Pierre's spelling of 8assecam8c8e)." This petition was of "the greatest consequence," for it required the quashing of Bourdon's will and reduction of Marguerite's share of the estate to one hundred écus. Baillargeon and his advisor never did explain how they arrived at this seemingly random figure, but they reiterated it.

In his second, more carefully drafted petition, Baillargeon stepped back from his original demand that Bourdon's will be quashed in its entirety. Baillargeon explained that he had no objection to the "pious bequests"—he was apparently thinking of those designated for the parish and the local Indian missions—included in Bourdon's will; indeed, he was disposed to increase them "out of the tenderness of his heart and in recognition of his stepfather [Bourdon], despite the grievous injustice that Bourdon had inflicted on him while he was dying." Baillargeon also had no objection to Bourdon's bequest to Noyon for the long-time services he had rendered to Bourdon, "especially during his last illness." And, finally, Baillargeon did not object to Bourdon's father receiving one-half of all his possessions; for, in view of the fact that Bourdon had no surviving children, his father was "a presumptive heir according to the law." Baillargeon's advisor clearly understood that French customary laws were relevant to the case he was arguing, although he was unable to adduce them verbatim or cite a specific article by name or number. Yet his argument here, referencing customary law, had some validity: Article CCCXI of the *Coutume* provided for inheritance by ascendants, namely parents and even grandparents should children die without leaving their own legitimate children as heirs, which had indeed happened to Bourdon.

The fundamental problem with Baillargeon's argument was that it neglected to mention that Bourdon had remarried, and, as we shall see, *that* changed everything. Then, somewhat contradictorily, Baillargeon took out after Bourdon's second wife, Marguerite 8assecam8c8e, and demanded to know by what right she should receive half of Bourdon's estate when "these possessions were truly the possessions of Baillargeon's mother, Domitile Ch8ping8eta, the first wife of Sieur Bourdon." Behind the verbose legal wrangling, it is abundantly clear that Baillargeon, during his teenage years, had been at daggers-drawn odds with his stepfather Bourdon and, especially, with Bourdon's young second wife, Marguerite. The *other* Illinois Indian woman—Domitile Ch8ping8eta, Baillargeon's mother—dominated Baillargeon's narrative as heroine.

Domitile, according to Baillargeon, had inherited "all the possessions" of her deceased husband, Antoine Baillargeon. This was of course not technically correct, for Baillargeon would have had a stake in his dead father's possessions whether or not his mother remarried. But ignoring this little detail, Baillargeon plunged ahead to paint a glowing portrait of his mother. She was an "energetic and industrious woman, who, far from carelessly running through what her husband had left *as all the other Illinois women did* [italics added], had, on the contrary, nurtured and fructified her possessions." Domitile Ch8ping8eta had commenced her widowhood (after the death of her first husband, Antoine Baillargeon) with a mere 500 or 600 livres, which—"according to the attached depositions"—she had husbanded and multiplied into 200 pistoles (2,000 livres) before she married Bourdon. As for Bourdon, he had always acknowledged that it was Domitile Ch8ping8eta who had provided him with the first capot ever to cover his wretched body, and that the wealth he had accumulated through trade was founded on her initial resources.

If a proper reckoning, *"un inventaire,"* of the Ch8ping8eta-Bourdon estate had been done when Domitile Ch8ping8eta died, Baillargeon argued, he would have received one-fourth, Bourdon one-half, and Baillargeon's half-sibling—the deceased child of Domitile Ch8ping8eta and Bourdon—one-fourth. Once again, Pierre failed to acknowledge that Bourdon, when remarried, had automatically created a new communauté. Baillargeon's arguments consistently gave short shrift to Marguerite 8assecam8c8e, whom he was hoping to brush aside as an obstacle to his claims. In any case, in Baillargeon's estimation, Domitile Ch8ping8eta's wealth would have swollen "in the hands of Bourdon," who at the time of Domitile's death was Baillargeon's stepfather and his tuteur.[10] But since no reckoning had taken place, the community of possessions (communauté) that had existed in the Bourdon-Ch8ping8eta marriage continued to exist as if Domitile had not died. And when this community was finally de facto terminated with the death of Bourdon, Pierre, given the earlier death of his half-sibling, stood to inherit the entirety of the possessions contained in the Bourdon- Ch8ping8eta communauté. This was all well and good, except for the fact that no final reckoning, commencing with a comprehensive *inventaire*, had terminated this communauté. And when Bourdon remarried—when he married Marguerite 8assecam8c8e—the old marital communauté was spontaneously rolled over and subsumed within the new one (*Coutume*, Article CCXLII).[11]

Baillargeon further argued that all of the real estate in the Bourdon-Ch8ping8eta communauté had come from Domitile Ch8ping8eta, and real estate must be deemed "patrimonial," meaning that a son could not be denied his claim to it unless reasonable cause could be adduced to disinherit him. In this last point, Baillargeon was suggesting that in some sense the real estate in question was of aristocratic origin, that it constituted a manorial fief, in which case an eldest son had certain preemptory rights according to the *Coutume*.[12] Baillargeon's patrimonial claim to the real estate from the Ch8ping8eta-Bourdon succession was total nonsense—but it was an ancillary element in his larger case against Marguerite 8assecam8c8e, Widow Bourdon, whom Baillargeon portrayed as a conniving, greedy woman, laying claim to possessions that should rightfully pass down only through the male line of succession. Baillargeon's fantasies about patrimonial succession were completely at odds with the entire thrust of the *Coutume*, which, when dealing with intergenerational transfer of wealth via succession, emphasized equal division of family assets among the children, regardless of age, sex, or marital status.

Baillargeon acknowledged that Domitile Ch8ping8eta and Bourdon had never gone through the formality of having a marriage contract drawn up, but noted that in the good ol' bygone years, folks in Kaskaskia had been ignorant of such legal intricacies, and that, furthermore, no one, that is, a proper notaire, had been available to draft such a contract. "Good faith had been the guide to their affairs, and they were not encumbered by legal formalities."[13] Everyone understood that a communauté of possessions had existed between Bourdon and Domitile—despite the absence of a marriage contract—and that that communauté, of which Baillargeon was the sole surviving heir, had persisted right on down to the moment of Bourdon's death. This meant that Bourdon's will had deprived Baillargeon of his "natural inheritance," and this "to satisfy a woman [Marguerite] who had no rightful claim to anything other than the *douaire coutumier* [customary dowry] from her marriage to Bourdon. Her marriage to Franchomme was not sufficient to create a second communauté, prejudicial to the first." The last sentence was in fact the kernel of Baillargeon's argument—that the Franchomme-8assecam8c8e sacramental marriage had not effectively created a civil community of possessions between the principals. Baillargeon and his advisor simply refused to acknowledge the existence of Article CCXLII of the *Coutume*, which specified precisely how communautés were rolled over into successive marriages.

Baillargeon's reference to an earlier, simpler, rosier, less complicated time in the Illinois Country, when naïve good faith between neighbors had guided all townsfolk in conducting their affairs, is intriguing. He was surely referring to the period before Commandant Boisbriant, with his administrators and officers, had arrived with notaries, law books, rules, and regulations. Baillargeon's remarks reveal a fissure in the community between the traditionalists, the long-time residents (some going back to Kaskaskia's origins in 1703), and the officious newcomers who wanted to take charge and put things in proper order. Not coincidentally, all five men who had sworn out depositions on Baillargeon's behalf on September 10 were members in good standing of the traditionalist faction.

Grasping at straws, Pierre decided to engage in some vernacular psychologizing, claiming that after Bourdon dictated his will, he had begun to have second thoughts about what he had done; indeed, that he had experienced *peines d'esprit* (mental anguish) in the days leading up to his death. Furthermore, those who had counselled Bourdon about the fateful clause in his will that favored his second wife (Marguerite 8assecam8c8e) were, Baillargeon claimed, ready to attest that they had been mistaken; that, had they had any idea about the size and scope of Bourdon's estate, they would not have advised Bourdon as they had.

Baillargeon then moved on from Bourdon's state of mind to his own mental state when he had signed his renunciation, on July 12, 1723, of all claims to the Bourdon estate in return for a defined quantity of goods and slaves. He had, Baillargeon claimed, signed the document *à contrecœur*, contrary to his true heart. Baillargeon acknowledged that no "physical violence" had been employed to force him to sign, but that such coercion was not necessary when it came to a person like Baillargeon, who was like a simple, ignorant child, and whom everyone agreed was the least self-interested person in the world. All the brain-numbing discussions about legal issues with which he was not familiar constituted a certain kind of mental and emotional coercion that rendered his signature on the renunciation document null and void.

Baillargeon's final plea was on behalf of his unnamed daughter—the coming child with whom his wife was pregnant at the time. She, or Baillargeon on her behalf, had every legal right to have Baillargeon's renunciation annulled, for Baillargeon had no legal authority to sign a document that adversely impacted the inheritance rights of his children; that is, the father had no right to alienate property that would eventually become the lawful inheritance of his offspring. This was in fact a legal argument of some merit within the context of French customary law, which consistently defended the property rights of children, both male and female. The *Coutume*, fundamentally, was all about transfer of family assets down through the generations—all generations, not simply the male line. Baillargeon summed up his case, demanding that Jacques Bourdon's will should be quashed and annulled, and that "the widow should be *assujettie* (subjected) to the law as any French woman would be."[14] Here, Baillargeon implied that Marguerite 8assecam8c8e's large claims against the Bourdon estate put her outside of the law, that she was indeed a bit of an outlaw *sauvagesse*, and that the rule of law must be applied to bring her back into line. Pierre and his advisor had only some vague sense of which law they were referring to, but in their "Factum" they several times referred to *le droit* (the law) and they insisted that society in Illinois Country should be a proper French society, governed by objective facts and established laws rather than by greed and personal caprice.

Baillargeon's attack on Franchomme's wife launched, for the first time in the short history of the Illinois Country, a serious legal debate. A war of wits and words was joined, and Franchomme became as passionately engaged as Baillargeon.

CHAPTER 5

Franchomme Prevails

T HE PROVINCIAL COUNCIL DELIVERED BAILLARGEON'S "FACTUM" (perhaps by special courier from Fort de Chartres to Kaskaskia) to Marguerite 8assecam8c8e in September 1723. She, Widow Bourdon and newly married wife of Franchomme, was faced with responding to Baillargeon's biting personal criticisms of her. She, naturally, turned to her French husband to handle this unprecedented case on her behalf. Surviving documents do not permit us to establish a precise timeline for these legal proceedings, other than to say that they all transpired within a six-week period between September 11 and October 22, 1723. Among the issues that slowed down the process was the four-hour ride between Kaskaskia and Fort de Chartres, where the Council sat and where the Illinois Country's only printed copy of the *Coutume* was available in Commandant Boisbriant's office.

Franchomme was a young man of wit and intelligence. Although he had been born and raised in a provincial village, he had obtained some formal education and even owned a small collection of books.[1] In other words, Franchomme was intellectually equipped to argue his wife's legal case before the Provincial Council. He began his response to Baillargeon's petition by flatly agreeing that the matter at hand was *à la dernière conséquence* (of the greatest significance). It certainly was to Franchomme, for if his new wife were reduced to receiving only one hundred écus from the Bourdon estate, the couple would be rendered pretty much destitute; Franchomme himself had arrived in America penniless. Franchomme then had a field day, slashing Baillargeon's "Factum" to ribbons, repeatedly adducing French customary law, article by article, to accomplish this. The *Coutume de Paris* had been briefly noted by name in earlier notarial records from the Illinois Country,[2] and Baillargeon's "Factum" had made general references to "French customary law." Franchomme's brief, however, is the earliest existing document from the Illinois Country to delve deeply into the *Coutume*, making it a valuable source for historians. Curious indeed that this delving would be done by a young French marine rather than by a *notaire* or an *avocat* (lawyer), making Franchomme's short life in North America all that much more remarkable.

During those six weeks in September and October 1723, Franchomme was absorbed
to the point of exhaustion paging through the *Coutume*, cover to cover, with, alongside it
on his desk, Baillargeon's "Factum." Having received some formal education in his native
parish of Montmeillant, and having come from the Ardennes-Champagne region, he also
would have had a general idea of the major provisions of French customary law; Champagne had its own set of customary laws, similar to but not identical to those of Paris and
the Île de France.[3] Baillargeon's claim that widow Bourdon's *douaire coutumier* amounted
to only one hundred écus was just plain nuts, Franchomme pointed out, for Article CCXL-
VIII of the *Coutume* states clearly that this dower amounted to one-half of the total succession, and that it was in play immediately upon the sacerdotal act of marriage. Franchomme then went on to ridicule Baillargeon's contradictory request that Bourdon's will
should be entirely quashed, except that it should not be; that is, Baillargeon wished to leave
Bourdon's bequests to Noyon intact, or perhaps even increase them a little. Franchomme
pointed out that these bequests raised legal problems, for Article CCXCVI of the *Coutume*
states that a husband cannot via a will or testament alienate *meubles* (personal property) or
acquired—meaning, not inherited by him—*immeubles* (real estate) from the communauté
in a manner prejudicial to his wife.

Franchomme thereupon set about examining just exactly what his wife, Bourdon's
widow, deserved to receive according to the *Coutume de Paris*. He stipulated that Baillargeon's "Factum," where it described Pierre's mother, Domitile Ch8ping8eta, was quite
true; everyone agreed on that. The woman had exhibited sterling qualities, and by virtue of
her industry the 600 livres she had received upon the death of her first husband, Antoine
Baillargeon, had increased to 2,000 when she married Sieur Bourdon, her second husband.
Franchomme further stipulated that Bourdon was destitute when he married Domitile
Ch8ping8eta. However, he argued that these facts had no bearing on the inheritance case
of his wife, Marguerite 8assecam8c8e. Franchomme pointed out with great precision how
Baillargeon had misconstrued the *Coutume*, attempting to cut Marguerite out of Bourdon's
succession. Baillargeon's fundamental error was to deny a legal reality—that the communauté of possessions from the marriage of Domitile Ch8ping8eta and Bourdon had been
automatically rolled over and subsumed within Bourdon's next marital communauté—that
with Marguerite 8assecam8c8e—as specified in Article CCXLII of the *Coutume*. Marguerite could not simply be pushed aside at Baillargeon's convenience.

Franchomme picked up Baillargeon's comments about an earlier, kinder, gentler, more
neighborly time in the Illinois Country, and possessing a native-born Gallic wit, he could
not resist mocking him: "It certainly appears by the author's tone in the 'Factum' that the
good faith, which, according to him, once ruled among residents of this region no longer
obtains, and that a spirit of chicanery has taken over." (Chicanerie is used more often in
French than its counterpart is in English, and has a more biting, pejorative tone to it.) But,
in addition to having some fun at Baillargeon's expense, Franchomme was driving home a

serious point: Baillargeon's criticism of the new order in the Illinois Country was an attack on the members of the Provincial Council, as well as on himself personally, and of course Franchomme's words were addressed directly to the Council.

So, Franchomme wrote in a most lawyerly fashion, "let us examine the communauté that had existed among Jacques Bourdon, Domitile Ch8ping8eta, and Pierre Baillargeon." It had begun with Bourdon and Domitile Ch8ping8eta's marriage in the amount of 2,000 livres, which had grown to 20,000 livres by the time Domitile Ch8ping8eta died. She left as heirs Bourdon, her husband, a child (who died shortly after Domitile Ch8ping8eta) that she had had by Bourdon, and Pierre Baillargeon, a product of her first marriage to Antoine Baillargeon. If a proper inventory had been compiled at the time of Domitile Ch8ping8e-ta's death, Franchomme acknowledged, Baillargeon would have received his fair share of the estate. But Franchomme complained that he was frankly put out having to deal with all the meaningless "verbiage" of Baillargeon's "Factum," and pointed out that two articles in the *Coutume* explained with great clarity the property issues involved in Bourdon's two marriages.

Article CCXX of the *Coutume* declared that no civil marriage contract was necessary to establish a communauté of possessions between married persons, for the communauté was created automatically and instantaneously at the moment the sacrament of marriage was performed; no written contract was necessary for the spontaneous generation of the marital communauté. The *Coutume*, which was essentially a compilation of civil, domestic law, was, in this instance, dependent upon a sacrament of the Roman Catholic Church, with the underlying assumption being that everyone involved was of the Roman Catholic faith. "A man and woman joined together in marriage hold in common their moveable possessions and their immovable possessions acquired during the marriage, and the community commences the day of the marriage and the nuptial benediction."[4] The learned jurist Claude de Ferrière (1639–1715) elaborated on this categorical statement in his *Nouveau Commentaire*: "This society [that is, the communauté of possessions] is contracted either by an express stipulation or by the existence of the customary law wherever the marriage occurs, *without* [emphasis added] any agreement on the part of the contractants."[5] So, despite the absence of written marriage contracts, communautés had existed in both of Bourdon's marriages, that with Domitile Ch8ping8eta and that with Marguerite 8assecam8c8e.

Franchomme specifically adduced Article CCXLII of the *Coutume* to the effect that the Bourdon-Ch8ping8eta communauté had been continued and subsumed within the Bourdon-8assecam8c8e communauté, although in referencing this article, Franchomme tacitly acknowledged that Baillargeon was eligible to receive *some* portion of the Bourdon estate. Then, throwing Baillargeon's words back in his face, Franchomme proposed that, yes, indeed, Bourdon had indeed been afflicted with a troubled spirit on his deathbed, but not because of anxiety over what he had inscribed in his will. Rather, Bourdon, on his deathbed, had feared that Baillargeon would indulge his ingratitude so far as to try to deprive Bourdon's widow (that is, Franchomme's wife) of what was rightfully hers, while forgetting all that Baillargeon owed Bourdon, who, as Baillargeon's stepfather, had always nurtured him.

Franchomme concluded his response to Baillargeon's "Factum" by requesting that the Council reject Pierre's claims, and that Franchomme's wife, Marguerite 8assecam8c8e, be left in peace to enjoy the possessions that were rightfully hers; and all the more so, because "a majority" of these possessions had been acquired since her marriage to Sieur Bourdon. Whether or not this was true is questionable, for it is unclear whether the bulk of Bourdon's wealth had been accumulated during his marriage to Domitile or during his marriage to Marguerite. And speculation is even difficult, for we do not know when Bourdon married Domitile Ch8ping8eta, when she died, or when, precisely, Bourdon married Marguerite. In any case, if Baillargeon obstinately persisted in his "unjust" demands, Franchomme wanted him to pay damages and interest. The Provincial Council in turn submitted Franchomme's response to Baillargeon on September 23, 1723. It had taken twelve days, with much riding back and forth between Kaskaskia and Fort de Chartres, for Baillargeon's petition and Franchomme's response to make their way through the Council's deliberative process. But the wheels of justice were turning, however slowly, in an Illinois Country, which after two decades of a helter-skelter legal regime, was finally being governed by royal administrators, active and well-intentioned, although with little formal legal training.

Baillargeon and his anonymous advisor agonized over Franchomme's biting response for a day or two, and then they decided just to let it pass, by simply not responding. Baillargeon did not wish to expose himself and his "author to any further insults from Francôme [*sic*]." The author in no way deserved the "gross insults" that Franchomme had heaped upon him, and, moreover, neither Baillargeon nor his collaborator had access to the sources necessary to verify Franchomme's legal citations. Unlike Franchomme, who was riding up the region's trunk road between Kaskaskia and Fort de Chartres to consult legal texts in Commandant Boisbriant's office,[6] Baillargeon and his advisor remained close to home in Kaskaskia. This situation obliged Baillargeon simply to throw himself on the mercy of the Councilors: "You are aware of the facts and the circumstances; you know Baillargeon's rights and the justice of his claims; you have the laws and your consciences. Have the goodness to adjudge to him that which belongs to him."[7]

The Councilors—Boisbriant, de La Loëre des Ursins, and Chassin—rendered a quick, preliminary and narrow judgment on September 25, 1723: Pierre Baillargeon was to permit Bourdon's widow (and Franchomme's new wife) to enjoy what belonged to her as a consequence of Bourdon's death, that is the *douaire coutumier* (dowry) defined as one-half of the inventoried estate. The other half of Bourdon's estate would remain for the time being in the custody of the executor named in Bourdon's will, namely, Sieur François Noyon. The Councilors made no mention about qualifying the various provisions in Bourdon's will, and they did not entertain the question concerning the validity of Pierre's signature on his renunciation document. More remarkably, they did not mention by name the *Coutume de Paris* or specify any of its provisions. However, three fundamental articles of the *Coutume*—CCXX, CCXLVII, and CCXLVIII—lay behind the Council's preliminary judgment: A communauté of possessions existed within a marriage from the moment of the nuptial benediction, even if no marriage contract had been signed; a wife had a right to the *douaire coutumier*, even if no marriage contract existed; the *douaire* consisted of one-half of the value of the communauté at the time a husband died. Whatever else happened, Widow Bourdon—Marguerite 8assecam8c8e—and now Franchomme's wife, was assured of receiving one-half of the Bourdon succession. The missing legal link in the Council's decision was how Article CCXLII regarding remarriages bore on this case; the Councilors were avoiding those complications for the time being. In any event, Baillargeon's attempt to have this Illinois Indian woman cut out of Bourdon's estate had been thwarted by the Provincial Council—and by Franchomme's articulate defense of his wife's rights, which of course weighed on him personally as her spouse.

The legal case concerning Bourdon's succession provoked much gossip on the dusty byways of Kaskaskia in late September 1723. Baillargeon, hearing rumors about which way the Council was leaning and fearing that his last plea had been too passive and ambiguous, decided to submit a final entreaty: He wanted it clearly understood that it would be "grievously prejudicial" to himself and other claimants to the Bourdon succession if the widow were to receive half the estate. He wanted the issue resolved definitively (*"un jugement décisif"*) and was only asking that his lawful rights be protected. He was throwing himself on the mercy of the Council and counting on its integrity to render him justice.[8]

The three Provincial Councilors broke out their printed copy of the *Coutume*, read from it selectively, scratched their heads, and set about ruminating over intricate issues of French customary law. None of these men was an avocat; indeed, avocats were prohibited in French Louisiana in the hope of fostering a less quarrelsome and litigious society.[9] In the absence of avocats, notaires were the highest-ranking legal officials in Louisiana. Notaires were hugely important cogs in the French legal machinery—as they remain to this day—vastly more important than notaries in England or America.[10] Both des Ursins and Chassin served on occasion as notaires, but it is not clear that either of them had undergone formal legal training of any kind. Rigorous qualifications and prohibitions defined the notarial profession in France. Royal notaires could be neither ecclesiastics—the Church had its own notaires, specialists in Canon Law—nor Protestants, and surely not Jews.[11] Candidates had to have achieved majority (twenty-five years), be of good moral standing, have the requisite intelligence, and serve a five-year apprenticeship with a senior notaire.[12] All of this was well and good in metropolitan France, but things were more slap-dash in the Illinois Country, where rules sometimes had to be bent in order to sustain a viable social organism in a tumultuous frontier environment. Chassin himself acknowledged in 1722 that "Jesuits . . . have up to now functioned as notaries. But now I have been assigned

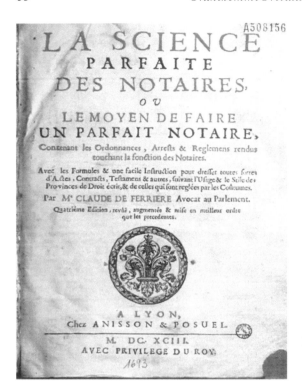

5.1. *La Science Parfaite des Notaires,
ou le moyen de faire un notaire
parfait,* textbook for royal notaries,
the highest-ranking legal officials in
French Louisiana. (Lyon: Anisson
& Posuel, 1693)

[apparently by Boisbriant] this duty, until the Company [Indies] sends over someone more expert than me."[13]

 In any case, the Councilors required a month to dope out the various legal complexities as best they could. The bitter controversy over Jacques Bourdon's will provoked the first thorough scrutiny of French customary laws in the Illinois Country. Such scrutiny was bound to have come sooner or later, for there was gathering awareness within the local governing elite that if French civil society and civilization were to thrive in the region—and that was their earnest hope—these laws had to be understood and implemented with as much exactitude as possible. The Councilors were forced to absorb the various charges and countercharges presented, place them within the context of their understanding of the *Coutume*, and finally render a verdict, which they did on October 22, 1723.[14] "Widow Bourdon will receive one-half of the possessions from the estate in accordance with the *Coutume de Paris*"—here, the Councilors noted the *Coutume* by name without adducing a specific article. Furthermore, considering that Jacques Bourdon had left no surviving children—a son by Domitile Ch8ping8eta had died as an infant—"we order that the other half of the estate shall be divided equally between Pierre Baillargeon and Bourdon's father, or other heirs of the late Bourdon." The Councilors were a bit sexist when they adduced Bourdon's father but not his mother, Marie Ménard, who was still very much alive and well at the time.

If anyone in Boisbriant's office at Fort de Chartres raised his voice and dourly noted, "But, ahem, Marguerite is not a French woman but an uncivilized *sauvagesse*," this issue was peremptorily brushed aside. Marguerite 8assecam8c8e had been Bourdon's lawful Christian wife, period. The cosmopolitan men deliberating in Boisbriant's office wished to bring human beings into the expansive realm of French civilization—not push them out, not exclude them. The Councilors all having been born and raised during the reign of the Sun King, Louis XIV, they understood intuitively that French civilization was the ne plus ultra, with an implicit imperative—"suffer others to come into our realm"—even if this imperative might sometimes require force of French arms. In the case at hand, however, this simply meant accepting Marguerite as a legitimate member of French society. This decision in effect recognized Marguerite's status as a *Régnicole* (see chapter 9), a naturalized citizen of France, subject to French laws and also beneficiary of such laws. Her situation—widow of a Frenchman and a baptized Roman Catholic—dictated this; her Indian background and the color of her skin did not matter whatsoever. The three Councilors were making case law history for the Illinois Country with this decision, proclaiming how Native American women could become French.[15] Very likely they, while working to resolve a particular, provincial problem, were quite unaware of the potentially wide-ranging implications of their decision; they were simply applying French customary law to a local situation in ad hoc fashion. Happily, all this occurred in the same year that Louis XV achieved his majority, although it is doubtful if anyone in Kaskaskia at the time knew that this occasion warranted a riotous celebration.

The three Councilors had faced the daunting task of resolving simultaneously three entangled successions—that of Antoine Baillargeon and Domitile Ch8ping8eta, that of Jacques Bourdon and Domitile Ch8ping8eta, and that of Jacques Bourdon and Marguerite 8assecam8c8e—a difficult chore, especially when none of the Councilors had been formally trained in French customary law. The Councilors decided to keep things simple by focusing first on the Bourdon-8assecam8c8e marriage and on Bourdon's death. Without specifically citing it, they relied on the most basic of the *Coutume's* many lengthy articles dealing with inheritance, Article CCXXIX: "Following the death of one spouse, the possessions of the said communauté will be divided in such a fashion that half will go to the surviving spouse and the other half will go to the heirs of the deceased." This decision meant that Marguerite would receive half of Bourdon's total estate, including both personal property and real estate. The Councilors then took into account Article CCXLII, which mandated that children from earlier marriages be included in succession settlements. Pierre Baillargeon, son of Bourdon's first wife Domitile Ch8ping8eta by her first husband Antoine Baillargeon, would therefore receive one fourth of the Bourdon estate. And Bourdon's father, Jacques Bourdon, would also receive one fourth, as the heir of Bourdon's deceased child by Domitile Ch8ping8eta, for Article CCCXI of the *Coutume* stipulated that ascendants (parents or grandparents) may inherit should their own children or grandchildren die without "heirs from their own bodies." At the time, no one in Kaskaskia knew whether Bourdon's father was still alive. As it turned out, he still had nine months to live,[16] although his wife, Jacques's mother, lived on until 1726.[17] It was ultimately left to other close Bourdon relatives to travel from Canada to Kaskaskia to claim the parents' share of Bourdon's estate (more on this below).

Despite clauses in Bourdon's will that left to Baillargeon part of the Bourdon estate, Baillargeon would be obliged to return everything that he had received from the late Bourdon, either in Baillargeon's marriage contract or in Bourdon's will, for the *Coutume de Paris* is categorical on this matter: An individual cannot simultaneously be legatee *and* heir of the same person (*Coutume*, Article CCC), and Pierre was an heir not a legatee. The Council further declared that Baillargeon's earlier renunciation of any right to the Bourdon succession be annulled, definitively quashed, because he was legally a minor. Although he was married and therefore had right to manage his own affairs, he had no right to alienate fundamental assets (Article CCXXXIX of the *Coutume*), even if he had agreed to do so in writing.[18] Regarding other bequests in Bourdon's will, they were to be honored only in so far as Widow Bourdon, Pierre Baillargeon, or other heirs (such as Bourdon's father), agreed to them.[19]

The Provincial Council's decree reveals that in the month between late September and late October 1723 the three Council members had been licking their fingers as they paged furiously through the *Coutume*, checking this article and that article. Without explicitly stating it, their authoritative decree in effect quashed Bourdon's will, overriding it with the *Coutume de Paris*, which henceforth would be the undisputed law of the land. The Illinois Country would be ruled by laws rather than by individual whim or caprice, which had been rife in Bourdon's sloppily composed will. All in all, the Councilors' decision was an equitable settlement, of which the various heirs of Bourdon's estate could be satisfied—or almost so.

News of the Council's decision reverberated through the region like echoes of a fusil shot wafting up and down the Kaskaskia River valley. Immediately following the decision, we hear for the first time directly from François Noyon, who, up to that point, had been an interested but invisible party in the legal process unfolding in Kaskaskia. Noyon did not wish to surrender what he had already received from the Bourdon estate until his "salary" for the two years he had lived with Bourdon was settled. He claimed that everyone in the community was well aware of his services to Bourdon during his final illness, and that everyone also knew of all that he had done on behalf of the estate since Bourdon's death. Moreover, Noyon noted that one of the costs he had had to bear, while attending the ill Jacques Bourdon, was that he had been deprived of an opportunity to go *à la mer* (New Orleans) on a profit-making trading expedition. Such expeditions for Kaskaskia traders were lucrative, indeed; they were in fact the essential basis of much of early Kaskaskia's wealth (see the Tessier estate in chapter 2). Noyon wanted his time, work, solicitous cares, and pains evaluated by arbiters so that he could receive fair payment for his efforts. In the meantime, Noyon was not forsaking his just demands to receive what Bourdon's will had granted him. Des Ursins decreed that arbiters would work in conjunction with Bourdon's heirs to address Noyon's demands, and that he would be permitted to keep only those things that were rightfully adjudged to him. Des Ursins obviously recognized the justness of many of Noyon's demands.[20]

Franchomme must have known precisely what Noyon was engaged in, for on the same day as Noyon's request, on October 22, 1723, he delivered to Councilor des Ursins a new request on his wife's behalf, attacking Noyon's claims. The considerable bequest to Sieur de Noyon made in Bourdon's will was "prejudicial" to Franchomme's widow, and she wanted the Council to quash it. Franchomme referred specifically to the Council's decree, which, in effect, had invited the widow, as well as the other heirs, to make such demands.[21] was on a roll. His slashing, sarcastic response to Baillargeon's "Factum" had destroyed Pierre's attempt to get Franchomme's wife disinherited, and now Franchomme wanted to maximize his wife's share of Bourdon's estate by disputing Bourdon's bequest to Noyon.

The Provincial Council sent des Ursins to clear up the Bourdon succession once and for all. The succession had become increasingly complicated as the Widow Bourdon, Pierre Baillargeon, and Sieur de Noyon had all taken possession, informally and extrajudicially, of portions of the estate. On October 26, 1723, des Ursins decreed that each of the three would have to return everything of which they had already taken possession. A complete inventory would then be compiled, after which Noyon would get his fair allotment, after which the widow (Franchomme's wife, Marguerite 8assecam8c8e) would receive her one-half share, Baillargeon his one-fourth share, and Bourdon's aging father the remaining one fourth.[22]

As it turned out, arbiters rejected Franchomme's attack on the validity of Bourdon's bequests to Noyon, deciding that Noyon deserved everything he had been granted in Bourdon's will, and then some, including thirty aulnes of black ribbon (one aulne being roughly equal to one yard), two pieces of Limbourg (coarse woolen fabric) cloth, a *chapeau fin* (Sunday-go-to-meeting hat), and a *fusil de façon* (fancy gun).[23] It is apparent the arbiters in this case were decidedly unsympathetic to Franchomme's request that Noyon be totally cut out of the Bourdon estate. Franchomme, representing his wife, did agree to sign off on the arbiters' decision, as did Baillargeon, who of course had a significant interest in the estate. Kaskaskia's commandant, Lieutenant Jean-Baptiste Girardot, and Antoine Carrière, a wealthy town resident (Census, no. 69), also signed the document, averring that they had been the fair-minded arbiters throughout the process.

Behind Noyon's valid claim that he had personally cared for Bourdon during his final two years lies a question that must surely have been occupying the minds of most everyone in town: What had Bourdon's young wife, Marguerite 8assecam8c8e, been doing during those two last years of his life, while Noyon was standing by Bourdon's sickbed? We shall see below that Marguerite had a tendency to disappear and reappear, wraith-like, which may account for her apparent absence at her dying husband's sickbed.[24] In times of stress, and her husband's slow process of death was certainly one such time, Marguerite may have repaired to her original home, the Kaskaskia Indian village, where she could find solace among friends and relatives. She had no idea at the time how she would fare when her husband's large estate would eventually be adjudicated, and how the local wheels of justice would treat a Native American widow of a Frenchman. She could not have imagined how the Provincial Council would deal with her, either. In any case, Bourdon's sickbed was located within a context of material possessions that he and his two Native American wives had acquired over two decades of life in Kaskaskia, and it was a very large and interesting mass of possessions indeed.

CHAPTER 6

Textures of Life

BOURDON'S VAST ARRAY OF MATERIAL POSSESSIONS and real estate provides a splendid introduction to everyday life in early Kaskaskia.[1] In the final *partage* of Bourdon's worldly assets, which occurred on October 26, 1723, Widow Bourdon—Marguerite 8assecam8c8e—received the principal residence, in which Bourdon died and in which she had been living since her marriage to him ca. 1715. This grand (by contemporary standards) residential complex became Franchomme's home after his marriage to Marguerite in September 1723, and it was surely larger and better staffed (with both African and Native American slaves) than anything he had experienced back home in Montmeillant. For the young French marine, life was more comfortable in North America than in Europe, even in the far-flung and rude village of Kaskaskia.

The dwelling house itself was large, "about forty *pieds*," erected of large, hewn timbers (*de colombage*), filled between with stones (*pirottée*) and mud packing (*bouzillage*); a double stone fireplace (apparently centrally located) was laid up with mud; floor and ceiling were finished with wooden planks, sealing up the interior, which had two interior dividing walls. As in rural France, major Illinois Country residences had one great room, usually called *la salle*, which served as living room, dining room, and kitchen.[2] Idiosyncratically, this room was called *la cuisine* in Marguerite's house, and contained, together with an array of cooking implements, pickaxes, a saddle and a bridle.[3] This space constituted what Americans now commonly call a country kitchen. The house's general layout, a center hallway with flanking rooms, was a fairly standard configuration for large houses in the Illinois Country over a very long period of time. This was the floor plan of Philippe Rastel de Rocheblave's resident in Ste. Genevieve during the 1760s, and the original configuration of the Pierre Ménard House, erected outside Kaskaskia during the first decade of the nineteenth century.[4]

Circumferential galleries were a prominent, even defining, architectural feature on many later Illinois Country houses, as can be seen in the Bolduc House in Ste. Genevieve, and at a practical level they affected the lifestyles of residents for many months of the year in the temperate climate of the region. Yet surrounding *galeries* do not appear in the description of Bourdon's residence, likely revealing that these Creole features of domestic architecture had not yet arrived in the Illinois Country from the Gulf Coast.[5] That is, stylistically, early

Kaskaskia houses were quite Canadian, which makes sense given the very large percentage of French Canadians making up the region's White population. Original thatched roofs on houses in the region soon gave way to split wooden *bardeaux* (shingles) made with white oak and chestnut.[6] The Bourdon residence was larger than the houses of either of Bourdon's two wealthy neighbors (Louis Tessier and Marie Rouensa), and the entire residential complex was appraised at 7,000 livres in 1723, compared to 4,000 for Tessier's in 1721 and 5,500 for Rouensa's in 1725.[7]

The lot on which the house stood was identified as an *emplacement*, a term interchangeable with *terrain* for describing residential properties in the Illinois Country. This may be seen in the final inventory of Marguerite 8assecam8c8e's share of the Bourdon estate, for it included a stable built of *poteaux-en-terre* (posts-in-the-ground) situated on an emplacement and a nearby barn situated on a terrain.[8] These words were exclusively reserved for properties located within the limits of the compact villages, and distinguished them from outlying plowlands that were designated "terres." Bourdon's residential emplacement was encircled by a stockade of *pieux* (stakes), and within the compound stood a free-standing stone bake oven and two small, ramshackle slave quarters; perhaps one for Africans and the other for Native Americans.[9] Although not mentioned, the compound likely included a kitchen garden, a well, and a poultry shed, all usual appurtenances to major residential properties in the Illinois Country.

The brief mention of Bourdon's stone bake oven is misleading, for this was an absolutely life-essential element of the residential complex; one might even say more important than the residence itself. Wheat bread was the staple of life for French settlers in the Illinois Country; it was the imperious manner of ingesting necessary carbohydrates, for *patates anglaises* (potatoes) did not arrive in the region until late in the eighteenth century.[10] Perhaps Bourdon's massive stone bake oven was indeed a more-or-less community oven, fired up (no quick or easy task) once a week to bake bread for anyone in the neighborhood who brought forth their *pâte* (dough) for baking into huge golden loaves. This would have reinforced Bourdon's position as a hybrid frontier seigneur in the village, providing his oven to his neighbors in a gesture of *noblesse oblige*.[11] There is no evidence that Bourdon levied seignorial fees for the use of his bake oven, although such medieval fees (*banalités*) were still collected, albeit rarely, back in Canada.[12]

The huge quantity of farm implements and household utensils, furniture, and fabrics on the Bourdon inventories was overwhelmingly of European provenance.[13] As in virtually all estate inventories from French Illinois, *robes de bœuf* (buffalo robes) make a signal appearance. Two earthenware crocks "of the Natchez" (*des Natchés*) filled with bear oil are a tantalizing entry in the Bourdon inventory,[14] for the language here suggests that Natchez Indian potters had manufactured these crocks. Natchez was an important waystation between New Orleans and the Illinois Country, and every river vessel ascending and descending the Mississippi stopped over there. As we saw earlier, bear oil for cooking was highly

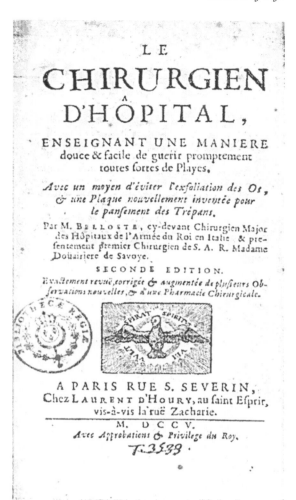

6.1. *Le Chirurgien d'Hôpital*, a surgical handbook owned by Jacques Bourdon. (Paris: Laurent d'Houry, 1705)

regarded throughout Louisiana, a province in which butter—favored in Canada, where most households were proud of their ornate butter molds[15]—quickly went rancid. The taste for bear oil had self-evidently come from Native Americans, and the Illinois language had a precise word for it: *mahkwapimi*.[16]

Franchomme's home contained a small library, while Bourdon's residence featured just one published book, *Le Chirurgien d'Hôpital: Enseignant une Manière douce et facile de guérir promptement toutes sortes de Playes*, written by one Monsieur Belloste (1654–1730), former surgeon major of the French royal army, and printed in Paris, on the Left Bank, rue St. Séverin, close to the Sorbonne, in 1705.[17] This volume had been brought up the Mississippi from New Orleans by the Illinois Country's first medical doctor, Jacques Le Prévost, a military surgeon. Le Prévost owned one of the first small—very small—libraries in the region, and after he died in 1722 Bourdon bought *Le Chirurgien d'Hôpital* for ten livres at the estate sale.[18] In purchasing this military medical handbook, Bourdon was demonstrating a sense of responsibility as the local militia captain in Kaskaskia. War with the Foxes was running hot in 1722, and who could predict when Bourdon might be forced to dress tomahawk wounds inflicted on one of his militiamen. Bourdon's ownership of such a book also set him apart from most of his neighbors (not, of course, Franchomme), the largely illiterate habitants of the village.

After Bourdon's death in 1723, Monsieur le Jeune Lalande (Jean-Baptiste, Census, no. 28) acquired *un livre de chirurgy*, together with an old pair of *tablettes* [?], from Bourdon's estate for fifteen livres. Lalande also purchased at the same auction *une paire de souliers* (a pair of shoes, likely moccasins) for thirty livres. Moccasins, perhaps ornamented by some Native American craftsman or woman, were clearly more valuable at Kaskaskia in 1723 than a surgical manual. By the late eighteenth century, *souliers sauvages* (Indian-made moccasins) were in demand in New Orleans, and a cottage industry developed in the Illinois Country that produced them for shipment downriver.[19]

Animate as well as inanimate possessions comprised the Bourdon estate. Of Bourdon's seven African slaves, Marguerite 8assecam8c8e received three, two men and a woman: Bambara (named after the Bambara Kingdom situated along the upper Niger River), La Fleure, and Aubas. It is not clear from the inventories whether the woman, Aubas, was the partner, either formally or informally, of either of the men. An enslaved African couple, Robin and Marie, made up part of Baillargeon's share of the estate, and yet another Black couple, Marman and Manon, likely also went to him; the inventories are unclear on this issue.

The Bourdon estate also included four Native American slaves: two women, Paniacicoa (of the Wichita Nation)[20] and Chonicoa, and two young men, Caracaroet (meaning, "Little Woodpecker")[21] and Aga. Chonicoa was living chez Nicolas-Michel Chassin, the storekeeper at Fort de Chartres, apparently functioning as a household servant. Chassin had married the Métisse daughter of Marie Rouensa and Michel Philippe, but a young couple of standing required a house servant of some sort (Census, no. 35). Both Chonicoa and Caracaroet were allotted to Marguerite 8assecam8c8e when the *partage* of Bourdon's estate was effected in October, while Paniacicoa fell to Pierre Baillargeon's lot. Aga had been rented out as a boatman to one Monsieur (Jacques?) Rollet for a commercial trip to New Orleans. He was absent from Kaskaskia in July and had still not returned in late October. In principle, he fell to the lot of the "Canadian heirs" (Bourdon's father or other collateral relatives), but should Aga either "die an accidental death or flee," the heirs would be compensated for Aga's value, which was estimated to be 1,000 livres. Aga was a young male; by way of comparison, Paniacicoa, an older female, was evaluated at 700 livres. Aga had still not turned up when the inventory for the Canadian heirs was drafted on November 8, 1723, and it seems likely that he never did reappear. One is permitted to hope that he successfully fled for his freedom, rather than died and been buried in an anonymous grave along the muddy bank of the lower Mississippi River.

Of the farm animals—horses, cattle, and pigs, though no sheep—in the Bourdon estate only four, all horses, were honored with names—Mazarin and Rougit went to the widow, Marguerite 8assecam8c8e, while Courtisan and Le Noir fell to Baillargeon. Three of these names denoted physical qualities—the reddish one, the courtly one, the black one—but Mazarin is an odd name to find at Kaskaskia. It may have derived from the fact that Franchomme's hometown of Montmeillant in Champagne was located near the prominent "Hôtel Mazarin, suggesting that Franchomme had named the horse after Bourdon's death"[22] Baillargeon's share included "one fourth of the pigs that are on the other side," while the widow, Marguerite, received a one-half share in the pigs.[23] What happened to the final fourth remains unknown, but the phrase "the other side" is instructive for understanding an important aspect of life at Kaskaskia. The expression referred to the unsettled and uncultivated region on the left bank of the Kaskaskia River, which served as a communal zone for free-ranging herds of pigs. The first Illinois census to enumerate livestock, that of 1732, shows pigs to have been the most numerous of domesticated animals in the region.[24] Pork was an important component in the diets of the Illinois habitants, and pigs that gorged themselves on the abundant supply of mast from the plentiful oak trees in the region provided the sweetest meat.

· · ·

The entire Bourdon succession process had become burdensome to the Provincial Council, whose members had never before dealt with any civil proceeding of such magnitude. To facilitate matters, La Loëre des Ursins came down to Kaskaskia on temporary duty from Fort de Chartres, receiving a per-diem allotment of fifteen livres; perhaps he took quarters in the Jesuit compound. Chassin's temporary duty in Kaskaskia must be viewed as a desirable assignment, for the fort and surrounding community were more remote and primitive than Kaskaskia. Kaskaskia was the economic and cultural, if one may say so, capital of the Illinois Country, despite the government's location at Fort de Chartres. Des Ursins also received an assistant, one Sieur de Laitre, to serve as *greffier* (clerk) to record the proceedings. The two men worked furiously on Wednesday, November 8, plowing through the various Bourdon-succession accounts.[25]

Bourdon himself acknowledged that when he had married his first wife, Domitile Ch-8ping8eta, he had been destitute, not even having a *capot* to cover his back. But once married he had demonstrated formidable entrepreneurial skills, and in partnership with his two Native American wives had enriched himself and his family. Bourdon certainly did not hew to Polonius's advice to Laertes, "Neither a borrower nor a lender be," for Bourdon was decidedly in both camps. His list of debts, though, was very short,[26] whereas his list of debtors was very long.[27] Bourdon owed Sieur (Jean-Baptiste?) Guion, who must have been a smithy, one hundred livres for a plowshare. Iron objects were dear in the Illinois

Country, for pig iron had to be shipped from France to New Orleans, and then laboriously taken upriver by *bateau*. Guion would have hammered the plowshare out of a glowing-red bar of iron that had been heated in a forge fired with locally produced hardwood charcoal.

Debts due to the Bourdon estate ran the gamut from the four livres that Louis Turpain owed for a down payment on a fusil, to the 670 livres that La Chêne, *habitant de Nouvelle Orléans*, owed for an assortment of unspecified items. Franchomme, husband of Bourdon's widow, was specifically designated to collect the debts on behalf of the estate. French marine officers and officials were major debtors of the Bourdon estate: Lieutenant Melique (Census, no. 64) owed 664 livres, Boisbriant 500 livres, d'Artaguiette 420 livres, and Chassin 400 livres. Eleven Illinois Indians—evidently accomplished hunters—were to settle their respective debts by providing bison flesh, deer pelts, and a buffalo robe.[28] The bison flesh was listed as "plats coste," that is *plats de côtes* or short ribs, which both Native Americans and many Frenchmen (apparently Bourdon himself) considered to be the best cut of the beast for human consumption.[29] During the 1720s bison could be hunted in close proximity to the villages of the Illinois Country, although by the end of the French regime (1763) this was no longer true.

Dettes des Sauvages (Indian debts, by name)[30]

Patchisita huit plats coste [plats de côtes]
Seyk8yrinta deux paut [peaux] de chevereille [chevreuil]
akanik8a un plats coste
Peressia un plats coste et deux paut de chevereille
Loutarde deux plats coste
8api8yrata une robe de bœuf
Tatakinchinga dix-sept plats coste et un font de graesse [fond de graisse]
Aremontessa quatre plats coste
8inguisuk8anga [**8inguissek8anga**] un plats coste
Moniguinrata cinq plast [*sic*] coste
8ynguibariata quatre plats coste

Translations

Patchisita eight short ribs (flat side or flank, plate cut, butchered chest and stomach muscles)
Seyk8yrinta two white-tailed deer skins
akanik8a one short rib
Peressia one short rib and two deer skins
Loutarde two short ribs
8api8yrata one bison robe
Tatakinchinga seventeen short ribs and a melting of tallow

Aremontessa   four short ribs
8inguis*u*k8anga [8inguissek8anga]   one short rib
Moniguinrata   one short rib
8ynguibariata   four short ribs

Indian names

Patchisita   "one whose rottenness or corruption is increasing"
Seyk8yrinta?   like *nisec8ara* "I enjoy someone's misfortune"?
akanik8a   *ahkanihkwa*, that is, the animate singular equivalent of *ahkanihkwi* "sewing awl."
Peressia   [*pileehsia*] In Le Boullenger's *Dictionary, piressia* means "raven"
Loutarde   French *l'outarde,* "(the) Canada goose" (not "bustard")
8api8yrata   "one with white tresses"
Tatakinchinga   *taahtakiihšinka* "he lies down"
Aremontessa   "little dog, puppy" (the "prairie dog" meaning not applicable to this area)
8inguis*u*k8anga [8inguis*s*ek8anga]   "well-pressed/sticking out-one"?
Moniguinrata   "bald/shorn-one"?
8ynguibariata   "one who hunts or walks well, good hunter"

This list of Indian debts to the Bourdon estate is a document of substantial importance at several levels, for it transports us into *la vie quotidienne* in early Kaskaskia in ways that other documents simply do not.[31] First, the interpersonal transactions implicit in the tabulation of debts reveal Bourdon's intimate relationship with Native Americans who were living in the Kaskaskia mission village, situated some three miles up the Kaskaskia River from the "French" village. These were two rather different communities, but by all appearances Bourdon (and Marguerite) moved with perfect ease between the two. Second, the tabulated debts reveal something about culinary tastes in Kaskaskia during the early 1720s—bison short ribs were clearly in demand. We can well imagine that they were cooked slowly over a hardwood fire, creating a dish perfectly palatable to Americans attending a weekend barbecue in the early twenty-first century. Whereas modern folks habitually wash down their barbecue with beer, there was no brewery in the Illinois Country at the time. A man of Jacques Bourdon's status would have preferred claret, imported from Bordeaux via Mobile or New Orleans, although the decade of 1720s witnessed a shortage of French wine in the Illinois Country. Franchomme's fellow marine officer, Terrisse de Ternan, a witty and inventive fellow, vinted a *barrique* (one barrique was approximately 300 liters) of wine from local, native grapes, but he ashamedly admitted that he and his friends were so thirsty that they swilled it before it had properly matured.[32] Bourdon did, however, have distilled spirits to spare, and they had made the long trip upriver from New Orleans by bateau.

Shipping alcoholic beverages up the Mississippi to the Illinois Country was rife with problems. In the autumn of 1722, a convoy of bateaux pulled up to the riverbank at Natchez for a stopover, and some of these vessels were loaded with barriques of eau-de-vie. Lieutenant Charles-Henri-Joseph de Tonty, nephew to La Salle's famous partner Henri de Tonty and a man of high status but low morals, was traveling with the convoy, and he siphoned off some of the liquor (apparently for his personal consumption), then cleverly filled up the depleted barriques with river water. One Paschal, *patron* (skipper) of the boat carrying the eau-de-vie, witnessed this and was enraged, for he, after all, was responsible for the security of his cargo. Helpless to thwart Tonty's shenanigans at Natchez, Paschal filed a lengthy and bitter protestation when the convoy arrived at Fort de Chartres, exposing Tonty's multiple delinquencies, which included gambling with the crew members.[33] Chassin took down a detailed deposition of the entire affair, although it's not known how the Provincial Council ultimately dealt with it. The incident did not stifle Tonty's career, for he went on to become commandant at Baie des Puants—"Bay of the Stinkers" (Winnebago Indians)—now Green Bay, Wisconsin.[34]

Bourdon as an entrepreneur was an importer and purveyor of two varieties of distilled spirits—generically known as eau-de-vie—one of which sold for thirty-two livres per pot (one pot being equivalent to approximately two quarts), and the other for forty livres. Either he was dealing in two different qualities of brandy or, more likely, the cheaper version of eau-de-vie was in fact tafia, a rough rum imported from the Caribbean Sugar Islands that was ubiquitous in colonial Louisiana. Bourdon's two milk cows, one "with the white mark on its back" and the other a "red one," were also profit makers, and milk was sold both by the pot and the chopine (one chopine being equivalent to a one-half pint or one-quarter pot, that is, one cup). The accounts unfortunately do not provide milk prices, but French-born-and-bred marine officers, like Melique and d'Artaguiette, were determined to have their café au lait in the morning, and for that creamy *lait* they owed the Bourdon estate. As in the dairy section of a modern supermarket, the tabulation places eggs and milk side-by-side, and the list of outstanding debtors includes the mining engineer, Philippe Renault (Census, no. 2), who owed the estate for precisely "three dozen plus three" *oeufs* from Bourdon's *poulailler* (hen house).[35]

Franchomme was charged with collecting the outstanding debts on behalf of the Bourdon estate, on the grounds that Franchomme's wife stood to receive much of it, and that, as a French marine officer, he was a man of integrity and honor. One does wonder how much time and energy he spent dunning Renault to pay for thirty-nine eggs, or Lieutenant Melique for three chopines of fresh milk from the deceased Bourdon's milch cows.

The Bourdon succession required that correspondence from Kaskaskia makes its way to the Bourdon family in Canada via the wilderness waterways. Fox Indians had made the Chicago portage too dangerous for the French to use by the 1720s, which meant that

6.2. Bourdon's dairy accounts. Milk was measured in pots (approximately two quarts) and chopines (approximately one pint). Notice also Renault's eggs on line 7. Kaskaskia Manuscripts, Randolph County Courthouse.

letters from the Illinois Country to Canada generally went down the Mississippi River to the Ohio—La Belle Rivière—then up the Wabash (Ouabache, "white shining river") to Fort Ouiatenon (near present-day Lafayette, Indiana). There, the heavy pirogue in which the letters had begun their voyage would have been exchanged for a lighter canoe, framed with spruce and covered with birch bark. The courier would then have proceeded up the Wabash to its headwaters, portaging near where Fort Wayne, Indiana, now stands into the Maumee, and thence downstream into Lake Erie and on to the St. Lawrence Valley. This trip demanded several months, and in our present case likely began in the spring of 1724, when ice on the rivers began to break up.[36]

Bourdon's father, Jacques père, died in July 1724, although he likely lived long enough
to get news of his son's death in the faraway Illinois Country. His mother, Marie Ménard,
certainly did, for she was not buried until February 1726.[37] In any event, Bourdon's younger
brother, Pierre, and his brother-in-law, François Bibo (Bibeau), took to the rivers and lakes,
and headed for the Illinois Country to collect Mother Bourdon's inheritance. Pierre Bourdon knew something about the water routes that headed west from Montreal, for he had
repeatedly signed on as an *engagé vers l'Ouest* in the years preceding his brother's death.[38]

Pierre Bourdon and Bibo departed Montreal for the Illinois Country in the autumn
of 1724, as hardy Canadians being neither discouraged nor impeded by the arriving cold
weather on the waterways. They arrived in Kaskaskia in late December, and on January 1,
1725, they set to work tending to their family's share of the Bourdon estate, which entailed
liquidating various inherited properties. Leonard Billeron dit La Fatigue (Census, no. 65)
purchased from the Canadians "terres in the prairie, and [curiously] half of the house, half
the barn, and half the lot situated in Kaskaskia."[39] This house and lot had been Bourdon's
secondary residential property, not his principal residence, the big house, which had passed
on down to Widow Bourdon and her new husband, Franchomme. La Fatigue paid 740
livres in *espèces sonnantes* (hard cash), specifically "not in playing card money," redeemable
in Montreal. *Cartes à jouer* (playing cards) were used officially in Canada from 1685 to 1729
for lack of a solidly backed printed currency, but cards were always heavily discounted relative to hard cash.[40] The cash payment to Bourdon and Bibo was eventually consummated
in Montreal, when La Fatigues's father, Pierre Billeron, received from Kaskaskia power
of attorney to make the payment on behalf of his son and his son's wife, Marie-Claire
Catoire.[41] Such financial transactions, spanning the intimidating distance between the
Mississippi and St. Lawrence valleys, were common in eighteenth-century French North
America.

Pierre Bourdon and François Bibo sold off the inherited enslaved humans as well as the
real estate, conveying to Nicolas Desvignes, on January 24, 1725, two Black people—one
male and one female—for a total of 1,300 livres; both slaves were identified as *pièces d'Inde*,
meaning they were African slaves in prime physical condition.[42] This slave sale of January 1725 is the first known example of the expression in the Illinois Country, but it soon
became widely used throughout the region on both sides of the Mississippi and persisted
throughout the eighteenth century.[43] These enslaved people—apparently Marman and
Manon[44]—seem to have been a couple—*homme et femme*—although there's no way to
determine if their union had been sanctified in a Christian ceremony. Desvignes appears
as a major slave holder in 1726 (Census, no. 66), owner of five Africans and two Native
Americans,[45] and Marman and Manon were surely two of the five Africans enumerated in
this household.

In any event, Pierre Bourdon and François Bibo wrapped up their affairs in Kaskaskia
in January and February 1725, and as soon as the spring thaw broke up the winter ice, they

were back on the rivers in their canoe headed north for Montreal. They were never to reappear in the Illinois Country, and the Bourdon name, so important in the annals of early
Kaskaskia, disappears from the local written records.[46] The fortune Bourdon had built up
in the two decades between the founding of Kaskaskia in 1703 and his death in 1723, did
not disappear, however. His widow, Marguerite 8assecam8c8e, had inherited the largest
share—one-half of the total of this fortune—and, as seen above, had married Nicolas Peltier de Franchomme within three months of Bourdon's death, sometime in September 1723.

By the autumn of 1723, Franchomme, Marguerite, and the ten-year-old Jean Saguingora, made up a household consisting of one Frenchman, one Illinois Indian woman, and
one Métis—plus perhaps four enslaved people, both African and Native American, whom
Marguerite had received from Bourdon's estate. To our modern eyes—as well as to those
members of Franchomme's family still living back in Montmeillant—this household appears unusual, but, although wealthier than most, it was quite an ordinary household in
Kaskaskia at the time. Marguerite is then invisible for several years in the local records. Curiously, she did not give birth to any child, and to the best of our knowledge she never did
by any one of her three White husbands—Bourdon, Franchomme, and finally Pierre Blot.
Records show that Franchomme purchased seven *pots* of bear oil for twenty livres in May
1724,[47] and, on November 9 of that year, he was a witness at the marriage of Louis Turpain
(widower of Marie Coulon) and Dorothée Michiper8a (widow of Charles Danis, Census,
no. 72), along with other French officers—d'Artaguiette, Legardeur Delisle, and Melique.[48]
Young marine ensign Franchomme was a dashing and popular figure in the Illinois Country
during the mid-1720s—his signature—"Peltier de Franchomme"—often ornamented (as
a witness) the marriage records of his friends and neighbors.[49] His own marriage contract
was, however, and as our next chapter reveals, of the utmost importance to him.

CHAPTER 7

The Marriage Contract
Center of Life

S UDDENLY, QUITE DRAMATICALLY, FRANCHOMME departed Kaskaskia and headed down the Mississippi to New Orleans around New Year's 1725. He was accompanied by several distinguished marine officers—Legardeur Delisle, d'Artaguiette, and Commandant Boisbriant—and, importantly, the notaire Nicolas Buffereau de Bellegarde.[1] Franchomme had absolutely vital legal business to conduct in New Orleans, and he needed help from his friends, especially Bellegarde, the notaire. These men were not merchants, and the group likely traveled by pirogue, rather than on the more cumbersome and slower bateaux. They moved swiftly downriver, avoiding the many pitfalls of Mississippi travel at that time—ambuscades by Chickasaw Indians at Chickasaw Bluffs (Écors-à-Prudhomme or Écors-à-Margot), lurking sandbars or deadly snags created by submerged trees.[2] The party arrived in New Orleans, still more town than city, in late January 1725.

On February 15, Franchomme submitted to the Superior Council, the highest governing body of Louisiana, a request to have a new marriage contract drawn up.[3] Franchomme claimed that he had been married "about a year ago [closer to a year and a half] at the Illinois post." A "young man named Sieur Buffereau," serving as notaire in Illinois at the time, had drafted the original contract, but this vital document had been consumed by rats. These vermin, Franchomme explained, were ravenous in Illinois, were a big nuisance, and had destroyed many official records—too bad for us historians—including his marriage contract. Franchomme did not need to explain the importance of marriage contracts in regions governed by the *Coutume de Paris*—including all of Louisiana—for every member of the Council knew that such contracts were the fundamental legal building blocks for creating, managing, and preserving family wealth. But Franchomme's marriage contract was of monumental importance to him, personally, because in it his wife, Marguerite 8assecam8c8e, had provided Franchomme with a gift-between-the-living (*donation entre vifs* from the Latin *donatio inter vivos*). The gift had been huge—20,000 livres—which of course came from Marguerite's one-half share of the estate of Jacques Bourdon. Franchomme's trip to New Orleans reveals the importance and sacrosanctity of marriage contracts,

7.1. *Plan de la Nouvelle Orleans* by Jacques-Nicolas Bellin, the metropole of French Louisiana was growing rapidly during the 1720s. Library of Congress.

which, like passports in the modern world, could not be easily duplicated. Franchomme was obliged to go in person to Louisiana's capital and petition the Superior Council directly.

The Council immediately ordered the notaire Bellegarde to present a deposition of facts concerning Franchomme's petition, including all the "terms and clauses that he can remember" of Franchomme's and Marguerite 8assecam8c8e's marriage contract.[4] Franchomme had been prudent to bring Bellegarde down to New Orleans from Kaskaskia, for Bellegarde supported Franchomme's contentions—and then some. Bellegarde swore that eighteen to twenty months earlier, meaning in September 1723, he, "functioning as notaire in Illinois," had indeed drafted a marriage contract between Franchomme and Marguerite Ouaquamo-quossa (a strange and confusing rendition of 8assecam8c8e), widow of Jacques Bourdon. Rats in the Illinois Country were numerous and voracious, and were of "prodigious size." Most of Franchomme's *meubles* (personal possessions), including his marriage contract, had been carried off or been eaten by these vermin, or both. The contract had been witnessed by high-ranking individuals—Boisbriant, d'Artaguiette, and Legardeur Delisle, among others—and was drafted in accordance with the *Coutume de Paris*.

To the best of Bellegarde's recollection, the marriage contract of Marguerite 8asse-cam8c8e and Franchomme had contained four fundamental provisions,[5] and a commu-

nity of possessions, both personal property and real estate, had been established between
them. Such a communauté of property was the financial basis of all marriages in regions
governed by the *Coutume de Paris*, including all French overseas colonies.[6] The *préciput*,
which was a sum independent of the communauté that either spouse would receive immediately upon the death of a partner, had been set at 3,000 livres.[7] Marguerite had retained
her right to renounce the communauté at the time of her husband's death, in the case that
Franchomme had contracted large and burdensome debts. Such renunciation would free
her of any and all debts contracted by her husband.[8] Marguerite had made a *donation entre
vifs* to Franchomme of 20,000 livres (a very large amount), "irrevocable and in the best
form, to be taken either from the property in the inventory [of Bourdon's estate] or from
other resources."[9]

   Former Illinois commandant Boisbriant added weight to Bellegarde's deposition by affirming that he had witnessed and signed Franchomme's marriage contract at Kaskaskia
in September 1723.[10] More marine officers followed suit in support of Franchomme's
cause—Pierre Diron d'Artaguiette, François Seimars de Bellile, and Legardeur Delisle, all
of whom had in fact signed the marriage contract as witnesses in Kaskaskia in September
1723.[11] One of the curious things about the Franchomme-8assecam8c8e marriage is everyone's vagueness about dates. In his original plea, Franchomme was not even clear about
precisely when his marriage had taken place; moreover, the absence of a parish marriage
record, which is also a bit odd, further confuses things. Vague as it was, though, everyone
agreed that the Franchomme-8assecam8c8e marriage contract had been executed in proper
form in Kaskaskia in September 1723.

   The unanimous and unqualified support of Franchomme's fellow officers meant that he
quickly carried the day with the Superior Council, and, on February 26, 1725, Michel Rossard Desbrosses (who signed his name simply Rossard), long-time chief greffier and notaire
of the Council, and highest ranking notaire in Louisiana, drafted a document that was in
effect a duplicate marriage contract for Franchomme and Marguerite 8assecam8c8e.[12] The
document could not, of course, technically *be* a marriage contract, for Marguerite 8asse-
cam8c8e, one of the original contracting parties, was absent. So, rather, the new document
(entitled "*Clauses de mariage entre Francosme et la veuve Bourdon*") reiterated all of the
pertinent portions of the original contract, which were then certified by four of the men
who had signed the original in Kaskaskia: Franchomme himself, Diron d'Artaguiette, Legardeur Delisle, and Buffereau de Bellegarde. That Franchomme could reassemble at New
Orleans in February 1725 the same group of signatories that had originally assembled at
Kaskaskia in September 1723 is extraordinary, virtually incredible given the vagaries that afflicted Louisiana in that era, with the daunting distances and multitudinous contingencies
that weighed on this possibility. The document was notarized by Rossard, and the elegant
paraph on his signature put a stamp of legality and finality on the document and its various
clauses, both in form and content.

Within days of Franchomme's departure for New Orleans in January, Marguerite 8as-secam8c8e fled French Kaskaskia, taking with her the Métis boy, Jean-Baptiste Saguinora. Likely in the absence of her husband she found the Kaskaskia Indian mission community, where she certainly had friends (and perhaps relatives), a more congenial place to live.[13] Adulterous wives were treated harshly in the Illinois Nation, and it is unlikely that Marguerite engaged in any sort of illicit liaison during Franchomme's absence from home.[14] As a consequence of her *évasion*, Sieur (likely Étienne) Hébert had moved into Franchomme's house to serve as caretaker in his absence; in March 1725, however, Hébert, for his own unknown reasons, abandoned this responsibility. The Provincial Council—which, since Boisbriant's departure for New Orleans, included Charles-Claude du Tisné, Boisbriant's replacement as temporary commandant in the Illinois Country—therefore ordered an inventory of Franchomme's possessions and found a new temporary tenant for his residence.[15] This tenant was Michel Vien—who, being only semi-literate, signed his name "Michelle"—a carpenter by trade; he promised to take responsibility for all of Franchomme's possessions until his return from New Orleans,[16] though no one could be sure when this would occur.

Through the many months of litigation over the Bourdon estate, Widow Bourdon, Marguerite 8assecam8c8e, had remained virtually invisible. But thanks to the inventory of Franchomme's (and her) possessions done in March 1725, she immerges briefly, and importantly, from the shadows. Women's activities are only rarely described in records from colonial Illinois, which makes this inventory especially valuable. Marguerite had walked away from the entire estate, leaving behind virtually everything, including both African and Native American slaves.[17] But, before she left, she attended to some domestic affairs pertaining to her household. On March 15, her slaves spoke to De la Loëre des Ursins and his greffier, Du Vernay, who were busy compiling the inventory, and told them that "Madame Franchomme" had given two fusils and twenty pounds of gunpowder to the Kaskaskia chief, Mamantoinsa. Mamantoinsa was an active and enterprising chief during the 1720s and has already appeared in historical literature.[18] Marguerite's expensive gifts to him reveal how close she remained to the power structure in the Kaskaskia Indian village and, indeed, how closely connected the French and Indian villages were through the agency of Native American wives like Marguerite 8assecam8c8e.

Jean-Baptiste Lalande, the younger (Census, no. 90), was also present when des Ursins and Du Vernay inventoried the Franchomme-8assecam8c8e household, and he informed the officials that Madame Franchomme had lent him a *couverte de Limbourg* (course woolen blanket) and twenty-three pounds of lead. Lasonde (Pierre Pillet dit Lasonde, Census, no. 79) then came forth, asking for a small pig that he had lent Madame, and Pottier fils—Jean-Baptiste Pottier, son of Jean-Baptiste Pottier père—who was about 10 years old at the time (Census, no. 70) wanted two small pigs, which, he claimed, Madame had promised to give him. The scene at the Franchomme property, while des Ursins and Du Vernay were compiling the inventory, thus provides us with precious vignettes of Marguerite's functioning as *maîtresse de la maison*, interacting with her enslaved servants, and haggling, borrowing, and lending with her French neighbors in Kaskaskia, as well as with Chief Mamantoinsa.

Immediately after having prevailed in his case before the Superior Council, Franchomme departed New Orleans and headed back up the Mississippi; he would never again set foot in Louisiana's capital. Franchomme was in a hurry, and he progressed upriver with remarkable speed, given that he started his trip at the very time that the Mississippi's waters were surging with spring runoff. By late June, he had reached Écors à Prudomme, a recognized location but not a proper settlement; the Guillaume Delisle map of 1718 shows a small French outpost at that site. Franchomme stopped over at Prudomme to help bury one of his pirogue-mates, "Étienne Guilleruite [?], native of near La Rochelle, [who] died June 28, 1725."[19] Guilleruite seems to have been a newcomer to Louisiana, but his hopes for carving out a new life in the colony were short-lived. Illinois Country settlements were utterly dependent on the riverine commercial artery connecting them to "*la mer*" (New Orleans and Mobile), but the brutal Mississippi River trips meant that paddlers and rowers often succumbed en route. We observed in chapter 2, for instance, Louis Tessier's death at Natchez as he was coming upriver from New Orleans.

Even in a place as remote and inconsequential as Écors à Prudhomme the ritual of inventorying a dead person's possessions was carried out. Franchomme formally witnessed the inventory of Étienne's pathetic list possessions—an old coat with the vest, a small sack of powder, an old shirt, an old hat, a worn pair of socks, worn *souliers* (very likely Indian-made *souliers sauvages*). These were the bare, essential accoutrements of a pirogue man. A bright spot in the otherwise gray inventory was ten pots of eau-de-vie, which was fuel for paddling, poling, and cursing a pirogue upriver. Jean-Baptiste Poudret[20] was in charge of the pirogue trip upriver, and he owed Étienne sixty-two livres in wages. The inventory was carefully carried (likely by Franchomme himself) upriver and deposited in the *greffe* (notarial files) at Fort de Chartres, but to whom the sixty-two livres in wages were ever paid will remain a small but intriguing mystery in the history of the Mississippi River valley.

Franchomme had been impatient to leave New Orleans and get back to his home in Kaskaskia, and his pirogue slipped, unannounced, onto the muddy riverbank near the Jesuit compound at Kaskaskia in September 1725. Disembarking, Franchomme went first in search of his family (his wife, Marguerite 8assecam8c8e, and the Métis boy, Jean Saguinora).[21] The three-member family had been riven by Franchomme's journey to New Orleans, but once reconstituted, they reoccupied the grand house—grand by the standards of that time and place—that Jacques Bourdon had built before he died in 1723. These first familial priorities Franchomme accomplished before the end of September 1725.[22] For the next several years, Franchomme led an uneventful domestic life as a good neighbor in the village of Kaskaskia, parish of the Immaculate Conception, standing as a witness at marriage after marriage. The most glittering of these marriages occurred in February 1727, when Étienne Hébert, captain of the milita at Fort de Chartres and native of the parish of Ste. Anne in Canada, married Élisabeth Philippe, daughter of Michel Philippe, lieutenant in the Kaskaskia militia, and of the late and great Marie Rouensa. Étienne Hébert and Élisabeth Philippe became a power couple in the budding parish of Ste. Anne, which included communities at Fort de Chartres, St. Philippe, and Prairie du Rocher.[23] Domestic bliss in Kaskaskia during the 1720s was, however, often shaken by periodic, jarring bursts of violence coming from the untamed hinterland that surrounded the Illinois villages, a hinterland through which hostile Fox warriors coursed at will.

CHAPTER 8

The Fox Scourge

THE KALEIDOSCOPIC COMPLEXITY of all the alliances and misalliances of upper Midwestern Indian nations during the late seventeenth and early eighteenth centuries is beyond the scope of our study, other than to observe that for decades, Illinois Indians and their French allies were at war with the Foxes (Renards or Mesquakies), and that this war was unremitting. Intertribal warfare was a deeply ingrained way of life among Midwestern Native nations, and the Illinois were proud of their martial successes. In 1694, Henry de Tonty, La Salle's lieutenant, reported from Fort St. Louis on the upper Illinois River (now Starved Rock) that local Illinois had provided a *procès verbal* (sworn statement), declaring that between 1687 and 1694 they had either killed or captured of their enemies 334 men and 111 women.[1] This grim affidavit provided no tribal affiliations, but Foxes were surely part of the tally. Deep enmity between the Foxes and Illinois was of longstanding duration, well antedating settlement of the French villages in the Illinois Country.

By early eighteenth century, the French were increasingly preoccupied with the Foxes. This preoccupation is visible in French imaging of North America, as may be seen on two of Guillaume Delisle's maps, that of 1703 and that of 1718. On the first, the Fox Nation does not appear, and the region southwest of Lake Michigan is dominated by Mascoutens; but on the second, the Foxes loom large in the region, their name being attached to "Renards R[ivière]" that flows eastward into Green Bay, while the Mascoutens are a much-diminished presence. As the Foxes rose to prominence in the region, they were not very neighborly neighbors, not at all persuaded that the meek shall inherit the earth. *The Fox Wars,* by R. David Edmunds and Joseph L. Peyser, is deeply sympathetic to the Foxes, yet large portions of the study describe Fox hostilities—perpetual hostilities—with surrounding tribes, virtually all of them: Mascoutens, Sioux, Ojibways (Chippewas), Hurons, Miamis, Ottawas, Kickapoos, Winnebagos, and of course the entire Illinois Nation, including the Kaskaskias.[2] In the western Great Lakes region, by the turn of the eighteenth century, it had become a truism that the Fox Nation was "both feared and hated by the other tribes, on account of its people's arrogance."[3]

During the 1720s, the grim give-and-take between the French and their Native American allies on the one hand and the defiant Foxes on the other continued unabated. The

8.1. Fox Country, detail of *Carte de la Louisiane et du cours du Mississipi* [sic], Guillaume Delisle, 1718. Library of Congress.

long-running Fox conflict was a fundamental and inescapable fact that weighed heavily on French settlements in the Illinois Country during that decade. Daily existence in the Indian-French villages of the region was fraught with persistent anxiety—for villagers and military men alike. Pressure from Fox Indians had been instrumental in pushing the Kaskaskia Indians out of the upper Illinois River valley during the early 1690s,[4] and three decades later the Foxes continued to foray down the entire length of the Illinois River, and beyond, into the Mississippi Valley. The French command in the Illinois Country did not relish conflict with the Foxes; it engaged in it as a necessity. Étienne Véniard de Bourgmont, father of a Métis son, was one of the great Indian diplomatists of the eighteenth century, and he brokered a sweeping ecumenical peace with western tribes in 1724. Bourgmont bemoaned the *fâcheuses* (unfortunate) consequences of French-Fox hostilities, but, nevertheless, he insisted that Fox aggressiveness had to be confronted with armed force.[5]

In 1722, Commandant Boisbriant mounted an expedition from Fort de Chartres up the Illinois River to assist Illinois Indians engaged against the Foxes. For decades, long before French villages had been established in the Illinois Country, the Illinois Nation had been at war with the Foxes.[6] According to Jean-Baptiste Diron d'Artaguiette, Boisbriant's waterborne force of French marines and local militiamen amounted to a hundred men. Two of the officers, Pierre Diron d'Artaguiette and Legardeur Delisle, were friends of Franchomme; each would sign his marriage contract in Kaskaskia in 1723 and each would support his petition to the Superior Council in New Orleans in 1725. Possibly, Franchomme himself participated in Boisbriant's 1722 expedition up the Illinois River but simply was not mentioned; he was, after all, only an ensign and a newcomer to the Illinois Country. When this rather imposing expedition reached Pimitéoui, word arrived that the Foxes had withdrawn northward up the Illinois River. Boisbriant then prudently decided against pursuing the Foxes deeper into their home territory and withdrew his forces back downstream to Fort de Chartres and Kaskaskia, leaving the Fox threat unscathed and intact.[7]

During the 1720s, and on into the early 1730s, French administrators in New Orleans never mentioned the Illinois Country without bringing up the vexatious issue of Fox hostilities.[8] This was a vicious, drawn out war, with no holds barred, no quarter given, and characterized by revolting (to us) practices on both sides of the conflict. All branches of the Illinois Nation were engaged on behalf of the French—or, more accurately, in hostility toward the Foxes—and in 1722, Chassin reported from Fort de Chartres that "the Peorias do well to avenge everything that they [Foxes] have done to them. They have taken and burned nine the first time, and twenty-eight the second time. This does not mean that we are not every day exposed to Fox attacks. They even had the effrontery to spend the night outside Kaskaskia, camping on the wheat field of a habitant, where they would have inevitably killed someone."[9]

Father Charlevoix described how Illinois Indians executed prisoners of war who had been condemned to death during the war; the lucky ones were enslaved. "The cry goes out to assemble the village. The condemned man is stripped naked. Two posts are planted in the ground and two cross pieces attached, one two feet off the ground and the other seven feet higher up. . . . The feet of the condemned are attached to the lower one, his ankles to the upper, and then he is burned. The entire village—men, women, and children—gather around, and each has the right to inflict on him any injury they can think of."[10] In 1723, Bernard Diron d'Artaguiette provided a somewhat different version of Illinois executions: "When they have condemned their prisoner to be burned, they tie him to a boat and burn him—today one part of the body and tomorrow another, and sometimes for three days and three nights. I have seen some of these unfortunates, who kept singing up to their last breath."[11] A sustained anthropological tradition has sought to explain the complex and often unsettling phenomena of torture and execution rites of Native Americans. Starting with Nathaniel Knowles seminal study, *The Torture of Captives by the Indians of Eastern North America*,[12] scholars have examined Native American torture practices by trying to go beyond depicting torture as mere blood lust, revenge, and retribution. Cornelius Jaenen explained how "torture of prisoners was a ritualistic function of warfare,"[13] and this analysis has been expanded by Gilles Havard in his discussion of how torture was "an integral part of Indian warfare," a continuation of war by other means.[14] Moreover, "Amerindian torture, in fact, had far more to do with the complex sequence of Amerindian mourning customs, religious ideas, and a community expression of aggression, as well as a means of revenge. To torture a captive gave the entire community—men and women, young and old—an opportunity to engage in a relationship with an adversary. Both the tortured and the torturers understood this."[15] The final sentence of d'Artaguiette's description of an Illinois execution—"I have seen some of these unfortunates, who kept singing up to their last breath"—lends credence to this analysis. Richard White has gone a step further and suggested that in exceptional cases even some *White* men became so deeply immersed in Native American culture that they grasped this larger dimension of Indian torture customs.[16]

To delve more deeply into these cultural complexities is beyond the scope of this study. Some historical context for blood-curdling events is, however, worth noting, even though this context is not suffused with the psychological subtlety of the anthropological approach to Indian affairs. We simply remind the reader that eighteenth-century French civilization did not consist solely of precious salons and powdered wigs, Rameau operas and Rococo architecture. At Fort de Chartres on October 16, 1732, a French marine, convicted of killing a fellow marine after a heated argument, was "hung and strangled until dead," after which his head was ceremonially bashed in in the presence of the assembled troops and habitants.[17] And, in 1757, Robert-François Damiens, who had launched a risibly incompetent attempt to assassinate King Louis XV, was drawn and quartered by horses on the Place de Grève in the center of Enlightenment Paris, the city of Voltaire and Diderot. His remaining torso was then ceremonially burned to the immense satisfaction of the assembled crowd.[18] Atavistic pleasure in witnessing physical pain is deeply ingrained in the human psyche.

At daybreak on April 12, 1724, Bohème (the Bohemian), "a married man living and working at Fort de Chartres was killed along with three companions, one of whom was 'l'Armurier' (gunsmith) by Fox Indians"; their bodies were taken into Kaskaskia for proper burial the same day.[19] And in May 1725, Joseph Lamy (Census, no. 76), *marguillier en chef* (chief church warden) in Kaskaskia was killed by "a party of enemies [Foxes] at two steps from the village."[20] Lamy, as the leading lay person in the parish, was honored with burial under his pew in the parish church of the Immaculate Conception. Lamy's death left his widow Marie-Françoise Rivard in financial straits, and she was forced to sell off her fine clothes, including a satin dress and silk stockings, to sustain herself and her children. Fox warriors were not content merely to defend their home territories west of Lake Michigan, for they were intent on pursuing an offensive war against French colonists in Illinois, taking the struggle *à l'outrance* right to village doorsteps.

More important than these isolated killings close to Kaskaskia was the annihilation in the spring of 1727 of an entire French squad led by Pierre Melique, a lieutenant in Captain Pierre Diron d'Artaguiette's company of detached marines. Melique (Census, no. 64) was an active and enterprising officer in his early fifties, and he showed every evidence of planning to become a permanent Illinois settler. He had been born and raised in Mont Didier, diocese of Amiens, a region of rich farmland,[21] and he was smitten by the equally rich land situated between the Mississippi and Kaskaskia rivers. Although officially posted to Fort de Chartres, Melique carved out a large plantation along the Kaskaskia River between the French village and the Indian mission (see d'Artaguiette map). During November 1726, he spent much time and energy sorting things out at this plantation, closing out his accounts with one tenant farmer, Joseph Gardon (Census, no. 42), and leasing the entire establishment, including two enslaved people (Native American?),[22] to a new tenant, Pierre Hullain (or Hulin, Census, no. 49).[23]

Having put his affairs in order in a region where lives were fragile and generally short, Lieutenant Melique lead his men against the Foxes early in the spring of 1727. News of his death and that of his seven men arrived in New Orleans in April, and unsettled the French command there, for officials feared that Foxes might sever the all-important link between Canada and Louisiana. The new governor, Étienne Perier, called Melique's death a "meurtre par les Renards [murder by Foxes]."[24] Perier studiously avoided using the standard French locution for describing combat deaths, *mort sur le champ d'honneur* (killed on the field of honor), for the governor was unable to conceive of Native American warfare as honorable; it was more like hunting down bandits. Foxes, on the other hand, would surely have honored Melique's "murderer" as a hero in their desperate war of survival against French colonizers.

· · ·

As Pierre Melique had been dispatched to face Fox warriors in the spring of 1727, so Franchomme was posted on the same mission in the spring of 1728; just as Melique never returned home, so too Franchomme never returned. As early as the autumn of 1727, Governor Charles de La Boisch de Beauharnois in Quebec was planning a major new offensive against the Foxes for the coming year. He wrote to Commandant Pierre-Charles Deliette[25] at Fort de Chartres that "It is reasonable to suppose that the people of Louisiana [the Illinois Country] will come to this war with more ardor than the Canadians, for they are much more exposed to the incursions of the Foxes, who alarm them continually and even kill them."[26] Jean-Paul Mercier, Seminarian mission priest at Cahokia, reported in January 1728 that Foxes had raided his mission, "killed two of our Indians and made off with three others; one escaped and [Mercier was much gratified to report] assured me that he had never lost faith in God." Mercier also reported that Foxes had struck the Illinois villages in October 1727, scalping two Illinois Indians and capturing one from the Jesuit mission at Kaskaskia. Providing reciprocity on this occasion, one of the Fox raiders had been captured and "burned in the village of Kaskaskia."[27] Mercier did not specify whether this grisly immolation pageant was played out in the French village or the Indian village (likely the latter), but, whichever, it brings us abruptly face to face with the ghastliness that could inform daily life in the region during the 1720s. If Franchomme and Marguerite joined the throng that witnessed the burning, would their sober faces have betrayed any sign of satisfaction at the horrific demise of a hated enemy?

Commissaire-Ordonnateur Jacques de La Chaise in New Orleans later described the circumstances surrounding the 1728 French offensive against the Foxes, which, ultimately, led to Franchomme's death: "The war against the Foxes continues unremittingly, and no good end is in sight for the French. Governor Perier will recount the news we have received, including that of the death of Sieur Franchomme, an officer who was part of the group of French, Canadians, and Indians commanded by Monsieur Deliette that set out [from Fort de Chartres] to join up with an army from Canada in order to strike the Indians."[28]

On June 7, 1728, Franchomme stood as a witness at the marriage of Susanne Pani8assa Kerami and Daniel Legras in Kaskaskia.[29] He then immediately set out as a member of Deliette's Illinois detachment, which headed north from Fort de Chartres, aiming to join up with Canadian forces led by Constant Marchand de Lignery, with plans to smite the Foxes.[30] The strategic plan called for the two French groups to assemble somewhere near Green Bay, on the western side of Lake Michigan, which was deep in Fox territory. But this rendezvous never successfully happened, apparently because Deliette's Illinois detachment encountered determined Fox resistance before getting to Lake Michigan. The Illinois contingent turned back, aborting the grand strategy, while the Canadians, advancing westward from Montreal, only got as far as Michilimackinac on their proposed route to Green Bay.[31] In July 1728, Governor Beauharnois heard that Foxes had struck Deliette's retreating Illinois detachment, killing five and seizing a sixth whose hands they cut off, proclaiming, "It is thus that we wish to deal with them."[32] One of the five Frenchmen killed in this engagement was likely Nicolas Peltier de Franchomme. Had he entertained an expansive conception of his duty as a French marine? Had he died for his king, or for the Bourbon monarchy, or on behalf of French or Christian civilization? Or had he simply paid the price for acting on a pulsing sense of adventure that carried him to places of whose dangers he had scarcely dreamed when he left his Ardennes home, traveled across France to La Rochelle, and sailed for Louisiana, a mythical land of infinite possibilities and imminent perils?

Fox pressure on the French Illinois villages was finally relieved following a bloody, lengthy, and ugly siege on the central Illinois prairie in 1730. Robert Grotton St. Ange led a contingent of French marines and militiamen from Fort de Chartres, and Nicolas-Antoine Coulon de Villiers did the same from Fort St. Joseph. Total French forces numbered fewer than 200 men, while allied Indians—Illinois, Potowatomis, Kickapoos, Mascoutens, Weas, and Piankashaws—numbered more than 1,000; the Foxes had indeed shown themselves masters at acquiring enemies. When, on a blustery, rainy night, the besieged Foxes attempted a breakout from their earthen fort, the French left the concluding dirty work to their Native American allies, who pursued the fleeing Foxes, tracked them down, and either slaughtered or enslaved them (mostly women and children). This is one of the darkest episodes in the entire recorded history of the Midwest. Triumphant over this victory,

Canadian Governor Charles de La Boische de Beauharnois was eager to press his advantage, and he proposed "annihilating" the Foxes.[33] The governor's language is fittingly unpleasant, for historians of the Fox wars agree that he was a decidedly unpleasant human being. His proposal has been labelled a policy of genocide, although the complicity of Native Americans (Hurons, Ottawas, and Potowatomis, as well as Illinois) begs the question whether genocide is an appropriate word for this ugly, bloody conflict.[34] Twentieth-century words do not always fit well when trying to understand and explain eighteenth-century events and people and motives

For Brett Rushforth, the most recent historian of Indian slavery in Canada, the Fox Wars were all about slavery; that is, capturing slaves from the Pays d'en Haut to be taken back to French settlements in the St. Lawrence Valley. "New France's appetite for Fox slaves originated with the bloody battles of 1712, when the French and their [Native American] allies captured large numbers of Fox women and children."[35] And, during "the Fox slaving spree of 1728–31," 400 Foxes were seized, and a large number wound up as enslaved people in French Canadian households,[36] although many were eventually manumitted.[37] In any case, Rushforth's charged vocabulary casts French Canadians as dedicated in their purpose of capturing Fox slaves, and that their pursuit was conducted with glee and gusto.[38]

If, indeed, the Fox Wars were, from the Canadian perspective, all about capturing slaves, this was decidedly not the case from the viewpoint of the Illinois Country settlements. Curiously, very few Fox slaves taken after the horrific 1730 siege wound up in Illinois French villages. Indeed, over the entire course of the eighteenth century, Fox slaves rarely appear in these villages.[39] This is strong evidence that French forces emanating from Fort de Chartres had a rather different motivation in waging war against the Foxes than did their counterparts from Canada. And this motivation was stark and simple: To prevent the utter destruction of the Illinois villages. From Fort de Chartres, Commandant Boisbriant tersely summed it up in 1724: "The Foxes lie in wait around our French and Native American settlements each summer, or, rather, all year long. This means that the inhabitants do not dare venture abroad except in groups."[40] Correspondence of Louisiana administrators during the 1720s, contains nothing about pursuing Foxes for the purpose of enslaving them. Rather, these audacious and stubborn aggressors were to be hunted and confronted, and put down hard enough to prevent them from threatening the Illinois Country villages, the agricultural products of which were important to all of French Louisiana.[41] When Lieutenant Pierre Melique and ensign Nicolas Franchomme sallied forth from Fort de Chartres to confront Fox warriors, and be slain by them, they did not die as slave catchers but rather as defenders of the Illinois Nation of Indians and of the French settlements in the Illinois Country.[42]

· · ·

Shortly before Franchomme's detachment set out up the Mississippi from Fort de Chartres, he sat down in his own home in Kaskaskia on March 6, 1728 and penned his last will and testament.[43] Article CCLXXXIX of the *Coutume* specifically acknowledged the validity of such wills, called "holographs" in English.[44] Franchomme was well aware of the mortal dangers he faced when he set out to wage war against the Foxes. Indeed, he had a clear premonition of his death when he drafted his will, and the document is suffused with the *angst* of a fragile human facing imminent death. In addition to routine provisions concerning remission of his sins and settling of debts, several clauses of Franchomme's will are unique and valuable sources about him and Marguerite 8assecam8c8e, and about their household in Kaskaskia:

> "Should I not return, I request that my wife [Marguerite 8assecam8c8e] pray for the repose of my soul, and that she comport herself in a manner pleasing to both God and man.
>
> If pursuant to the marriage contract that I had drafted '*à la mer*' [New Orleans] during my last trip there (the first contract having been lost) my heirs lay claim to some possessions that came from my wife, I declare clearly to them that this is neither my wish nor my desire, for it is not natural that anything she has given me, and which I've used during my life, should go to my heirs after my death, and that she should be left to beg for her bread.
>
> Since my wife [Marguerite 8assecam8c8e] has no relatives to whom she is obliged,[45] I beg her to do all that she can for little [Jean-Baptiste] Saguingora to make sure that he does not join up with the Indians. I exhort her to instruct him in our religion as best she can, which I myself would have done if I had lived longer. I further exhort her to treat the slaves as gently as she can, as she has seen that I have done; and, as I have often recommended, to provide them with the necessities of life, both with regard to food and clothing, insofar as it is possible.
>
> I request that Monsieur de Vincennes[46] should have all of my books [unfortunately not listed by title or author], paying for them whatever he should judge to be appropriate.
>
> Kaskaskia, Friday, March 6, 1728. Nicolas Peltier Franchomme"

These are touching and fascinating statements, hugely important as historical sources for early Illinois history. Franchomme addresses his wife directly, begging her to comport herself well. This was a very odd request to insert in a will and reinforces an impression of Marguerite 8assecam8c8e dating back to her flight from Kaskaskia in 1725, while Franchomme was conducting important business in New Orleans. She was an impulsive, willful woman, who occasionally required—at least in Franchomme's opinion—admonishment in order to serve as the proper wife of a French marine officer. Yet, at the same time, she was a sober and intelligent person, and Franchomme entrusted to her hands and brains some serious business. Indeed, although he does not use the word *exécutrice*, Marguerite 8assecam8c8e clearly was to serve in that capacity. Franchomme felt no responsibility to name, for example, a fellow French officer to handle his estate, and he frankly acknowledged that most everything he owned, had come from Marguerite via the critical donation clause in their marriage contract.

The longest, and most interesting clause in Franchomme's will was devoted, in one way or another, to racial, religious, and cultural matters. As the imperious Marie Rouensa did not want her Métis children to associate with Indians, thereby becoming less French, less Roman Catholic, and less like herself than she wished, Franchomme wanted Jean Saguingora, a fifteen-year-old Métis boy, to be raised French and Catholic by his Illinois Indian stepmother.[47] Marie Rouensa was a big favorite of the Jesuits and was emphatically Roman Catholic, but we know nothing about Marguerite 8assecam8c8e's religion other than that she was nominally Catholic. She was a member of the power elite in Kaskaskia, but her relationship with the local Jesuits, who were of course also major power players in the community, remains unknown. Marguerite married three times in the parish church of the Immaculate Conception at Kaskaskia, which means that she had been earlier baptized and given the Christian name Marguerite. Nevertheless, in his will Franchomme evinces some anxiety about Marguerite's knowledge of Roman Catholicism, and, indeed, perhaps her commitment to that faith, for he instructed her to educate Jean Saguingora in "our religion as best she can."

The 1726 Kaskaskia census (Part II) lists four slaves, three Africans and one Native American in the Franchomme-8assecam8c8e household, all of whom were passed down to Marguerite 8assecam8c8e via the Bourdon succession.[48] As we saw above, the succession papers reveal the names of three African slaves, two males and one female—Bambara, La Fleure, and Aubas. The census lists only one enslaved Indian, who was either the male, Caracaroet, or the female, Chonicoa, whom Marguerite had also inherited from Bourdon.[49] Franchomme did not differentiate enslaved humans by race or color or origin in his will, but he specifically entreated Marguerite to deal with them *le plus doucement* (as gently) as possible. This is a very rare, in fact unique, admonition to discover in a last will and testament from colonial Kaskaskia, and it suggests that Marguerite was not always a gentle mistress when dealing with her enslaved people. In this particular situation, we are faced with an elusive yet informative instance of a Frenchman admonishing his Native American wife to go easy on her enslaved people—elusive because it involved relationships between a man and his wife and their slaves that we cannot fully decipher, and informative because it demonstrates the complexity of coping with and understanding slavery, skin color, and human relations in 1720s Kaskaskia.[50] Franchomme had not experienced slavery when growing up in northern France, and it is conceivable that he was not entirely comfortable with the system of human bondage that he experienced in Kaskaskia as Marguerite's husband.[51] We will never know the truth of this matter.

Commandant Pierre-Charles Deliette's detachment returned to Fort de Chartres from the guerrilla war zone southwest of Lake Michigan and spread the word about Franchomme's demise at the hands of Foxes; death struck the young officer in late July or early August

8.2. Franchomme's personal effects as auctioned off at Fort de Chartres, August 6, 1728, included moccasins and deerskin shot pouch. Kaskaskia Manuscripts, Randolph County Courthouse.

1728, four or five months after he had prudently written up his final will and testament. Franchomme had, in addition to his home in Kaskaskia, small quarters in the officers' barracks at Fort de Chartres. In these barracks, Nicolas-Michel Chassin, member of the Provincial Council, oversaw the sale of Franchomme's personal effects—that is, those articles not being part of his marital communauté—on Friday, August 6, 1728.[52] Franchomme's widow, Marguerite 8assecam8c8e, was not present, remaining at home in Kaskaskia, and no boisterous crowd gathered for the auction, despite the fact that auctions, traditionally held on Sundays after Mass, were often festive social occasions in the Illinois Country. In this case, an aura of pathos hung over the sale of the dead man's possessions. Only four persons were present—Chassin, and three of Franchomme's fellow marine officers: Deliette, Terrisse de Ternan,[53] and St. Ange fils.[54] All items auctioned off were sold to one or another of these four men: Terrisse bought for ten francs a set of leggings, a pair of moccasins, and a black deerskin shot-pouch decorated with porcupine quills; St. Ange garnered a black (ostrich?) plume and a gunpowder sack for twenty-one francs; and Terrisse took away a worn but *fin* (high-quality) hat with a silver band for twenty francs.

But the gallant Franchomme should not be remembered through the prism of the paltry physical remnants of his life as a French marine at Fort de Chartres. Rather, one should image him at the very outset of his North American venture: Seventeen years old, arriving in the small harbor at the east end of Dauphin Island in 1720, standing eagerly on the foredeck of the *Duc de Noailles,* madly waving his black-plumed hat, musketeer-style, to his cousin, Jean Jadard de Beauchamp, who awaited him on the sandy shore; by nature, he was not a violent, grasping invader, but rather a young, inquisitive, big-hearted knight errant. Begun brightly, Franchomme's Louisiana venture ended darkly eight years later, with an early death at age twenty-five, and with an anonymous grave somewhere on the northern Illinois prairie, his body likely mutilated by Fox warriors. We shall see that his widow, Marguerite 8assecam8c8e, lived on, marrying yet another Frenchman and adding further details to our story about Native American wives and their French husbands. These women and men were also of interest to French officials in New Orleans.

CHAPTER 9

Aubains and Régnicoles
Blood and Culture

MÉTISSAGE (INTIMATE RELATIONS) BETWEEN Native American women and Frenchmen had been a glowing topic of discussion since Louisiana's earliest days, even before the founding of New Orleans in 1718.[1] This debate continued during the 1720s, and the Illinois Country was at the very center of it. Late in the year 1728, Father Jean-Antoine Le Boullenger departed Kaskaskia and headed down the Mississippi to New Orleans.[2] He was en route to visit his sister, Marie-Anne, who was cloistered in the Ursuline Convent there,[3] but he also had serious questions concerning Indian-French marriages that he wanted to discuss with legal authorities in Louisiana's capital. Le Boullenger was particularly vexed by two cases involving family assets and inheritance practices. The first was that of Guillaume Pottier, whose Illinois Indian wife, Marie Apechic8rata (seen in chapter 2), was pregnant with—in Guillaume's adamant opinion—another man's child. Pottier himself was eager to pursue an official declaration of bastardy against the child when it was born; obviously, no thought was given to trying to terminate the pregnancy.[4]

The Marguerite 8assecam8c8e case also occupied Father Le Boullenger's thoughts as he arrived in early December 1728 in New Orleans, where he intended to discuss Native American wives and widows with the Superior Council. Marguerite was of particular interest because she had had no children by either of her husbands, Bourdon or Franchomme, and she had been left with a substantial estate, including real estate and enslaved people.[5] Father Le Boullenger knew Marguerite well, for they had lived in the same small village together for at least a decade, and she was part of the elite coterie of Illinois Indian women married to Frenchmen. Le Boullenger had also witnessed Marguerite's flight from "civilization" when, at the time of Franchomme's journey to New Orleans during the first few months of 1725, she had disappeared from the French village of Kaskaskia, apparently repairing to live with Indian friends (possible relatives) in the nearby Kaskaskia Indian village. In the autumn of 1728, just months after the death of her second husband, no one could predict how

Marguerite might handle, or mishandle, her estate. Le Boullenger's trip to New Orleans was all that much more important because Illinois's Provincial Council, which had laboriously adjudicated Jacques Bourdon's succession in 1723, had withered up and disappeared by the end of 1725. It was therefore in New Orleans where all matters of legal weight had to be resolved for all Louisiana, which included the Illinois Country.

Arriving in New Orleans, Le Boullenger proceeded immediately to *Procureur Général* (Attorney General) Jean-François de Fleuriau and painted a complicated picture of matrimonial affairs in the Illinois Country.[6] Fleuriau digested the priest's story, ruminated over the issues, and drafted talking points for the Superior Council, "Questions à décider concernant les alliances matrimoniales des français et les sauvages" (Issues to Decide Regarding French and Native American Marriages). Fleuriau then added his proposals for dealing with the situation in a document titled "Exposé du Procureur Général de la Louisiane sur les remonstrances de R.P. Boulanger [*sic*], Jesuit curé des Kaskaskias aux Illinois" (Response of the the Attorney General of Louisiana to Remonstrances Made by R.P Boulenger). Fleuriau took Le Boullenger's concerns about *métissage* in the Illinois Country seriously. Indeed, the detail and specificity with which Fleuriau addressed Illinois Country issues suggests that Le Boullenger worked closely with him in composing the "Exposé," for it was the priest who had deep, first-hand knowledge about the region.[7]

The Council, having digested Fleuriau's "Exposé," completed a first draft of a decree on December 8, 1728,[8] and ten days later produced the final version along with an *Arrêt* (Decree) to be *publié et affiché partout* (published and posted everywhere), so that no one in Louisiana could remain ignorant of it.[9] The three-page document pertained exclusively to situations in which Frenchmen were married to Native American women, especially those of the Illinois Nation, and particularly in those marriages that had produced no children. The Councilors conceded right off that the "Black Code, which prohibits marriage of White and Black people, in no way prohibited French marriages with Indian women."[10] The decree spelled out with great clarity that these Native American wives had, for all intents and purposes, become French: "They have been married with the customary ceremonies of the Church; they enjoy the same benefits as their husbands, and assume their status and condition; they live under the laws of the country [French Louisiana], and are subject to its ordinances and regulations. This means that they have attained a position of *naturalité* [naturalization], have become Régnicoles, and are eligible for all the benefits of the [marital] communauté." Although the decree deals explicitly only with childless marriages, by logical extension, if these marriages had produced Métis children, these children would have assumed the same status as their mothers, meaning as lawful, naturalized French citizens, that is to say, Régnicoles. And as such these children would have enjoyed full inheritance rights under the *Coutume de Paris*. In the Illinois Country, this had been routinely the accepted practice, as in the case of Catherine 8abanakic8e's children (as seen in chapter 2), and those of Marie Rouensa.[11]

But childless Indian-French marriages raised an altogether different issue. Assuming that the French husband died first, his surviving Native American wife would receive the entire estate if a mutual donation clause had been included in their marriage contract. If such a clause had not been included, or, more likely, no marriage contract had ever been formalized, the Indian wife would receive one-half of the estate "according to the *Coutume de Paris*" (Article CCXXIX), and the deceased husband's heirs the other half. The authors of the decree, working for the Superior Council in New Orleans, were no doubt familiar with the basic tenets of the *Coutume*. In their minds, the issue arose about what should occur when an Indian widow herself died: "Are her relatives, who are Indians, permitted to carry off to their villages her possessions, to take her enslaved people and livestock, and dispose of her agricultural land, residences, and other assets?" The decree's answer was quick and categorical: Absolutely not. These possessions had been accumulated within the context of a lawful French-Christian marriage, under French customary law, and within the confines of French civil society—and by all rights they should remain there. Simply put, French possessions, whether personal or real, should not devolve upon *Aubains* (persons who were not assimilated into French society)[12] and were not Régnicoles (lawful citizens of Louis XV's realm).[13]

The position of the Councilors here may be interpreted as racist, but more plausibly their motivations were economic, for they were concerned with the future viability of French Louisiana. Conditions in the colony during the 1720s were tenuous, as the Indies Company's exaggerated hopes of creating a booming colonial economy foundered. Within three years, the Company would abandon its misplaced adventure in Louisiana and retrocede control of the colony to the French crown in 1731.[14] The Councilors in New Orleans, understandably, could not abide seeing assets, both material and financial, dissipated into the wilderness outside the confines of established French settlements, thereby sapping the economic strength of Louisiana, and, ultimately, of France itself. In the dog-eat-dog world of eighteenth-century commercial and colonial competition, the Councilors were most likely thinking in economic terms rather than racialist, mercantilist rather than racist.

Interestingly, the Council's decree of December 1728 specifically adduced Article XXIII of the royal letters patent of August 23, 1717, which had officially conveyed the colony of Louisiana to John Law's *Compagnie des Indes* (known, since 1719, as the *Compagnie d'Occident* or *d'Ouest*).[15] The Article states that Europeans professing the Roman Catholic faith could immigrate to Louisiana and assume the status of proper *Régnicoles*. No Native Americans of any tribe appear in this Article, and thus they were omitted from the pool of those eligible for Régnicole status. But it is hard to argue that this was for racial reasons when European Protestants and Jews were also excluded from eligibility as proper Régnicoles, for both groups were officially outlawed in French Louisiana.[16] The officials working at Versailles who drafted the royal letters patent in 1717 simply could not get their skulls around the prospect of Jews, Protestants, or unassimilated Indians becoming fully naturalized citizens of France. These peoples just would not fit, for they were too eccentric, too distant from the center, that is, the center of traditional Gallic Roman Catholic and French civilization.

Officials of the Bourbon monarchy at Versailles had absolutely no knowledge of the Indian-French marriages that were the foundation stones, the sine qua non, of society in the Illinois Country at the time, and they had not digested—or even contemplated—the cultural and legal ramifications of those marriages when they drafted their letters patent of 1717. By 1728, however, the Superior Council in New Orleans was faced squarely with the issue of Native American wives, and therefore, necessarily, succession issues, in the Illinois Country. For the Councilors, practical, legal problems demanded realistic solutions, and these solutions could, indeed, be implemented using existing provisions of French law. Nothing needed to be invented and no racial arguments needed to be adduced, deployed, or even implied, meaning that there is nothing inherently racist, or even racialist, in the language of the Council's practical decree.[17]

French law, with an authority bred of antiquity and proven utility, that undergirded the Council's decree was the *Coutume de Paris,* and the apposite Article was CCCXVIII. Claude de Ferrière, one of the most eminent and erudite jurists of the Old Regime, provided extended commentary on this article:

> There are several reasons why a person cannot inherit, even though they may be the closest relative to the deceased: The first is the *incapacité des effets civils* [loss of civil rights]. [Ferrière provides a variety of possibilities, such as perpetual banishment from the kingdom for a criminal offense.] The second is illegitimate birth, such as [is the case of] bastards, to which one may add *Aubains. . . . Aubains* are incapable of inheriting in France, and their successions belong to the King, to the exclusion of any Seigneur. Nevertheless, legitimate children of *Aubains* born in the Kingdom are capable of inheriting.[18]

Ferrière's last sentence could certainly be construed as pertaining to Indian children of Native American couples living in French Kaskaskia, although none such couples were enumerated on the 1726 census; and, of course, such a situation would never have remotely entered Ferrière's French brain.

The Superior Council's decree of December 1728, promulgated in Louisiana, was, significantly, more generous and open-spirited than either the *Coutume* or the royal letters patent of 1717, both of which emanated from metropolitan France. Likely with encouragement from Father Le Boullenger, the Council's decree officially transformed Illinois Indian wives, who had been born and raised Aubains, into naturalized French citizens, Régnicoles, by virtue of their marriage to and intimate association with their French husbands.[19] Once again, the Council in no way, either explicitly or implicitly, construed this in racial terms; the Councilors dealt with what was a difficult situation—fraught with cultural, social, and financial complexities—in a strictly practical fashion. If we are trying to understand the early denizens of the Illinois Country, we would be well-advised not to obsess over racial issues; they most certainly did not.

The Council wrapped up its decree with a series of interim provisions, "while waiting for what the King [Louis XV] wishes to do." Native Americans—that is, Aubains—would be excluded from French successions; successions of Native American women dying without children would by default go to Law's Compagnie des Indes, which exercised sovereign rights in Louisiana until 1731; Indian widows would have their *biens fonds* (basic possessions) placed in the care of tuteurs for proper management; the widows would receive an annuity, based on one-third of the proceeds from the *biens fonds*, while the other two-thirds would be conveyed to their children or other heirs. This provision harkened back to Commandant Boisbriant's appointment of a tuteur for Louis Tessier's widow, Catherine 8abanakic8e, in 1721, which we saw above in chapter 2. Finally, until the king's government pronounced the final word, no Frenchman would be permitted to contract a marriage with a Native American woman. All of this is infinitely interesting to those of us who study French colonial Louisiana, but it turned out to be, at the time, utterly fatuous. None of these provisions was ever enforced or implemented—except the first—and it would be virtually impossible to determine precisely how this was handled in various succession cases.

Finally, no evidence exists that King Louis XV ever weighed in on any of this, which, as pointedly stated, was necessary for any of it to become settled law. Even before the founding of New Orleans in 1718, the regency government of the duc d'Orléans in Versailles had taken up the issue of Indian-French marriages and admonished officials in Louisiana—that is, along the Gulf Coast, mostly at Mobile—to prevent marriages between Frenchmen and Native Americans "insofar as it is in their power,"[20] which, of course, it most assuredly was not. It is highly unlikely that a copy of the Superior Council's December 1728 decree ever arrived to be posted and read in the Illinois Country, and in that region the prohibition on Indian-French marriages fell flat on its face. Jennifer Spear has rightly emphasized that Roman Catholic clergy in French Louisiana were generally more tolerant of racial mixing than French civil administrators.[21] At Kaskaskia, Father René Tartarin scorned any attempt to prevent mixed marriages, and they continued, although in diminishing numbers over time (see Census).[22] One of these, fittingly, was Marguerite 8assecam8c8e's third, and final, marriage to a Frenchman, Pierre Blot, which is explored in the following chapter.

CHAPTER 10

Marguerite 8assecam8c8e's Last Dance

MARGUERITE 8ASSECAM8C8E HAD SUITORS within weeks of Franchomme's death; her substantial worldly assets and apparent good looks made this inevitable. Pierre Blot, who seems to have come to the Mississippi frontier just for the hell of it, prevailed in the competition for the widow's hand, and Marguerite and Blot married at Kaskaskia in August 1729.[1] Blot was born and raised on the Île d'Oléron, oyster capital of Europe, just off the southwestern coast of France. He likely sailed out of nearby La Rochelle—a major seaport for the trans-Atlantic trade—for Louisiana, and eventually caught passage on a bateau headed from New Orleans to the Illinois Country. Pierre arrived in his new land with significant financial resources, and when the estate of Jacques Prévost, Surgeon Major of the Troops, was auctioned off in September 1722, Blot was an active bidder, acquiring among other things "two dress shirts" for forty livres.[2] Two years later, he purchased a house at Fort de Chartres for 1,000 livres in cash, plus a pair of silk stockings, but then he reoriented his life, moved to Kaskaskia, and met Marguerite 8assecam8c8e.[3] His life would never be the same.

As for Marguerite, she collected French husbands as easily as she gathered nuts from the large black walnut tree that stood in the center of the village outside the parish church. She married three times and took as successive husbands a French Canadian and then two Frenchmen; there apparently had been no chance that she would have changed the course of her life and found a new man from within the Illinois tribe. One obvious consideration was the absence of such men who qualified as Régnicoles, which Marguerite did, in every which way. Indeed, the Superior Council's decree makes no mention whatsoever of Illinois Indian men; it was only Illinois women who were transformed into Régnicoles as lawful wives of Frenchmen.

It was fitting that Father Tartarin, who decidedly approved of Indian-French marriages, did double duty in the case of the Blot-8assecam8c8e marriage, drafting the civil marriage contract and officiating at the sacramental marriage ceremony.[4] Marriage contract signings were of huge importance in the Illinois Country parishes, for they brought together friends and relatives to deal with crucial issues concerning family, finances, religion, life, and death.[5] Tartarin conducted the affair in the *presbytère* of the parish of the Immaculate

Conception in Kaskaskia "at about 10:00" in the evening of August 24, 1729.[6] Marriage contract ceremonies were usually conducted in the home of the bride-to-be, and the use of Kaskaskia's *presbytère* in this case is notable. This was perhaps done because conducting the ceremony in Marguerite's house—which had been the home and hearth of Nicolas Peltier de Franchomme only a year earlier—might have appeared unseemly. Tartarin identified Marguerite 8assecam8c8e simply as "Marguerite, widow of Peltier de Francôme," her Native American name not appearing in the document.[7] What with her marriage to a third Frenchman, her Régnicole status, which had commenced with her marriage to Jacques Bourdon ca. 1715, was progressively rising. How Marguerite herself understood her evolving status as she moved from pure Indianness at her birth through three marriages to full citizenship within Louis XV's colony of Illinois, a curiously cosmopolitan frontier, is something upon which we may only speculate.

Tartarin, perhaps because, in drafting the marriage contract, he was serving in a role generally reserved for notaires, took pains to spell out, syllable by syllable, that his written words precisely reflected the terms of "la coutume de la ville, prévôté, and vicomté de Paris."[8] Sacramental marriage ceremonies between consenting adults did not require witnesses, only the two principals and the officiating priest. On the other hand, an honorable *promise* to marry had to be in writing and validated by four witnesses, and this promise always occupied the first clause of a marriage contract drafted under the *Coutume;* it was in effect a formal engagement to be married.[9] Blot and Marguerite 8assecam8c8e "mutually promise by those present to take one another in name and in law by legitimate marriage, celebrated before our mother holy Church, Catholic, Apostolic, and Roman. And this to be done as soon as possible with the advice and consent of relatives and friends." The family members and close friends who appear in marriage contracts were customarily divided into two distinct groups: Those who were physically present to support the bridegroom and those who similarly were there to support the bride.

The Blot-8assecam8c8e marriage contract includes four witnesses, each of whom is interesting enough to invite a bit of examination. Blot was represented by the elegant French Canadian, François-Marie Bissot de Vincennes, commandant at the new post of Vincennes on the Wabash. Vincennes himself married a Métisse at Kaskaskia in 1730,[10] but was burned alive at the termination of Governor Bienville's disastrous 1736 campaign against the Chickasaws; Blot's second witness was Michel Philippe, lieutenant in the militia company of the parish of the Immaculate Conception and widower of the formidable Marie Rouensa. Marguerite's witnesses were Jean-Baptiste Pottier and Pierre Baillargeon. Jean-Baptiste's brother Guillaume was married to an Illinois woman, Marie Apechic8rata (whom we have seen in chapter 2), and our well-known Pierre Baillargeon was married to a similar woman, Domitile Chacateni8a8a. No Native woman stood forth that evening as a specified "friend or relative" of Marguerite 8assecam8c8e, but Indianness nevertheless suffused Father Tartarin's presbytery, what with the presence of the bride herself, and of

Domitile Chacateni8a8a and Marie Apechic8rata. We have seen that back in 1723, Baillar-geon and Franchomme—the latter on behalf of Marguerite 8assecam8c8e—had engaged in a bitter dispute over the succession of Jacques Bourdon, Marguerite's first husband. But Baillargeon's service as a witness at Marguerite's marriage in 1729 suggests that this bit-terness had been put behind them. Marguerite and Baillargeon's wife, Domitile Chacat-eni8a8a, were almost certainly friends, and Domitile had likely served as an intermediary to heal the breach generated by the 1723 succession dispute. Elite Illinois Indian women, wives and widows of Frenchmen, may often have served to mitigate social tensions in the racially diverse community.

A mutual donation clause stood at the core of the Blot-8assecam8c8e marriage con-tract: "Because of the mutual affection and devotion that the future spouses have for one another, they agree to a donation pure and simple between the living [that is, the spouses] that is irrevocable."[11] Whichever one of the couple survived the death of the other would immediately inherit the entire estate, all personal and real property, to have and to hold for herself or himself for as long as they lived. However, this donation clause would be rendered automatically null and void should the couple produce legitimate children, in which case all of the possessions, personal and real, would remain within the estate, the communauté established when the marriage was celebrated. And any child or children produced by the marriage would eventually share in the division of this communauté.[12]

Blot and Marguerite 8assecam8c8e affixed their respective marks to their marriage con-tract, with Tartarin identifying Marguerite's mark as that of Franchomme's widow. The fact that Claude-Charles Dutisné, commandant at Fort de Chartres, rode down to Kaskaskia for the occasion and ornamented the contract with his signature suggests that the marriage of a French marine's widow to Blot was an affair of some social significance in the Illinois Country.[13] Although Tartarin's sacramental record of the Blot-8assecam8c8e marriage has not survived, we may assume that the sacrament was performed within a day or two after the signing of the marriage contract on Sunday evening, August 24, 1729, for this was the prevailing habit in the universe of French civilization and the *Coutume de Paris*.

Marguerite 8assecam8c8e Blot led, for the last two decades of her life, a comfortable life in Kaskaskia. The Fox threat to Illinois Country settlements had been crushed on the northern Illinois prairie in 1730, and the next two decades were the salad days of French Illinois: The population was growing, agriculture was expanding, flour production was ris-ing, and trade with New Orleans was thriving. Although childless, the Blot-8assecam8c8e household stood out as one of the more prosperous in Kaskaskia, as revealed in the compre-hensive 1732 Illinois census compiled by Robert Grotton de St. Ange père, commandant at Fort de Chartres.[14] Jean Saguinora had left Marguerite 8assecam8c8e's household to make his own way in the world as a boatman on the Mississippi.[15] Blot and Marguerite owned three enslaved Africans and three Native Americans, revealing that Blot had brought three slaves into their marriage in 1729, adding to the three Marguerite already owned—what

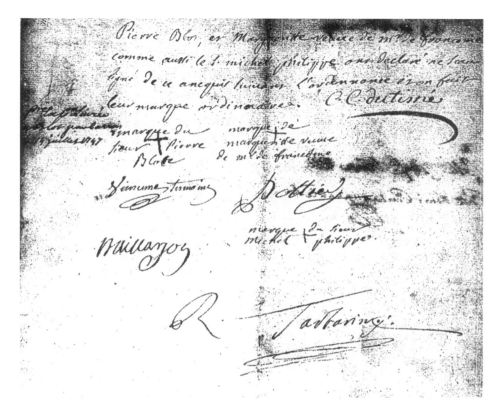

10.1. Marriage contract (*contrat de mariage*) of Pierre Blot and Veuve de Mr de Francôme, April 24, 1729. Kaskaskia Manuscripts, Randolph County Courthouse.

remained of her allotment in human property from Jacques Bourdon's estate—as enumerated on the 1726 census.[16] Adding diversity, Marguerite's three successive husbands hailed from different regions of the Bourbon empire, and would, respectively, have spoken rather different versions of the French language. How Marguerite adapted to language difficulties that undoubtedly existed in her various households is an interesting but imponderable question.

The marriage of Blot and Marguerite 8assecam8c8e was a union of more of less financial equals. This had manifestly not been the case in her earlier marriage to Franchomme, who had arrived in North America as a destitute teenager. Of course, Franchomme did bring into the match his panache as a royal marine officer and a trumped-up aristocratic name. Blot and Marguerite, in addition to their residential plot in the village, owned a two-arpent strip of plowland land in Kaskaskia's common field.[17] Blot was a small agricultural entrepreneur, owning and operating three horse-driven gristmills, at which he could mill his own wheat, and likely that of his nearest neighbors.

Within the family's slave holdings were two Indian women, and they likely worked alongside Marguerite 8assecam8c8e, the *maîtresse de la maison*, helping with her domestic affairs, which included cooking, mending clothes, feeding the livestock, and slaughtering the succulent acorn-fattened pigs come autumn. Surely a good deal of intimacy character-ized relations among these three Indian women as they managed the household, which must have been endowed with a fair amount of Indianness in everything from cuisine to clothing to daily routines.[18] Although born and raised on the seacoast of southwestern France, Blot adapted to this environment—geographically American and Midwestern, al-though those terms ring strange for describing Kaskaskia during the 1720s and 1730s—with aplomb and success. It was, after all, his initiative in courting Marguerite that had begun the building of this successful household, the foundations of which were laid down in their marriage contract of August 1729.

Having no children to raise, with the dreariness of winter months in a Midwestern ag-ricultural economy, and without much to do other than mend clothing and agricultural equipment, Marguerite and Blot had time and energy to have a go at opening their own business. The brothers Joseph and Pierre Lacourse had purchased from Jacques Lalande and his wife, Marie Tetio, *une maison* situated on the street leading directly from the front door of the parish church to the right bank of the Kaskaskia River, that is, close to the very heart of the village. The entrepreneurial brothers had developed within this house *un bill-ard*, that is, a billiard parlor and on-site drinking establishment, the first such entertainment center known to have existed in the Illinois Country.[19] The brothers Lacourse then sold the parlor—but not the house in which it was located—to Blot and his wife Marguerite "8ssec-ome8oir," notaire Jean-Baptiste Barrois's idiosyncratic version of 8assecam8c8e. One likes to imagine Marguerite reigning as *barista* in the establishment, maintaining a modicum of order on Saturday nights when tafia flowed freely and parishioners had to be disciplined enough to appear in respectable condition at next morning's Mass.

Finally, for whatever reasons, Blot and Marguerite sold the billiard parlor back to the La-course brothers on April 15, 1737, for 1,000 livres.[20] The bill of sale does not spell out what precisely constituted the parlor—surely, though, the table, the cue sticks, and the balls, but perhaps also a bar for serving liquid refreshments. Nor was there any clarification as to whether the parlor, situated in a house, yet discrete from the house, was deemed *meubles* (personal property) or *immeubles* (real estate). In either case, since it was certainly property, which Article CCXX of the *Coutume* decreed was jointly owned by the spouses, Blot and Marguerite. Article CCXXV gave husbands control over such acquired properties, with the power to sell them without his wife's consent. But in this fascinating case, the bill of sale has a sidebar explicitly stating that Blot accepted Marguerite as his partner (*"de luy autorizée pour l'effet des présentes"*). In keeping with this authorization, Barrois repeatedly spelled out Marguerite 8assecam8c8e's Indian name (idiosyncratically, "8assecome8oir"), never referring to her as Madame Blot and making it clear that Blot and Marguerite were indeed the co-equal grantees of the billiard parlor.[21] The traditional monarchial model of French society, even with the important leveling influences of the *Coutume*, provided husbands with much power within the household, yet Marguerite's marriage to Blot was very much one of financial equals.[22]

Blot and Marguerite 8assecam8c8e were, by 1740, each into their fifth decade on earth, when they decided to sell one of their female African slaves, Aubas.[23] Pierre, although energetic and entrepreneurial, seems to have been a poor money manager, and the couple likely needed some ready cash. Aubas—also Umbas and Unbas—first appears in written records in 1723, when she was listed among the enslaved people in Jacques Bourdon's succession papers[24]; and, as we have seen, she was allotted to Marguerite in the settlement of that succession. Aubas appears, though nameless, in the slave holdings of Marguerite and her second husband, Nicolas Peltier de Franchomme, on the 1726 census (see Part II); and again, nameless, she appears in the slave holdings of Marguerite and her third husband, Blot, on the 1732 Illinois census.[25] Marguerite and Aubas had worked together as part of the same household for seventeen years. The separation of these two women—one African and one Native American, one slave and one free—with the sale of 1740 surely provoked some emotional distress, although they continued to live in close proximity to one another in the intimate francophone village of Kaskaskia.

Like an old soldier, Marguerite 8assecam8c8e just faded away. No burial record for her has survived, but very likely she was not buried under the floor of the parish church, as had been the older, more famous Illinois woman, Marie Rouensa. Marguerite was not the active parishioner that Marie Rouensa had been, and she had never become a favorite of the Jesuit fathers in Kaskaskia. Marguerite's final appearance in civil records can be seen on June 3, 1741, when she and her husband Blot sold for 800 livres a plot of land that included a decaying grist mill. They had no children, and Blot lived on for another eight years or so—again, no burial record has survived—in the company of a few enslaved household servants. He also sold a Native American slave to Jean-Baptiste Richard in 1748.[26] From what sources we have, Blot was a good enough though unremarkable man, whose claim for inclusion in an account of early Illinois history is based almost entirely on his marriage to a remarkable Indian woman.

The prolonged disposition of the large estate amassed, over several decades, by Domitile Ch8ping8eta and Jacques Bourdon has been one of the principal issues driving this study. With Blot's death, that estate, one-half of which was carried on after 1723 by Marguerite 8assecam8c8e via Bourdon's succession, dwindled to an anonymous end.

The Critical Decade

NO OBJECTIVE OBSERVER COULD have reasonably predicted at the time the Illinois Country was incorporated into Louisiana in 1717 what the region would look like ten years later—or even if the Indian-French colony would survive at all.[1] No governmental structure existed, the grinding war of attrition with Fox Indians continued, serious wheat cultivation was only just beginning, and the essential commercial lifeline on the Mississippi River between Kaskaskia and the Gulf Coast was tenuous, threatened as it always was by both human (Chickasaw Indians) and natural (riverain hazards) forces. There is now no consensus among colonial historians about how most accurately or usefully to define the third decade of the eighteenth century in the Illinois Country, and which particular issues should be focused on in order to make that decade more comprehensible to students of American colonial history. What may be said with certainty is that the Kaskaskia of 1717 was radically different from that of 1726, when the first census of the community was compiled (Part II).

A century ago, the great Clarence W. Alvord defined the 1720s in the Illinois Country in economic terms as "The Era of Speculation."[2] Alvord based this definition on three well-established facts: The *Compagnie des Indes* had control over all of Louisiana (including the Illinois Country) during that decade; the *Compagnie*'s purpose in Louisiana was to speculate on the province's economic future; and the *Compagnie* brought the engineer and entrepreneur Philippe Renault (Census, no. 2) from France and sent him to the Illinois Country with the expectation that mining—lead, but also, in everyone's perfervid hopes, gold and silver—would make venture capitalism bear handsome fruit. The land grants that Boisbriant and des Ursins, representing the *Compagnie*, conveyed to Renault on June 23, 1723, reveal the grandiose plans for the Illinois Country that the French mining engineer entertained: "One [grant] on the Meramac River, where his [smelting] furnace is located; one at Pimitéoui on the Illinois River; one at Mine La Mothe [named after de La Mothe Cadillac]; and the last at the Grand Marais, next to the Illinois Indians near Fort de Chartres."[3] Renault's major, enslaved labor mining enterprise in the Meramac River valley, of what is now southeastern Missouri, was to be the *Compagnie*'s major investment in the

Illinois Country, and the mines, in the florid imaginings of French investors, would help to float the *Compagnie*'s entire Louisiana enterprise.[4]

It all came to naught. Even before the *Compagnie* threw in the towel on its Louisiana venture in 1731, returning economic control of the colony to the French crown, Renault's grandiose plans to extract glittering mineral wealth from Illinois had foundered. Though neither gold nor silver were ever found, rich veins of lead were indeed present in the Meramec Valley, and small-time individual entrepreneurs did continue to work them for modest profits, but neither Renault personally, nor the *Compagnie* corporately, ever cashed in on Illinois mines during the 1720s.[5] Renault returned unceremoniously to France in 1741, his former life in the Illinois Country a fading memory and his reputation as a mining messiah in tatters. At the time, Renault's abandoned lead mine in the Meramec Valley was reportedly being exploited sporadically by Native Americans.[6]

During the 1720s, however, another form of investment, which Alvord quite overlooked, was slowly and persistently making headway in Illinois Country settlements, and this quiet enterprise had nothing to do with the dazzle of Renault's dream of mineral wealth. Yet it turned out to be the harbinger of all the succeeding "amber waves of grain" that have swept the American Midwest down to the present day. As noted in the Introduction, by ca. 1720, habitants at Kaskaskia were systematically plowing with charrues and sowing with wheat, maize, and oats, the rich alluvial land located on the peninsula between the Kaskaskia and Mississippi rivers. Individual, habitant/entrepreneurs, with no direct help from either the *Compagnie* or the Bourbon crown, were investing in land, equipment, blood, sweat, tears, and often in enslaved people, to make this investment pay off, as it began to do in the early 1720s. It is noteworthy that Marguerite 8assecam8c8e's share of the Bourdon estate included quantities of wheat, maize, and oats, apparently all brought in with the 1723 harvest from Kaskaskia's grain fields.[7]

Expansion of arable agriculture in the Illinois Country was swift and dramatic, as the rudimentary statistics available to us clearly demonstrate. The 1726 census lists 2210 terrains *défrichés* (cleared parcels of plowland) measured in square arpents (one arpent equivalent to 0.85 acres), while the 1732 census lists 266 linear arpents by width (one arpent equivalent to 192 feet), which, when multiplied by the standard forty arpents of length, produced 10,640 square arpents of plowland.[8] A whopping five-fold increase over a six-year period. Enslaved Africans (and some Native) were soon deployed as agricultural laborers in Illinois Country settlements, working shoulder to shoulder with White habitants in the grain fields. The increase in their total numbers between 1726 and 1732 (129 to 165) was significant, although not commensurate with the rapid increase in acreage of plowlands.

When Governor Étienne Perier and Commissiare-ordonnateur Edmé-Gatien Salmon drafted a "Mémoire sur le païs des Islinois" in 1731, the French administrators spelled out with great lucidity the strategic geo-economic situation in French North America and how the Illinois Country fitted in to it: "This country [Illinois], which by its fertility can supply grain, meat, and other foodstuffs to the colony, can be sustained only by commerce. . . . Transportation between this post and Canada is very difficult, whereas it is very easy with New Orleans via the river St. Louis [i.e., the Mississippi]."[9] When Bienville was reappointed governor general of Louisiana in 1732, Louis XV singled out the importance of the Illinois Country: "We cannot hope that this crop [wheat] will ever succeed [in lower Louisiana]. But we also have this advantage that it succeeds well at the Illinois."[10] French administrators were absolutely smitten with the prospect that a French overseas colony could become a major producer of foodstuffs. This had never before occurred in the history of French overseas colonies, which were chronically short of an adequate food supply.

This revolution in agriculture did not signify that Kaskaskia ceased to be a major Mississippi-Valley fur-trading entrepôt, which the village had been since its founding in 1703. On the last manuscript page of the comprehensive 1732 Illinois census, the enumerator— likely Commandant Robert Grotton de St. Ange—noted that "numerous voyageurs, about fifty of them, are always coming and going."[11] St. Ange did not enumerate any individuals from this group on the census, but these voyageurs were nevertheless important components in the Illinois economy. Some of them were engaged in the important flour trade with New Orleans,[12] but many—voyageurs and the more free-wheeling *coureurs de bois*—were heading northward, up the Mississippi and the Missouri rivers and on into their distant tributaries, in pursuit of furs and skins. The Illinois Country plays a major role in Gilles Havard's encyclopedic, exhilarating volume, *Histoire des coureurs de bois, Amérique du Nord*.[13] Throughout the eighteenth century and on into the nineteenth, Kaskaskia remained a fur trading outpost, attracting men like the French Canadian Pierre Ménard (1766–1844), who was both a trader and a planter, a ubiquitous combination in the eighteenth-century Mississippi Valley.

· · ·

In mid-summer 1723, widow Marguerite 8assecam8c8e Bourdon and ensign Nicolas Peltier de Franchomme were the two most eligible unmarried citizens of Kaskaskia—she, attractive and about to inherit a fortune, and he, a French officer with an ostrich plume in his musketeer-style *chapeau*.[14] The mutual attraction was obvious and immediate. After having been married to Bourdon, there was no way on earth that Marguerite was going to step backward—financially and socially—and marry an Indian man; no known Illinois Indian widow ever did that, for in their eyes that would have constituted a clear reversal of fortune. As for Franchomme, the ethos of the village of which he had just become a resident was reflexively tolerant of Indian-French liaisons and marriages, while he, personally, was far too much an eighteenth-century cosmopolitan to have scruples about marrying an Indian woman.

Historical studies of Indian-French marriages usually dwell on what have now become famous in the literature as *mariages à la façon du pays*, informal (though often more-or-less permanent) liaisons between Indian women and fur traders.[15] This book does not touch on this subject in any way, for it deals exclusively with *mariages à la façon de la Coutume de Paris*—that is, the marriages of Marguerite 8assecam8c8e and others in her cohort of Illinois Indian women who married Frenchmen and lived in the village of Kaskaskia during the 1720s. These marriages were not only sanctified by a Roman Catholic priest, but were governed in civil contracts under the appropriate provisions of the *Coutume*—the signing of the marriage contract was just as important as the holy sacrament. The voluminous collection of documents generated by the adjudication of Jacques Bourdon's estate, which he shared with Marguerite 8assecam8c8e, permit us to delve as deeply into the Franchomme-8assecam8c8e marriage as any other Indian-French marriage in the history of the Illinois Country, perhaps in the entire history of French colonial North America—and deeply into how the *Coutume* governed the marriage, how the marriage reflected Kaskaskia society at the time, how French civil authorities and priests viewed Indian-French marriages, and how Marguerite's domestic life unfolded over the decades.

Marguerite, although eluding sharp focus, emerges in these documents as a preeminent survivor, successfully navigating successive marriages to three Frenchmen. From the moment of her marriage to Bourdon ca. 1715, through her marriage with Franchomme during the 1720s, and finally to that with Blot in the 1730s, Marguerite's life in Kaskaskia was largely governed by the *Coutume*. She must have been aware of that fact as she followed, step by step, during the autumn of 1723, Franchomme's extended legal battle against Baillargeon to protect her share of the Bourdon estate. The congeries of French customary laws, which constituted the *Coutume*, provided legal structure for her life and protected her in ways not available to traditional Illinois Indian women; simply put, being a Régnicole (a lawful subject of Louis XV's realm) improved her situation in life. The genial *Roi bien aimé*, who during his long reign was never able to accomplish much for his subjects closer to home, would have been delighted that a woman in a faraway corner of his empire was enjoying some benefit of French civilization.

· · ·

The issue of race in American life and American history, whether it appears on television, in the popular press, or in academic studies, is inescapable. We are gobsmacked with the issue, and its prominence in scholarly work is accelerating. Sue Peabody, in her seminal study of racial attitudes in Old Regime France, observed that it was not until the 1760s that "racial stereotypes became entrenched in public discourse."[16] Taking exception to that observation, Guillaume Aubert has argued that racialization—conceptual formations of distinct racial categories—was clearly discernible in France and the entire French Atlantic world well before that date, although he gave short shrift to Louisiana.[17] Cécile Vidal's recent book about New Orleans is a full-throated lament about racialization and racism in the early city, featuring race, or some close cognate—racism, racialism, racialized, racialization—

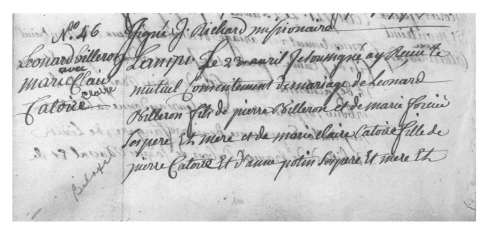

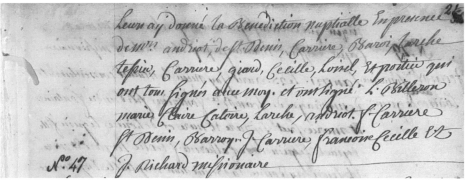

c.1. Marriage record of Marie-Claire Catoire and Léonard Billeron, Biloxi, April 23, 1721.
New Orleans, St. Louis Cathedral parish records, Marriages 1720–30, no. 46.

on virtually every one of its four hundred pages.[18] Sophie White has brought the topic of racialization directly into Illinois Country historical discourse, and acknowledges that "the ascendancy of a hegemonic protobiological difference in the colony as applied to Indians" was complicated "and that there was no smooth transition to racialization."[19] Historians doggedly pursuing evidence of racialization, a necessary preliminary to racism, certainly have an easier task tracking it down in lower Louisiana than in the Illinois Country, and when examining African-White relations rather than Native American-White.

Gary Nash observed in his widely used study of race in colonial America, *Red, White, and Black: The Peoples of Early America,* that a scarcity of European women persuaded some European men to "overcome their racial prejudices . . . to consort with women of another race."[20] Viewed through the prism of early Kaskaskia sources, that statement is risible. If, when Franchomme was courting Marguerite 8assecam8c8e in the summer of 1723, someone had mentioned "race" in his presence, he, as a product of a rural French parish, would have assumed that they were discussing the breed of magnificent horses — Mazarin and Rougit, Courtisan, and Le Noir — that stood out as part of Bourdon's large succession. Aubert has demonstrated that in the eighteenth century, within higher levels of French officialdom, "race" was beginning to take on some vague semblance of its nineteenth-century meaning regarding diversity among human beings.[21] But rustic Franchomme would never have heard, in his life on either side of the Atlantic, the word "race" applied to human beings, and it is simply inconceivable that he would have considered Marguerite as "racially" inferior to himself. Moreover, it is laughable to suppose that Franchomme had to overcome a distaste about intimacy with Indian women (*pace* Gary Nash) before courting and marrying Marguerite. This insouciance regarding intimacy with Indian women was the norm throughout Upper Louisiana, at Arkansas Post as well as in the Illinois Country proper.[22]

Marie-Claire Catoire appears on the 1726 Illinois census as the wife of Léonard Billeron dit Lafatigue (Census, no. 65). One of the more remarkable characters in the history of colonial America, Parisian-born Catoire spent her youth as an orphan in the infamous Hôpital Général de la Salpêtrière.[23] Arriving as a refugee on the Gulf Coast in 1721, she married Billeron, a French Canadian, on April 23, moved to the Illinois Country, and spent her entire adult life there, first at Kaskaskia and then at Ste. Genevieve, dying in January 1773. During Catoire's energetic half century of life in the region, enslaved Native Americans were ever-present as servants in her household, and she lived on intimate terms with them every day of her adult life.[24] In January 1768, she sat down with quill and ink at a black walnut table in her vertical log house in Ste. Genevieve and inscribed a document that prepared for the eventual manumission of two enslaved Native Americans, Susanne and Joseph.[25] Catoire's ragged script betrayed the grace in her heart, as she explained that these enslaved humans had a two-fold obligation to secure their everlasting freedom. First, they were obliged to serve Catoire and her son Billeron for the duration of their lives. Second, after manumission, the Indians were to commit themselves to the Roman Catholic religion and to "*la nation française.*" The last phrase is revealing, and also charming in its naivete, for it demonstrates that Catoire was utterly oblivious of the fact that she was living in a Louisiana that France had formally conveyed to Spain in 1762 with the Treaty of Fontainebleau. In any case, in return for their freedom, Marie was requiring that Susanne and Joseph adopt full-fledged Gallo-Catholic identities, which would serve them well both in this world and the next.[26] It is worth remarking that in French Canada, although the grand policy of wholesale Frenchification of Native Americans foundered, many enslaved Indians were casually, without documentation, absorbed into the local population.[27] In 1733, Governor Charles de La Boisch de Beauharnois wrote to his superiors at Versailles: "Ordinarily, owners of Panis [enslaved Native Americans], after having obtained several years of service from them, free them verbally. It would be useful to assure their status if this were done in front of a notaire."[28]

Catoire may rightly be accused of harboring, deep in her soul, hegemonic Roman Catholic and proto-nationalistic sentiments, with which she was determined to inculcate her enslaved Native Americans before they became fully free citizens of Ste. Genevieve. But there is not a scintilla of "racialization" in her manuscript of manumission; thinking in racial terms lay outside of her conceptual realm, which had been realized over a lifetime of intimate association with Native Amerians. Catoire's attitude regarding her enslaved Indians thus provides us with a cautionary tale: Not carelessly to employ twenty-first-century words when dealing with Indian-White relationships, or perceptions, in the colonial Illinois Country. The authors of this book conclude that in the Kaskaskia of the 1720s, French villagers did not entertain thoughts about "hegemonic protobiological differences" between themselves and Native Americans because such thinking was quite beyond the framework of their mental structures; they did not think in those terms simply because they were incapable of thinking in those terms.[29]

PART II

Illinois Country Generations
The 1726 Census

THE 1726 CENSUS OF the Illinois Country is a rare and essential document for understanding the region during the 1720s. It takes us into the emerging mid-Mississippi valley settlements, enumerating heads of households, wives, children, and the enslaved, both African and Native American.[1] Research into the names at once illuminates many of their brief histories in the region and sometimes the journeys that ultimately brought them to the Illinois Country. Infants baptized by the Jesuit priests in Illinois villages just after the turn of the eighteenth century had grown, married, and had children of their own. For example, Pierre Baillargeon, son of Antoine and Domitille Ch-8ping8eta, was baptized in 1701—prior to the priests' migration with their flock to the Metchagamia River.

The death of Baillargeon's father and his mother's remarriage to Jacques Bourdon eventually led to the legal dispute over Bourdon's estate. Baillargeon, his wife, Domitille Chacateni8a8a, their two children (plus three engagés and five enslaved persons) made up one census household in Kaskaskia. Agnès Philippe (Census, no. 35), eldest daughter of Marie 8canic8e Rouensa and Michel Philippe, was baptized in 1706 in Kaskaskia, and in 1722 she married the Royal Indies Company storekeeper, Nicolas-Michel Chassin, who had left France five years earlier. The couple had two children in the first years of marriage. Marie La Boissière (Census, no. 11), baptized at three months of age in 1708, was the daughter of a (manumitted?) Native slave mother and a poor Frenchman. Though Marie La Boissière's parents were not married,[2] this birth status did not affect marriage prospects: she married a militia officer in Kaskaskia in 1723, and had a daughter by the time of the census. Cécile Brunet (Census, no.14) was the daughter of Élisabeth Deshayes of France and Jean Brunet dit Bourbonnois of Canada. She was baptized at age two in Kaskaskia in 1712. Her older sister Élisabeth had been born and baptized in Mobile, and made the trek upriver with her parents; Cécile's birthplace is not known. Cécile married French Canadian Toussaint Loisel in early 1724 and baptized a son in 1726.

We draw conclusions from these earliest pages of sacramental records with care, for the ink has faded, the different priests' spellings are both irregular and inconsistent, the pages have been damaged, and the entries are extracts, mere notes, varying in their formats and not even in chronological order. There are no contemporaneous civil—notarial[3]—records until the arrival of commandant Boisbriant in 1719. A deeper local context is thus missing for many of the early names. Still, the attempt to assess the make-up of the population in the villages is useful.

Sacramental records document a mostly French-Native American settlement: Just over twenty French-Native couples appear in the extant sacramental records up to late spring 1719. The records during that time are sprinkled with French names, but only one Canadian-French couple, Bourbonnois and Deshayes (Census, no. 80). Eleven of the French-Native couples from before 1719, around half, reappear in later records.[4] On the 1726 census, fourteen French-Native couples were counted among a total of almost sixty in which both spouses could be identified.[5]

The arrival to Kaskaskia of Frenchwomen (from Canada and from France) married to Frenchmen (from Canada and from France) was a trickle until about 1720; just five French-women appear in sacramental records. Canadians Catherine Forestier and her husband Gabriel Beaudreau, an explorer in a lead-mining venture with his brothers, stayed in Kaskaskia for an unknown period of time between 1708 and1714. Forestier and Beaudreau had left Canada with their two children, and the third was born en route and baptized in Detroit in 1708.[6] Reaching Kaskaskia, Catherine Forestier stood as godmother to Pierre Chabot, son of Pierre Chabot and Symphorosa Mer8tap8c8e, in November 1709. Élisabeth Deshayes was godmother to the daughter of Marie 8anic8e Rouensa and Michel Philippe in June 1712. Marie Tetio, likely Canadian-born, was the mother of Jacques Lalande, baptized in February 1715. Françoise La Brise was godmother to Tetio's son Jacques. These two women, La Brise and Tetio, were an enduring presence in Kaskaskia's early decades. Canadian-born Marie-Magdelaine Quesnel was godmother of Paul Tessier, son of Louis and Catherine 8abanakic8e.[7] The evidence of women and children—some of them newborns—on the move, south from Canada or north from the Gulf coast, alters our perspective that the waterways were an exclusively male domain, and corrects the misconception that there were no Frenchwomen at all in Kaskaskia before Boisbriant arrived.[8]

The origins of a majority of the male heads of households, in the column "maîtres," could be confirmed. Roughly forty men came from Canada, and thirty from France and several additional European countries. Another thirty remain with unconfirmed birthplace. Forty-four men reported no wife during the gathering of census information,[9] but several of them indeed had a wife at the time, easily confirmed by sacramental and notarial records. Sixty-five men reported themselves as married; unfortunately, even the most thorough research across decades of records did not reveal the names of seven of the reported wives. The unidentifiable wives had neither known ante-nuptial contracts nor sacramental marriages with their husbands in the Illinois Country (or Canada or New Orleans/Mobile), they did not serve as witnesses at other family members' marriages, they were not godmothers (often identified by name and as "wife of"), they did not inherit known estates or leave named heirs, and they were not named in business transactions that their husbands conducted. In other words, their inclusion in the census may be the result of misunderstanding or transcription errors, but the possibility must be considered that some men lived with Native women and had children in unsanctioned relationships.[10]

Married couples in which both spouses were born in Canada number fewer than ten. Marie-Magdelaine Quesnel's journey illustrates one way that Canadian women might have come to the Illinois Country. Quesnel married Antoine Carrière in April 1718 in Montreal; it is unclear if Carrière had already established himself in the Illinois Country. Carrière's mother and brother Jacques were present at the sacramental ceremony (Census, no. 69). Several months later, Antoine appeared at the office of the Montreal notaire Pierre Raimbault with his supplier, Pierre Lestage, to draw up an agreement for Carrière to trade 549 livres of merchandise with the Ottawas, located in villages to the west, near the post of Michilimackinac. Carrière must have been confident of his ability to fulfill his obligation, for he put up his widowed mother's house in Montreal on the rue St. Paul as a guarantee. Whether he personally returned to Montreal to pay the debt is not clear, for in less than a year Carrière and his wife were in Kaskaskia.[11]

More wives were born in France (twenty-three) than in Canada (between four and seven), or were Native or Métisse (around seventeen). In the Company of the Indies' efforts to fulfill its promise to populate the colony, young unmarried women were sent from France to find spouses and settle in Louisiana. Several ships, including the *Mutine* and the *Baleine*, arrived on the Gulf coast in 1719 and 1721, carrying exiles and "girls sent from Paris by Order of the King." The *Marechal de Villars* carried twenty "girls from the poorhouse of La Rochelle."[12] A number of the young French women accepted the prospects from the Illinois Country and married while still on the coast, before ascending the Mississippi.[13]

Approximately a dozen women who were born in France married men who were born in France, and a few married couples or families migrated from France to Louisiana. Fourteen wives appeared in the records with combined Christian (baptismal) and Native names, for example, Catherine 8abanakic8e and Marie Apechic8rata;[14] four wives had identified Native mothers. All wives, no matter their origins, were enumerated in the *maîtres* column. By the time of Bernard Diron d'Artaguiette's 1723 summary count of the population of Cahokia, Kaskaskia, and Fort de Chartres, French-Native couples were likely a minority in the French villages. The greater population of Illinois Indians resided outside the villages in which the census was taken. D'Artaguiette estimated 700 warriors, spread among the Kaskaskia, Cahokia, and Metchagamia settlements, or approximately 3,500 people in total.[15] The 1726 census officially enumerated 512 persons in the French villages. This count included the enslaved but excluded some of the marine garrison, and others whose names appear scattered through the sacramental and notarial records. Even if the census is an undercount and the estimate of local indigenous people is an overcount, the French villages contained far fewer people.

Confirming the presence of individual children counted in the census was complicated. No children's names were written in the document, but approximately ninety-six children were identified through sacramental and notarial records. Forty-one children of the ninety-six—or forty-three percent—had a Native American mother. Mothers born in France or Canada had a total of fifty-five children. At Fort de Chartres and its surroundings, the children of French and Canadian mothers numbered fourteen girls and eight boys among thirteen households, and Métis children in four households were six girls and one boy. At Kaskaskia, the children of Frenchwomen numbered fifteen girls and eighteen boys, and there were eighteen girls and sixteen boys with Native mothers among ten households. Illegitimate and natural-born children account for several of the enumerations, and manuscript records show that, at least legally, they were treated equally in matters of succession with the children born of legitimate marriages.[16] In two instances, the fathers of such children were charged with their upbringing.

The first ships that brought enslaved Africans to Louisiana arrived in New Orleans between 1719 and 1721, meaning that adult African slaves in late 1724 in the Illinois Country were born elsewhere, and this is a profoundly important and provocative fact about the populations of the Illinois Country. Because the census did not distinguish the gender and ages for the enslaved populations, it is probable that some of the 129 enumerated represented a new generation, born in Louisiana; in 1721, for example, there were two baptisms in Kaskaskia of infants born to Black slaves, both married couples.[17] No previously published version of this census has attempted to name the enslaved.

Cécile Vidal has argued that the persistent shortage of White laborers led French settlers, especially in lower Louisiana, to regard African slaves as essential to improving the economic production of the colony, and to ask the Company to send more.[18] It is not surprising that the Company representatives in the Illinois Country (Boisbriant, des Ursins, and Renault, Census, nos. 1 and 2 below) held roughly one-third of the enslaved Africans, and the Jesuits nine. Enslaved Native Americans surely were present in all the iterations of the Kaskaskia village before its final move to the Metchagamia river. Sixty-six Native slaves were counted in the 1726 census, a number of them in households managed by Native wives.

Further characteristics illuminate the picture of slaveholding in the early Illinois Country. The older, agricultural village of Kaskaskia had a slight majority (twenty-eight of forty-eight) of households that held slaves, the Jesuit compound included. In the newer settlements around Fort de Chartres, just seventeen of sixty-one households (excluding the two Company establishments) reported one or more enslaved persons. In all locations, habitants with more arpents of cleared land tended to have slaves, and almost no villagers with ten or fewer arpents of land did, suggesting slaves' labor was applied above all in agriculture.

Single men tended not to be slaveholders (they had less land and often had fewer financial resources), but some married couples with children also were not. Overall, sixty-three of the 110 households (includes the Jesuits and the government) held no slaves at all, yet slaveholding had a significant presence. However, 1720s Illinois Country had only a few families that might compare to the capital, New Orleans, where slaveholding evolved to confirm, and to some extent confer, social status in a growing plantation economy.[19]

Certain omissions do not diminish the value of the census; however, they beg caution in interpreting its surface form. Above all, the census represents a moment (or several months) of time. For example, men who are single on this census might marry in the next months to a woman who reached marriageable age or lost her husband after the information was gathered. Internal evidence reveals four additional important points about the census. First, the information was compiled well before 1726, because the names of persons deceased in the first part of 1725 appear as living. Joseph Lamy (Census, no. 76) died in May 1725, and Marie 8canic8e Rouensa, wife of Michel Philippe (Census, no. 77) in June. An even earlier date is suggested by the entry for Étienne Veniard de Bourgmont (Census, no. 20) whose presence in the Illinois Country can be dated to the last weeks of 1724, at his return from his famous diplomatic mission on the Missouri River. He passed through the Illinois Country on his way to New Orleans, and sailed on to France, never to return.[20]

Second, some names appear more than one time in the overall list. This makes using simple addition to reach the total population inaccurate. The top official at Kaskaskia was Jean-Baptiste Girardeau/Girardot, ensign in the *troupes de la marine* (Census, no. 63). Girardot had been appointed to the role of commandant by Boisbriant, and likely was responsible for the collection of census information at Kaskaskia. Two separate efforts that were loosely coordinated could explain the duplication of several names, although it is also possible that the duplication was intentional, as several men owned land both in Kaskaskia and near the recently-constructed Fort de Chartres.

Third, even though the census showed no divisions according to village, as later censuses did, associated real property transactions and land grants indicate two groups of names, moving generally from Fort de Chartres and the surrounding areas (perhaps including Cahokia) south to Kaskaskia. The Kaskaskia residents were listed following the priests (Census, no. 62), proceeding from commandant Girardot to the ranking officer lieutenant Melique and Leonard Billeron dit La Fatigue, who later served as royal notary.

Fourth, several connections in the sources between "neighbors" on the census suggest that they may have been neighbors in fact, and these relationships are described in the text or in the notes. Previous published versions of the 1726 census that transform it into an alphabetized list have lost these tantalizing connections.

In the identifications that follow, the names in bold are spelled as they appear on the original draft document, without altering the order but with numbers added for easier reference. Variant spellings that occur in other records have been generally preserved in identifications and in the notes, and *sic* is not used. Only male heads of households appear in the original census.

Under the Coutume de Paris, widows could be heads of household, but the fourteen widows in this census had all remarried, most bringing children from the previous marriage into the new one.[21] The lone identified free Black man was enumerated as an engagé, not a maître. He in fact signed at least one contract as an engagé, but the census categorized him as head of household. This somewhat contradictory status, both an engagé and a head of household, may reflect his unusual situation.

A category for freed slaves would appear in censuses much later.[22] In 1726, the census scribe recorded no names for wives, children, engagés, servants, or slaves. Painstaking examination of multiple original sources[23] has brought to light many of the persons associated with each household. As a result of this broad investigation, several names are different from previously published versions of the census.[24] The names of persons most probably in each household are set in italics—head of household, wife, children, and slaves. For genealogical context, prior marriages and later remarriages (where known) of the census spouses are given, as are first marriages, and sometimes second, for their children.

Children born later than the census enumeration of their parents and siblings are included, but not underlined, to complete the picture of each family. The notes often show the earliest appearance of each census adult, and additional information sometimes appears, but is not exhaustive. Doubtless some omissions have occurred, though, due to the incompleteness of the sources, to judgment, and to inevitable human error.

A table showing the number of each type of resident in each household follows the descriptions. A total for each category is also included.

maîtres (husbands, wives, and children)
engagés ou domestiques (contract employees/indentured servants and domestic
     servants)
esclaves nègres (African slaves, no gender or age distinctions)
esclaves sauvages (Native slaves, no gender or age distinctions)
bet. corn. (horned livestock-cattle and oxen)
chev.x (horses)
terrains défrichés (cleared agricultural plots)

1. Habitation de Mr⁵ De Boisbriant[25] et Laloire[26]

Pierre Dugué de Boisbriant (born in Canada) was commandant, and Marc-Antoine de la Loëre des Ursins (born in France) held the title of Director and Principal Commissioner for the Royal Indies Company. From 1719 to roughly April 1726 des Ursins worked with the commandants on company matters. By the close of 1724, the Company storehouse and offices had moved inside the new fort walls, leaving property outside the fort described as a *habitation*, or residence complex. In December 1728, four years after the departure of Boisbriant, commandant Pierre-Charles Deliette sold a portion of this property (no slaves appear in this sale), including a house and stable on two arpents of land, a barn, a mill, and a well.[27] The Broutin map, circa 1734, showed a "prerie" of Mr. Ste. Therese,[28] Boisbriant's nephew, who inherited some of the remainder of his uncle's land.

Slaves: *Pierre (André?) Perico* (born ca. 1708), *Creolle*, and *Pierrot*, named in testimony to the Provincial Council in August 1725.[29]

Remi, born November 13, baptized November 14, 1723, godfather Remi Buisseret, godmother Marie-Marguerite Moulé[30]

Jean-Baptiste, age 20, and *Marie-Catherine*, baptized December 27, 1723. Godparents were Mr. de Ste. Therese, Mme. Chassin (Agnès Philippe, Census, no. 77), Mr. de la Loëre des Ursins and Mme. St. Ange (Élisabeth Chorel). Directly following their baptisms, Jean-Baptiste and Marie-Catherine were married by the Jesuit curé, Nicolas-Ignace de Beaubois.[31]

Marie-Jeanne, born January 10, baptized January 11, 1724, godfather Mr. de St. Ange, godmother Jeanne Balis (Bailly? Census, no. 25)[32]

2. M. Renaud

Philippe-François de Renault, Director of the Mines

In 1723 Boisbriant and des Ursins granted four parcels of land to Philippe-François de Renault, Director of Mines of the Company of the Indies,[33] one identified as "on the Mississippy at the place called the Great Marsh, joining on one side to the Illinois Indians established near the Fort Chartres."[34] On Broutin's 1734 map, the village of Mr. "Renaud" lay on the north side of the Metchagamia prairie.[35]

In August 1723, Renault drew up two contracts for laborers, one with André Chabernon,[36] and the other with Jean Martin and his wife, Marianne René Charbonnet.[37] In 1719 a Marie Charbonnet arrived in Louisiana at age fourteen, on the *Marechal de Villars*, one of a group of girls sent from a poorhouse of La Rochelle where she had lived from the age of one.[38] A Jean Martin, member of the troops, was on the same ship. Charbonnet and Martin married May 19, 1722 at Fort Louis (Mobile, AL).[39] In the Illinois Country, Martin signed on as a laborer with Renault for one year. The agreement stated that his wife would serve as a wet-nurse if needed, and she could mend fabrics.[40] The couple could have been enumerated here with a child, or with Chabernon as the third person.

3. La Croix sa fe. et cinq enfants

François Lacroix,[41] born October 17, baptized October 28, 1677, Beaupré, Canada, int. January 12, 1770[42]

m. *Barbe Monmainier*, Widow Mercier, born in France ca. 1674, resident of Beaupré,[43] Canada, died by June 1733[44]

    Agnès, m. 1726 Louis Boisset [45] (rem. 1737 Jean-Baptiste Chauvin[46])

    Barbe, m. 1732 Henry Saucier[47]

    François[48]

    Marie-Louise, born ca. 1704, int. Ste. Genevieve, 1790[49] m. before July 13, 1733, Jean-Baptiste Ste. Gemme Beauvais[50]

    Marie-Josèphe, born ca. 1712, parish St. Joachim in Québec,[51] int. St. Louis 1779,[52] m. 1733 Jean-Baptiste Sébastien Gouin dit Champagne[53] (rem. 1756 Alexander Langlois[54])

rem. 1739 Jeanne L'Enfant, widow of Belhumeur and Pajot[55]

    On June 4, 1723, Jacques David, royal notaire of Montreal, drew up a permission document on behalf of governor of New France (*Lamerique Septentrionalle*), Philippe Rigaud de Vaudreuil, for François Lacroix, of Beaupré, his wife and five children to leave Montreal at the first favorable opportunity to establish themselves in the Illinois with the Seminary priests at Cahokia. The permission granted was for two canoes. According to the King's decree of 1716, the party was prohibited from conducting any trade with Native peoples along the way. Rations of up to four pots of eau-de-vie per person were permitted, but for personal consumption only. The same day, Ignace Martin and Louis Lemieux, donnés of the Seminary, applied for and were granted similar permission, for one canoe with six men.[56] Surely the Lacroix family and the donnés traveled together.

4. Rollet sa femme et deux enfants

François-Xavier Ripaux Rollet,[57] born October 30, baptized November 4, 1695, Grondines, Canada,[58] died by October 1752[59]

m. *Domitille Apanik8e*[60]

Marie-Catherine, m. 1741 Louis Gaut[61]

Domitille, m. 1748 Jean-Baptiste Baron[62]

rem. July 27, 1745, Marie Becquet[63]

rem. June 12, 1747, Marianne Fouillard[64]

5. Neau et sa femme

Charles Nault,[65] born La Chevrotière, Canada, died January 1740[66]

m. *Suzanne Ch8perikinga,*[67] died by 1732?[68]

Marie-Jeanne, baptized April 6, 1724[69]

rem. 1736 Françoise Becquet[70]

6. Giard

Antoine Giard, born and baptized March 28, 1682, Montreal, Canada,[71] died by April 18, 1747[72]

7. Prée sa fe. et deux enfans

Jean-Baptiste Du Pré, master blacksmith, born February 9, baptized February 20, 1669, Québec, Canada, died November 1, 1727[73]

m. November 23, 1700 at Québec, *Françoise Marchand,*[74] born Canada, died by January 29, 1726[75]

Jean-Baptiste, baptized August 18, 1701, in Québec[76]

Pierre, born and baptized June 10, 1706, in Lachine, died by 1732[77] m. 1728 Marie Che8kaokia, Widow Cécire (rem. 1732 Mathurin Pineau[78])

Marianne, born and baptized February 17, 1710, Montréal,[79] m. before January 29, 1726 royal notaire Jerome Rousilliet (rem. 1741 Toussaint Vaudry[80])

8. Richard

Jean Ricard

A Jean Ricard "le petit anglois" (the little Englishman) was noted as a servant in a letter by the Seminarian Thaumur de la Source dated March 2, 1724, at Cahokia.[81]

9. Bontems sa fe. et un enfant

François Cécire dit Bontemps,[82] born December 15, baptized December 20, 1676, Lachine, Canada,[83] died by February 15, 1728[84]

m. ca. 1724[85] *Marie Saka8ie*, born ca. 1703, int. December 7, 1743 (rem. 1728 Pierre Du Pré,[86] rem. 1732 Maturin Pineau[87])

Marie-Josèphe, m. 1739 Antoine Cheneau dit Sanschagrin [88]

Marie-Françoise, born December 30, 1725, baptized January 1726[89]

10. Nieuport

Pierre Nieuport, born Canada, died by 1743[90]

11. Baron sa fe. et un enfant

Joseph Baron,[91] baptized March 1696, Boucherville, Canada,[92] died by January 1758[93]

m. April 12, 1723, *Marie Laboissière*, baptized June 9, 1708, age three months, Kaskaskia,[94] int. Ste. Genevieve, 1768,[95] (rem.1759 André Deguire dit La Rose[96])

Suzanne, born ca. 1724, int. December 26, 1746 m. 1745 Joseph Metoth[97]
Cécile, born ca. 1737 [98] m. 1760 Jean-Baptiste Deguire dit La Rose[99]

12. Darbonne sa femme et un enfant

D'Arbonne, a cadet of the troops, born Paris, ca. 1680[100]

13. Chapu et sa femme

Mathurin Chaput, baptized June 12, 1693, Pointe-aux-Trembles, Canada, died before November 27, 1728[101]

m. January 14, 1724 *Hélène Danis,* int. St. Louis, November 29, 1784 (rem. 1728 Ignace Hébert[102])

14. Loisel et sa femme

Toussaint Loisel, Pointe-aux-Trembles, Canada, baptized March 17, 1690,[103] died by March 1739[104]

m. February 8, 1724, *Cécile Brunet,* born 1710, baptized November 24, 1712, Kaskaskia, int. December 24, 1743[105] (rem. 1739 Antoine Huneaux[106])
    Toussaint, born and baptized February 6, 1726,[107] int. December 11, 1746[108]
    Joseph[109]

15. Hébert et sa femme[110]

Étienne Hébert, born Cap St. Michel, baptized Boucherville, Canada, April 18, 1689,[111] died by November 21, 1735[112]

m. January 5, 1721, *Françoise Bareau,* Widow Chesne,[113] died by February 1725
    rem. *Marie-Louise Coignon,* widow of François Chesne[114]
    rem. February 11, 1727, Élisabeth Philippe[115]
    Slaves : *Marie-Jeanne,* baptized December 30, 1723, born to two Black slaves of Étienne Hébert. Godfather Jean-Baptiste Le Comte, godmother Marie-Jeanne Tabouret[116]

16. Sans Chagrin sa femme et deux enfants[117]

François Hennet dit Sans Chagrin, born Switzerland, died December 25, age ca. 50, burial in the church December 26, 1746[118]

m. 1721[119] *Marianne (Marie-Jeanne) Charpin,*[120] born France, died by April 15, 1734[121]
    Marie-Anne, died by 1736[122] m. Pancrace Alberman (rem. 1734 Jean Chabot[123])

François, m. 1746 Marguerite Becquet[124]
Catherine, baptized February 8, 1724[125]
Madeleine, m. 1740 Michel Le Jeune[126]
Joseph, m. 1752 Élisabeth Roy[127]
Genevieve, died by November 1748[128] m. Charles Cadron[129]
Marianne, m. 1751 or 1752 Jean-Baptiste ?[130]
Jacques, m. 1757 Marie-Françoise Eloy[131]
Maturin[132]

17. Fabus

Jean Fabut dit La Jeunesse[133]
Jean Fabus, died by May 29, 1728, m. Denise Manisure [134]

Jacques Fabut was present in 1725 at Fort de Chartres[135] and was the deputy guardian of François Hennet's minor children in 1734.[136]

18. Timonier

Timonnier signed several contracts as a witness in 1726. He appeared on the 1730 list of owners of pigs and their identification markings, and in 1732, he sold his house at Fort de Chartres.[137]

19. Du Trou et sa femme

Denis Du Trou, born St. Sulpice, Diocese of Paris [138] died in 1731[139]
m. November 25, 1720, at Biloxi, *Marie-Josèphe Grace,* born St. Hubert, Artois, France
rem. ? Marie-Josèphe Larmeau/Larmuseau[140] (rem. Hubert Finet[141])

20. Bourgmont

Étienne de Veniard de Bourgmont[142]
Bourgmont's signature does not appear on any of the extant manuscripts in the Kaskaskia collection from 1724 to 1726.

21. Baptiste, nègre

Jean-Baptiste André[143] He was noted as an engagé rather than a maître. In March 1725, Baptiste contracted to work for Melique for one year as a "domestique" (servant) in the house and garden, for the pay of a calf at the end of the year.

22. Joseph L'Espagnol, sa femme et deux enfants

Joseph Quebedeau dit L'Espagnol, died by February 26, 1745[144] (France?)

m. *Marianne Antoinette Beau* (France?[145])

   Marie-Josèphe, born Paris, France, m. February 26, 1745, Mathurin Pineau[146] (rem. May 19, 1749 Alexandre La Ville, soldier, cobbler[147] rem. June 5, 1764, Claude Tinon, soldier, Toulon, France[148])

   Mathurin, baptized February 10, 1724[149]

   Marie-Françoise, m. 1745 Nicolas Provost dit Blondin[150]

23. Ant.e l'Espagnol

This may be the Antoine who was an employee of La Renaudière, and accompanied Bourgmont's expedition to look for ores.[151] Charlevoix devoted a paragraph to Antoine, the Spaniard, whom he described as a former prisoner from the 1707 siege of Pensacola by the British and allied Native groups. Antoine was later sent to assist in the mines of the Illinois Country.[152] Debts of Antoine L'Espagnol were expressed in lead rather than furs or flour.[153]

24. Biron et un enfant[154]

Henry Biron, baptism May 28, 1705, Ville-Marie, Canada,[155] died by August 1726[156]

m. May 1, 1724, Marie Maurice Medar, Widow Etevenard dit Beausoleil[157]

   Agnès Etevenard[158]

25. St. Jean et sa femme

Jean Hubert dit St. Jean, died by April 20, 1738[159]

m. *Jeannette Bailly,* born in Leimart(?), Holland[160] (rem. 1738 Jean-Baptiste Le Comte[161])

26. La Forest

La Forest dit Provençal[162]

27. Becquet sa fe. et deux enfants

Jean-Baptiste Nicolas Becquet, locksmith, France

m. *Catherine Barreau,* France[163] int. January 24, 1760? [164]

   Catherine, baptized December 30, 1723, died 1726[165]

   Françoise, m. 1736 Charles Neau[166]

Jean-Baptiste, born and baptized October 24, 1725,[167] died 1797 in St. Louis[168] m. 1757 Marie-Françoise Dodier

Marie-Marguerite, born ca. 1728 m. 1746 François Hennet[169] (rem. 1764 Gabriel Dodier), died 1813 in St. Louis[170]

Marie, died by June 12, 1747[171] m. 1745 François-Xavier Rollet

28. La jeune Lalande

See Census, no. 90 for likely the same man, Jean-Baptiste Lalande, listed with his wife and family. Lalande appears two times, perhaps, as suggested by Margaret Brown, because he owned property in two locations.[172]

29. Pradel

Jean Pradel de la Masse, Perche, Limousin, France. Pradel was lieutenant under Bourgmont at Fort d'Orléans, and he returned to Fort de Chartres by October 1724.[173]

30. Barselone

Corporal Barselonne owned a house where a blacksmith named Levé (Leveillé?) lived. Barselonne's name appeared on the list of villagers who owned marked pigs.[174] Sacramental records do not contain his name.

31. Du Sablon et sa femme

Jacques Guillotteau Du Sablon,[175] Du Sablon took part in an auction of the effects of a deceased villager in 1723, and he was party to a contract in June 1726. He owned pigs marked by a crescent on the left ear. No wife's name was located in the records. In 1728 he signed the settlement of Michel Aco's inheritance received from Aco's mother's (Marie 8canic8e Rouensa) estate.[176]

32. Des Essarts

Onezime Pierre de Lessart, born La Rochelle, France[177]

Slave: *Jean-Baptiste,* baptized January 13, 1724 born to a married slave woman belonging to de Lessart, sergeant of the troops, godfather Jean-Baptiste La Source? godmother Madeleine Cordier.[178]

33. Robillart et sa femme

Louis Robillard, died by 1762[179]

m. May 15, 1721 at Biloxi (*Marie-)Magdelaine Cordier*,[180] born in France, d. May 10, 1779, Pointe Coupée[181] (rem. 1762 Guillaume Le Moine dit Le Normand, Census, no. 57, at Pointe Coupée[182])

    Marie-Magdelaine, born ca. 1729 m. Antoine Rivière dit Bacané, rem. René Kiercereau[183]

    Marie-Josèphe, m.1747 Louis Gremillion [184]

    Charles, m. 1762 Marie Porciau[185]

34. Dragon

A *Pierre de Vacogne dit Dragon* was a soldier in 1724.[186] A Dragon also owned pigs.[187]

Jacques Le Vicomte also used the *dit* name Dragon. He married Marianne René Charbonnet, Widow Martin, in 1726.[188] In 1723 Martin was engaged by Renault, see Census, no. 2 above.

35. Chassin sa fe. et deux enfants

Nicolas Michel Chassin, garde magasin (storekeeper) for the Royal Indies Company and member of the Provincial Council,[189] died by October 29, 1730[190]

m. November 2, 1722 *Agnès Philippe*,[191] baptized January 22, 1706,[192] died by January 28, 1743[193] (rem. 1737 René Roy, surgeon major[194])

    Agnès, m. February 11, 1737, Jean-François Moncharvaux[195]

    Magdelaine, m. July 16, 1741, Jean-Baptiste Mallet, trader of Fort de Chartres[196]

    Charlotte, m. 1745 Antoine Henaux[197]

Slave: *Bibianne*[198] Also, a male Native slave, age fourteen or fifteen, is mentioned but not named, in a lease agreement with Baron in 1726.[199]

36. La Jeunesse dit Le Gros

A Legros dit La Jeunesse owed money to the estate of Etevenard in May 1724. In October 1725 a land transaction in the village noted Gros La Jeunesse as a neighbor.[200]

37. La Plume et un enfant

Antoine Pellé dit La Plume, born Diocese of St. Omer, France, master pit-sawyer,[201] died 1744[202]

Slave: Jeannot[203]

38. Bellegarde et deux enfants[204]

Jacques Bougnolle/Boulougne de Bellegarde, died by November 26, 1727[205]

m. Catherine Bechet, died 1737[206] (rem. 1727 Pierre Onezime de Lessart[207])
   Jeanne, m. 1737 Michel d'Amour de Louvière[208]
   Marie, died in New Orleans by February 1773, m. 1737 Jacques Philippe, son of Michel and Marie 8canic8e Rouensa[209] (rem. Charles Phlibot[210])

39. Langevin et sa femme[211]

René Grudé dit Langevin, born ca.1691[212] Louplande, diocese of Le Mans, France, died by 1739[213]

m. April 11, 1725, *Marie Barbe Colleret de Blée,* born in Germany[214] (rem. 1739 Louis Le Vasseur[215] rem. Joseph Boisdore[216])
   René[217]
   Marie, m. 1751 Philippe-François Suvin dit La Forme, a French soldier[218] (rem. 1760 Paul Labrosse)
   Catherine

40. St. Pierre sa fe. et un enfant[219]

Pierre Dirousse dit St. Pierre Laverdure

m. February 24, 1721, at Biloxi, *Catherine Delaunay*[220]
   François, died 1792[221]   m. 1750 Marie-Josèphe Turpin[222]

41. Lantrulu et sa femme

A Lambert dit Lenturlu was a soldier in New Orleans in December 1731. Lantrulu was an owner of pigs in the Illinois Country, marked by a fleur-de-lis on the right ear. No record found of a wife.[223]

42. Gardon sa fe. et un enfant

Joseph Gardon dit La Jeunesse

m. *Marianne Tabouret,*[224] born in France

43. Antoine et sa femme

Antoine Camus Tambour (drummer), born France, died by 1736 [225]

m. *Blanche Vigneron,*[226] born France, died July 31, 1740 (rem. by 1736 Louis Thomas[227])

44. Canarel et un associé

Nicolas François Caignerel and *François Poupard dit Rencontre*[228]

45. Robin et un associé

On October 19, 1724, a *Robin* purchased an old blanket of dog hair from the effects of a hunter named Le Gras, who was assumed lost in the woods.[229] His associate is unknown.

46. Daniel

Olivier Daniel of Fort de Chartres agreed to work for the master locksmith Jean-Baptiste Becquet at Kaskaskia for one year, including cutting the wood for his forge, beginning in November 1725. He requested one pair of French shoes from the first convoy to carry shoes as part of his payment.[230]

47. Capitaine et sa femme

His given name, and his wife's name, remain unknown. He purchased land at Fort de Chartres in 1725, and had a house and a barn.[231]

48. St. Jacques sa fe. et un enfant

Jacques Bernard dit St. Jacques, born at Nantes, France[232] died by 1732

m. June 22, 1721, New Orleans, *Denise Aleaume dite Voillot,* born in France ca. 1703, died by 1730[233]

49. Pierre

Pierre Hullin[234]

50. Gouverneur et Brun

Jean Henniquin dit Gouverneur and *Jean Lefebvre dit Le Brun*[235]

51. Belhumeur et sa femme

Étienne Poujart dit Belhumeur,[236] died by November 1738

m. *Jeanne L'Enfant,* born at diocese of Anger in Anjou, Picardy, France[237] (rem. 1738 Jean Payo, soldier[238] rem. François Lacroix[239])

52. Moreau ? sa fe. et un enf[240]

Ambroise Moreau dit Sansregret appears in a land transaction at Fort de Chartres in February 1726.[241] Ambroise Moreau and his wife, Jeanne Paul, traveled from France to Louisiana on the *Marie* in May 1719, sent by order of the king.[242] Ambroise was noted in several records as being unable to sign, but Jeanne signed her name in an unpracticed hand on a contract in 1733.[243] The couple lived a long life in the Illinois Country, with Jeanne Paul noted as "Madame Sansregret." Both died in 1760 at about age eighty, buried at Prairie du Rocher.[244]

53. Dauphiné sa femme et deux enfants

Antoine Sorel dit Dauphiné, born ca. 1687, int. January 23, 1747[245]

m. July 15, 1721, New Orleans, *Lucie Rollet,* died by December 8, 1733[246]
    Marianne, m. 1735 Estienne Motet dit La Pensée[247]
    Marie-Josèphe, m. 1740 André Thomas des Jardins[248]
    Françoise, baptized April 10?, 1726[249]
    Élisabeth, m. 1750 François Larche[250]

rem. by 1746 Marie-Barbe Le Vicomte[251]

54. Beausejour et son camarade

François Le Conte dit Beausejour[252] His *camarade* could not be identified. On the pigs document, Beausejour and "Tomas," see below, were listed jointly as owners of pigs.

55. Thomas

Louis Thomas[253]

56. Bellerose

François Robert dit Bellerose, soldier and habitant[254]

57. Le Normand[255]

Guillaume Le Moine dit Le Normand, born ca. 1698, Havre de Grace, Notre Dame parish, bishopric of Rouen, France, captain of the bateaux for the Company,[256] int. August 8, 1771 in Point Coupée[257]

m. 1722 Thereise Latreille Le Doux[258]

rem. 1725 Marie Saumerine[259]

rem. 1742 Marie Gaynard/Gonnard [260]

rem. 1762 (Marie-)Madeleine Cordier, Widow Robillard (Census, no. 33), at Pointe Coupée[261]

58. Texier sa fe. et un enfant

Pierre Texier, baptized February 8, 1675, Montreal,[262] died by April 6, 1731[263]

m. *Marie-Jeanne Gaudié,* died January 1, 1741 (rem. 1739 Claude Benetôt dit Duchemin[264])
    Pierre, died by 1775[265] m. 1751 Magdelaine Turpin[266]
    Jacques
    Marie-Josèphe[267]

59. La Pointe sa fe. et 1 enfant

Augustin La Pointe, born Côte St. Michel à Sillery, Canada, baptized July 10, 1677, Québec[268]

m. Marthe Mer8ki8etam8c8e ca. 1714, died by 1720[269]
    Marie, baptized April 14, 1715 [270] died August 18, 1748, buried the same day inside the church to the right of the door on entering the church[271] m. 1731 Joseph La Roche[272]

rem. *Suzanne Kaskaskic8e* ca. 1720
    (son) baptized December 20, 1720[273]
    Catherine, born and died 1722[274]

Slave: *Ladrieu,* "a young Black slave"[275]

60. Ignace Hebert

Ignace Hébert, baptized June 8, 1694, Varenne, Canada[276]

61. Le Vieux Turpin et deux enfants[277]

Jean-Baptiste Turpin, baptized Montreal, November 23, 1685,[278] int. New Orleans, August 16, 1731[279]

m. Marguerite Fafard dite Couc, May 5, 1710 at Fort Pontchartrain (Detroit)[280]
    Jean-Baptiste, born and baptized December 14, 1710,[281]died 1736[282]
    Marie (natural daughter), m. 1735 Gabriel Metote[283]

62. Deux P. Jesuittes et

deux curés missionnaires

In 1724, the Jesuit **Joseph-François de Kereben** served both the soldiers and habitants at Fort de Chartres and the Metchagamias in their village.[284] **Jean-Antoine Le Boullenger** served the Kaskaskia Indian village, and **Nicolas-Ignace de Beaubois** was at the French village of Kaskaskia. In 1725, Kereben continued the same assignment, interrupted by a several-month journey to Pimitéoui early in the year.[285] Father Jean-Charles Guimmoneau[286] returned to Kaskaskia from Montreal at the beginning of 1725. Beaubois traveled to New Orleans with Bourgmont in the last days of 1724, and then sailed to France to plead the case of the Jesuits' needs before the directors of the Company of the Indies. Le Boullenger served both villages in his absence. Only Beaubois and Le Boullenger were noted as curés, both at Kaskaskia.[287] The *engagés ou domestiques* enumerated in the second column are likely the donnés, one of whom, Zebedée Le Jeune, was buried in 1727.[288] The second might be Simon Lucas, Frère Simon, who witnessed the marriage of two slaves of Thuillier Devegnois in 1728.[289] Jean-Paul Mercier was one of the Seminary priests at Cahokia during this time. Mercier had accompanied Bourgmont to the Missouri in 1723, and remained there for a time after Bourgmont left.[290] Also at Cahokia was René Thaumur La Source.[291]

Slaves
    Françoise (married former slave Antoine Sanssouci in 1724)[292]
    Louis and *Thérèse*[293]
    Catherine, born April 12, baptized April 15, 1724, to married Black slave parents Louis and Thérèse, godfather Pierre(?) Dulude, godmother Françoise La Brise[294]
    Michel[295]

63. Girardeau sa f. et un enfant

Jean-Baptiste Girardeau/Girardot, born April 2, 1683, St. Pierre Parish, Moulins, France,[296] died by July 17, 1730, ensign of the troops and commandant at Kaskaskia[297]

m. November 9, 1722, *Thérèse Neveu,*[298] born April 19, baptized April 20, 1700, Repentigny, Canada,[299] died by 1745[300] (rem. Louis du Tisné[301] rem. Pierre-René Harpain de la Gautrais[302])
    Marthe, died September 15, 1725[303]
    Jean-Pierre, born December 1, baptized December 2, 1723[304]
    Pierre, baptized July 30, 1726, m. 1761 Madeleine Loisel[305]

Slave: *Marie*, age 13, baptized January 6, 1724[306]

64. Melique off[er] LaJeunesse sa femme et un enfant ses fermiers

Lieutenant Pierre Melique,[307] born ca. 1675, Mont Didier, diocese of Amiens, France[308] died by June 1726 or 1727[309]

(Catherine)[310]

> *Françoise,* natural daughter, born ca. 1721 m. 1736 Louis Sionneau[311]
>
> Tenant farmers: *Gardon dit La Jeunesse* and *Marianne Tabouret* (Census, no. 42), mentioned in January 1725 as Melique's tenants.[312]

65. La Fatigue sa fe. et 2 enfants

Léonard Billeron dit La Fatigue, born February 5, baptized February 6, 1695, Montreal,[313] died by February 1738[314]

m. April 23, 1721 at Biloxi *Marie-Claire Catoire,* born ca. 1701, France,[315] int. January 13, 1773 in Ste. Genevieve[316]

> *Léonard,* born ca. 1722, m. 1758 Catherine Normand dite La Brière[317]
>
> *Pierre,* born ca. 1724, m. 1751 Élisabeth Aubuchon[318]
>
> Joseph, born ca. 1726
>
> Marianne, born ca. 1728, m. January 7, 1748 François Vallé[319]
>
> Jacques, born ca. 1732[320]

66. DesVignes[321] sa fe. et deux enfans

Nicolas Thuillier Devegnois, baptized April 3, 1689, Montreal,[322] died by 1748[323]

m. November 17, 1721, *Dorothée Mercier,*[324] widow of Pierre Chabot (rem. 1756 Antoine Gilbert dit Rotisseur, voyageur[325])

> *Pierre Chabot,* baptized February 16, 1721[326]
>
> *Jean-Baptiste,* born September 4, baptized September 5, 1723[327]
>
> Françoise, m. 1747 Jacques Godefroy[328]
>
> Marie-Rose, m. Jacques Seguin dit Laderoute 1750[329] (rem. 1770 Joseph Fortin[330])
>
> Joseph, baptized January 1726[331]
>
> Jacques, m. 1761 Marie-Anne Seguin[332]
>
> Marie-Louise, m. 1764 Pierre Seguin dit Laderoute[333]
>
> Marie, m. Charles Lefevre (rem. 1770 Jean-Marie Legras[334])
>
> Élisabeth, m. Antoine Bienvenu, died by 1766[335]

Slaves[336]

> *Jeannot*[337]
>
> *Jean-Baptiste* and *Marie,* married 1728[338]

François and *Marie Charle,* married 1728, these two marriages witnessed by Frère Simon, signed Simon Lucas, and "by all the French, assembled for mass"[339]

Two slaves unnamed (possibly *Marman* and *Manon*[340]), purchased from the estate of Bourdon, "given by Rev. Chabot"[341]

67. La Lande L'aisne sa femme et quatre enfants

Jacques Lalande,[342] baptized July 20, 1690, Montreal,[343] died by March 6, 1737[344]

m. *Marie Tetio,* died by 1744[345] (rem. 1739 Jacques Lefevre Duchouquet[346])
    Jacques, baptized February 10, 1715[347]
    Élisabeth, baptized November 20, 1717[348]
    Marie, baptized November 20, 1717[349]
    Étienne, baptized July 14, 1721[350] m. 1744 Jeanne Perthuis[351]
    Gabriel, baptized July 14, 1721[352] twin of Étienne, died by 1740[353]

Slaves: No records for slaves were found in the years immediately surrounding this census. Tetio remarried, and in 1740, the estate from her first marriage was inventoried. Two slave couples appear in the estate papers: Marabou and his wife Acciga, and Coneoy (?) and his wife Margot. Their estimated values at 1,800 and 1,600 livres suggest that they may have been old enough to have been in the household for some time.[354]

68. Du Longpré sa fe. et deux enfants

Étienne Philippe Du Long Pré,[355] born ca. 1668, Canada, died by September 17, 1734[356]

m. *Marie Ma8e8ensic8e,*[357] died by January 1740[358] (rem. 1735 Charles Huet dit Dulude[359])
    Marie-Philippe, born January 17, baptized January 21, 1714,[360] m. 1730 François Morganne (Bissot) de Vinsenne[361]
    Jacques, baptized? September 9, 1718[362]

Slave: *Marion, pièce d'Inde,* given in dowry to Marie by her parents at her marriage to Vinsenne in 1730.

69. Carriere sa femme et deux enfants

Antoine Carrière, born ca. 1686, Canada, died by 1739[363]

m. April 20, 1718, at Lachine, Canada, *Marie-Madelaine Quesnel,* born ca. 1700[364]

(rem. 1739 Jean-Baptiste de Monbrun de St. Laurent[365])
    Antoine, baptized October 21, 1721[366]

Celeste-Thérèse, baptized November 20, 1723[367] m. Louis Boré[368]
Marie-Madeleine, twin of Celeste, int. December 5, 1723[369]

Slaves:

Jean-Baptiste, son of married parents *Pierrot* and *Marie,* born and baptized June 22, 1721; godparents were Jean-Baptiste Pottier and Magdelaine Quenel[370]
Unnamed parents and male child, baptism, March 9, 1726[371]

70. Le Vieux Potier sa fe. et quatre enfants[372]

Jean-Baptiste Pottier, born April 8, 1682, Lachine, Canada,[373] died by April 1735

m. *Françoise La Brise,* died by April 1735[374]
Jean(-Baptiste), baptized March 3, 1715,[375] int. November 30, 1746[376]
Marie-Françoise, baptized November 10, 1717,[377] m. 1737 Joseph Buchet[378]
Marie-Catherine, baptized June 18, 1719,[379] died by November 1740,[380] m. 1736 Joseph Moreau[381]
Jacques, baptized February 2, 1721,[382] int. September 5, 1723[383]
Toussaint, baptized November 22, 1723, died and int. December 6, 1746,[384] m. 1745 Catherine de Lessart[385]
Jeanne, m. 1740 Jacques Millet[386]
Louis,[387] m. 1752 Marie Kiercereau[388]
Joseph, int. December 5, 1746[389]

71. Deslaurier sa fe. et un enfant[390]

Pierre Du Roy dit Deslauriers, born ca. 1663[391]
Thomas, a natural son[392]

72. Le jeune Turpin[393] sa fe. et quatre enfants

Louis Turpin/Turpain, baptized Montreal, May 15, 1694,[394] died 1751[395]

m. Marie Coulon, born ca. 1702, int. February 24, 1724[396]
Louis, baptized September 20, 1720, int. November 9, 1722[397]
Élisabeth, born February 14, 1724,[398] int. October 2, 1726, age 3[399]

rem. *Dorothée Michiper8e,*[400] widow of Charles Danis, September 11, 1724, died by Jan 11, 1747[401]
Marie-Anne Danis, baptized October 4, 1718,[402] m. 1734 Philippe Chauvin dit Joyeuse[403]
Charles-Pierre Danis, baptized January 30, 1720[404]

Michel Danis, born September 29, baptized October 1, 1723,[405] m. 1745 Marie-Barbe Pillet[406]

    Marie, born ca. 1733

    Marie-Josèphe, baptized February 14, 1733[407]

    Louise-Françoise, born ca. 1737

    Jeanne, born ca. 1739

    Thérèse, born ca. 1741, m. 1762 Paul Jusseaume[408]

rem. 1751 Hélène Hébert

Slaves:

Etsaca, Black slave of the Widow Danis, and *Léveillé,* Black slave of the Danis children, had a child in 1726, baptized Germain[409]

Marie-Françoise, baptized 1726, Native slave mother, unnamed French father.[410]

73. Baillargeon sa femme et 2 enfants

Pierre Baillargeon, baptized April 17, 1701, likely at the Rivière des Pères settlement[411]

m. *Domitille Chacateni8a8a*[412]

    Marie, int. 1725[413]

    Dorothée, born March 4, baptized March 5, 1724,[414] int. October 4, 1790, age sixty-six,[415] m. by May 1739 François Alarie[416]

Slaves: *Marie,* born April 18, baptized April 22, 1724, and her unnamed parents, Black slaves[417]

Paniacicou, Robin, and *Marie,* inherited from Bourdon estate.[418]

74. Collet

Pierre Collet, born in Canada[419]

75. De Launay sa femme et deux enfants

Joseph de Launay/Delaunay, born and baptized April 10, 1689, Québec,[420] died by June 11, 1729[421]

m. January 16, 1723, *Élisabeth Brunet,* born October 17, 1707, Mobile,[422] (rem.1729 André Deguire dit La Rose[423]) died by December 1757[424]

Élisabeth, born and baptized December 23, 1723,[425] m. Antoine Aubuchon[426]

Joseph, died January 1726[427]

Joseph, born ca. 1727[428]

Philippe, born ca. January 1729[429]

76. Lamy sa fe. 3 enfants et son neveu[430]

Joseph Lamy, baptized Sorel, Canada, August 21, 1685,[431] died May 6, 1725[432]

m. May 12, 1722, at New Orleans. *Marie-Françoise Rivart*, born New Orleans[433] (rem. 1726 Jean-Baptiste Thaumur La Source[434])
    Joseph-Marie, born August 26, baptized 27, 1723[435]
    Marie-Françoise Charlotte, born ca. 1725, m. 1743 Charles La Chapelle[436]

Slaves: *Marie*, born July 23, baptized July 24, 1723, to two unnamed slaves of Lamy[437]

77. Michel Philippe sa fe. et 6 enfants[438]

Michel Philippe, born ca. 1669, Canada,[439] died by January 6, 1746[440]
    m. *Marie 8canic8e Rouensa*, widow of Michel Aco, int. June 25, 1725[441]
    Pierre Aco, baptized 1695[442]
    Michel Aco, born and baptized February 22, 1702,[443] died by 1739[444]
    Jacques, baptized July 26, 1704[445] died by Feb 1747,[446] m. Marie-Anne Bolougne[447]
    Agnès, baptized January 22, 1706[448] died by May 29, 1744, m. 1722 Nicolas Chassin[449] (rem. René Roy, surgeon[450])
    Élisabeth, baptized June 22, 1712[451] int. January 3, 1747[452] m. 1727 Étienne Hébert[453] (rem. 1735 Alexandre Duclos[454])
    Marie-Josèphe, baptized January 28, 1714[455] m. 1727 Joseph Lorrain[456]
    Joseph, baptized November 7, 1715[457]
    Ignace, baptized July 27, 1719[458]

Slaves: *Michel*, born January 17, baptized January 30, 1724, son of two unnamed parents, Black slaves of Michel Philippe, officer of the militia, godfather Michel Philippe, godmother Élisabeth Philippe[459]

Joseph-Marie, born January 14, baptized January 20, 1724, son of a Native slave woman belonging to Michel Philippe, father unknown. Godfather Michel Vien, godmother Marie Laboissière[460]

Pierrot and *Brinbelle*, married Black slaves[461]

Carodit and *Gotton*, married Black slaves

Chenenchenan, Native slave *garçon*[462]

78. St. Pierre sa fe. et deux enfants

Pierre La Chauvetau dit St. Pierre, born diocese of Périgueux, France

m. June 15, 1723, *Marguerite Clairjon,* widow of Henry Metivier, born La Rochelle, France, died January 1726[463]

 Henri Metivier, born March 13, baptized May 3, 1719 [464]

 Marie Metivier, born September 7, baptized September 8, 1721[465]

79. La Sonde sa fe. et un enfant[466]

Pierre Pillet dit Lasonde, died by 1769[467]

m. *Magdelaine Truelle Boisron/Boiron,* born in France[468]

 Jean-Baptiste, baptized July 29, 1721, int. August 29, age ca. 6 weeks[469]

 Jean-Baptiste, int. November 4, 1722, age ca. 3 months[470]

 Antoine, baptized April 19, 1724[471] m. 1758 Marie-Louise Graveline, widow of Augustin Langlois[472]

 Marie-Louise, m. 1743 Alphonse Reaume[473] (rem. 1751 Jean-Baptiste Marquis[474])

 Marie-Barbe, m. 1745 Michel Danis[475]

 Madelaine, m. 1747 Jean-Baptiste Millot[476]

 Angélique, died September 7, 1776[477] m. 1755 Jean-Baptiste Crely[478] (rem. Gabriel Aubuchon)

 Louis,[479] m. 1767 Marie Barbeau[480] (rem. Marie-Thérèse Le Compte[481])

 Dorothée, born ca. 1739, died September 7, int. September 8, 1764, age 25[482] m. 1759 Jean-Baptiste Olivier[483]

Engagé: In late 1725, an Antoine Taupart signed an agreement to work for Lasonde.[484]

80. Bourbonnois sa fe. et trois enfants

This is a foundational French family in the Illinois Country. Bourbonnois and Deshayes arrived in Kaskaskia by 1712, well before the first commandant.

Jean Brunet dit Bourbonnois, born April 6, 1673, Montreal[485]

m. 1704 at Mobile *Élisabeth Deshayes,* France[486]

 Élisabeth(-Angélique), born Mobile, October 17, 1707,[487] died ca. 1757[488] m. 1723 Joseph Delaunay[489] (rem. 1729 André Deguire dit La Rose[490])

 Cécile, born 1710, baptized November 24, 1712,[491] int. December 24, 1743[492] m. 1724 Toussaint Loisel[493] (rem. 1739 Antoine Heneaux[494])

 Marie, born November 23, 1712, died by April 22, 1771 in Ste. Genevieve, m. September 15, 1727, New Orleans, Bertrand Cardinal,[495] (rem. May 10, 1728, New Orleans, Pierre Aubuchon[496])

Slaves: In 1746, citing article 50 of the *Code Noir* regarding manumission, Brunet and De-shayes petitioned to have their slave Catherine and her son Jean freed upon their deaths. The request was approved by officials in New Orleans in 1748.[497]

81. Leonard Bosseron sa fe. et quatre enfants

Antoine Bosseron dit Leonard, born Canada, died by February 5, 1726[498]

m. *Suzanne Padoukiquoy/Pani8assa/*[499] *Kerami*, widow of Pierre Milleret[500] (rem. 1728 Daniel Legras[501]) died October 28, 1747[502]
   Marianne Milleret, born ca. July 1712, baptized January 26, 1713,[503] m. 1726 Jean-Baptiste Texier Lavigne[504]
   Pierre Milleret, born October 14, baptized October 18, 1713[505]
   Antoine Bosseron dit Leonard, baptized August 7, 1717[506]
   (Jean-)Augustin Bosseron dit Leonard, baptized August 28, 1719[507]

Slaves: *Pierre*, born June 2, baptized June 3,1723, to two unnamed slaves of Bosseron, godfather Pierre Chêne, godmother Isabelle Levre (?).[508] The 1726 estate inventory after Bosseron's death gave no names for his slaves, but listed two couples *pièces d'Inde* each with two male children, and one Native slave about thirty years old. One of the Black slaves was noted as ill, and perhaps it is she who was buried in July, two months later.[509]

82. Mercier sa femme et un enfant[510]

Jean-Baptiste Mercier, born Canada, died by March 1740[511]

m. May 16, 1718, at Beaupré, Canada, *Marie Baret*, born Canada[512] (rem. by 1742 Michel Arsenau[513]), died January 26, 1751, age 55[514]
   Jean-Baptiste, baptized July 23, 1719[515]
   Unnamed daughter, int. October 18, 1722, age 11 months and 5 days[516]
   Jean-Baptiste, baptized December 26, 1723, m. Marie-Josèphe Tessier[517]
   Jacques, baptized April 29, 1726[518]
   Madeleine, m. 1744 René Roy[519] (rem. 1745 Louis Robert[520])
   Marie, m. before 1762 Joseph Bellecour[521]
   Étienne[522]
   Marie-Jeanne,[523] m. Charles Cadron, militia captain at St. Philippe[524]

83. Ollivier et sa femme[525]

Jean Olivier[526]

m. *Marthe*, widow of La Boissière[527]
   Marie Olivier, baptized August 4, 1715 (mother: Petronilla Mansakime[528]) m. Étienne Guevremont[529]

Françoise Olivier, baptized November 30, 1717 (mother: Marta Accica[530])
Jean-Baptiste Olivier, baptized March 28, 1720 (mother: Marthe Pad8ca[531]) m. Dorothée Lasonde[532]
Françoise Olivier, baptized June 22, 1721 (mother: Marthe Axiga)[533]
Dorothée Olivier, m. 1748 Nicolas Boyer[534]

84. Glinel[535] sa fe. et deux enfants

Pierre Glinel,[536] born February 27, baptized February 28, 1693, Quebec, died by November 1754 [537]

m. 1721 *Marianne Mac8tensic8e*,[538] widow of Pierre Roi,[539] died by November 1754[540]
    Marie-Louise Roi, baptized August 25, 1717[541]
    Genevieve Roi, baptized October 2, 1719[542] int. September 19, 1721[543]
    Marie-Josèphe Glinel, baptized October 8, 1723[544]
    Unnamed daughter, age 2 months, int. January 26, 1727[545]
    Étienne, birthdate unknown[546]

85. Potier le Jeune sa fe. et un enfant

Guillaume Pottier,[547] born January 23, baptized January 28, 1693, Lachine, Canada[548] died by November 11, 1728[549]

m. *Marie Apechic8rata*[550] (rem. Raimond Quesnel[551])
    Marie-Marguerite, born May 30, 1719, baptized Kaskaskia April 21?, 1720[552]
    Guillaume,[553] baptized March 9, 1721[554] died February 23, 1748[555]
    Marguerite, born and baptized January 15, 1724[556]
    Charles, born 1727?[557]

Slaves: In the estate division in 1728, an unnamed *pièce d'Inde* (Black) male slave was in the widow's portion, and a female Native slave was in the portion of Charles. This may have been Auipie "Arrow," whose name appears in a 1741 lease of the land, and who was the slave of Charles Pottier.[558]

86. La Renaudiere sa fe. et deux enfans

Philipe de la Renaudière, clerk of the mines for the company of the west, born France

m. *Perrine Pivert*,[559] born France
    Charles, baptized July 3, 1721[560]
    Marie-Françoise, baptized September 7, 1723[561]

87. Melet et sa femme[562]

Pierre Disené dit Melet, born St. Bonnet, Poitiers, France, died 1726[563]

m. April 22, 1724 *Françoise Rabut,*[564] born ca. 1696, Paris, France,[565] widow of Pierre Durand[566] (rem. 1726 Antoine Bienvenu[567])
    Françoise, m. January 8, 1743, Charles Brazeau[568]

88. Cadouin et sa femme

Nicolas(-Michel-François-Marie) Cadrin,[569] baptized May 26, 1688, Ile d'Orléans, Canada,[570] int. November 10, 1727[571]

m. January 8, 1724,[572] *Marie-Jeanne/Marie-Anne (Boisjoly) Fafard,* baptized June 3, 1714, age 3,[573] (rem. 1728 Jean-François Becquet[574] rem. Joseph De Couadie[575])

89. Beaujoly[576]

Pierre Fafart/Fafard dit BoisJoly, born Canada, ca. 1667[577]

90. La Lande le jeune sa fe. et 3 enfants[578]

Jean-Baptiste Lalande,[579] baptized Montreal, July 18, 1694[580]

m. December 11, 1721,[581] *Catherine 8abanakic8e,*[582] widow of Louis Texier[583]
    Marie-Rose Texier,[584] m. 1732 Pierre St. Ange,[585] (rem. 1741 Nicolas Boyer[586])
    Paul Texier, baptized April 6, 1719,[587] died ca. 1740[588]
    Marc-Antoine Lalande, born October 7, baptized October 20, 1723[589]
    Jean-Baptiste Lalande, born September 25, baptized September 29, 1725[590]
rem. 1734 Charlotte Marchand, Montreal,[591] died 1772, age ca. 60[592]
    Charles, baptized June 6, 1735[593]
    Charlotte, m. 1749 Jacques La Course[594]
    Louis, born February 25, 1744[595]
    Élisabeth, m. 1760 Charles Bienvenu dit Delisle[596]

Slaves: A total of thirteen slaves were listed (most without an indication about whether they were African or Native) on the 1721 estate inventory of Louis Tessier,[597] first husband of Catherine 8abanakic8e: Baptiste and his wife, an unnamed twenty-year-old male, an unnamed woman with a two-year-old son; an unnamed boy of thirteen to fourteen years, an unnamed ten-year-old girl, plus six Black slaves, men and women, out on lease. Jean Baxé was named in the estate of Paul Texier (Tessier) in 1744.

91. Franchomme off.er et sa femme

Nicolas Peltier de Franchomme, baptized January 4, 1703, Montmeillant parish, France

m. autumn 1723 *Marguerite 8assecam8c8e,* widow of Jacques Bourdon (rem. 1729 Pierre Blot)

Slaves: *Bambara, La Fleure, Aubas* (Black); *Caracaroet* (Native)[598]

92. La Rigueur et sa femme[599]

Jean de Tharade dit La Rigueur,[600] died by January 1740.[601] In his will, he left money to his goddaughter, Dorothée Olivier.[602] He had a sugar business on the "little river."[603]

93. Bienvenu le jeune[604]

Antoine Bienvenu, born and baptized November 22, 1703, Ploemeur parish, France[605]

died in New Orleans by 1773,[606] married 1726 Françoise Rabut, Widow Melet.[607]

94. Adam

Joseph or *Estienne Adam,* born Canada[608]

Jean Adam Solingue, born Flanders[609]

95. De Noyan

François de Noyon,[610] baptized September 2, 1678, Boucherville, Canada[611]

96. Gautier(?) et sa fe.[612]

Jean(-Baptiste) Gautier Saguingora[613]

m. *Marie-Susanne Capei8ssec8e* (?)[614]
    Marie, born and baptized January 6, 1702[615]
    Domitille, baptized at 3 or 5 days, November 14, 1703[616]
    Jean, baptized at 9 days January 11, 1713[617]

OR POSSIBLY **Charles Gaussiau (Gossiaux),**

Charles Gossiau, mason, born Avesne en Gainau, diocese of Cambray, France

married September 13, 1723, *Jeanne Bienvenu,* parish of Pleines, diocese of Cannes [618]

97. Hebere et sa fe.

Étienne Hébert, see Census, no. 15

98. Boisseau sa femme et deux enfants

Antoine Boisseau, born Canada ca. 1680[619]

No record found with the name of his wife.

    Thérèse Boisseau, born ca. 1711, died May 12, 1771,[620] m. February 1727
    François (Nicolas) Blot dit Charron[621] (rem. 1740 Pierre Hubert Lacroix[622])

99. Liberge

Guillaume Liberge, baptized May 1, 1700, Quebec[623]

Guillaume Liberge was sentenced to pay 3,000 livres damages to La Renaudière, 300 to the church, and to raise the child Liberge had with Renaudière's wife, Perrine Pivert. Liberge was a voyageur who traveled between the Illinois Country and New Orleans and was killed by Indians during one of his voyages.

100. St. Cernay

Raimond Brosse dit St. Cernay[624]

101. La Bonte Tailleur[625]

A soldier named La Bonté had died in late 1722.[626] Perhaps the identification of "tailor" distinguished him from the soldier.

102. Cailloux sa femme et deux enfants

Pierre Cailloux[627]

103. Portié et sa femme[628]

Christophe Pottier, born at diocese of Bourges, France

m. May 20, 1724, *Agnès Anard,* widow of Marc Clement[629]
    Agnès Clement, m. 1729 Augustin St. Yves[630]
    François Clement
    Catherine Clement, died 1747 m. 1737 Louis Normand La Brière[631]

104. St. Jean sa fe. et quatre enfants[632]

See above, Census, no. 25. St. Jean and his wife Jeanne Bailly took in at least one orphaned child.

105. Pignet armurier

Yves Pinet, born France?[633]

106. La Vigne

Jean-Baptiste Texier dit Lavigne, born Canada[634]

107. Du Lude

Charles Huet dit Dulude, baptized November 2, 1696, Boucherville, Canada[635]

108. Poudret l'aine

Jean-Baptiste or Vincent Poudret, born Canada[636]

109. Du Lude voyageur

Jean Huet dit Dulude,[637] baptized May 19, 1688, Boucherville, Canada[638]

Slaves: Marie, a Native woman ?[639]

110. Villeneuve sa fe. et un enfant

Claude-Pierre Maréschal dit Villeneuve, died by September 1729[640]

m. April 1, 1721 at Biloxi, *Marie-Anne dite Rose Goneau/Gono*[641] (rem. 1729 Charles Gossiaux[642])

   Pierre[643]

Census Counts

	Maîtres	Engagés ou domestiques	Esclaves nègres	Esclaves sauvages	Bet. corn.	Chev.x	Terrains défrichés
1. Habitation de Mr De Boisbriant et Laloire	0	2	22	0	8	4	100
2. M. Renaud	1	3	20	0	3	11	80
3. La Croix sa fe. et cinq enfants	7	0	1	0	8	2	5
4. Rollet sa femme et deuxenfants	4	0	0	0	0	1	5
5. Neau et sa femme	2	0	0	2	6	0	30
6. Giard	1	0	0	0	10	1	4
7. Prée sa fe. et deux enfans	4	0	0	0	0	0	4
8. Richard	1	0	0	0	0	0	3
9. Bontems sa fe. et un enfant	3	0	0	0	0	1	2
10. Nieuport	1	0	0	0	0	1	4
11. Baron sa fe. et un enfant	3	0	0	0	1	0	4
12. Darbonne sa femme et un enfant	3	0	0	0	0	0	4
13. Chapu et sa femme	2	0	0	2	3	0	6
14. Loisel et sa femme	2	0	3	1	4	2	0
15. Hébert et sa femme	2	0	4	0	11	6	60
16. Sans Chagrin sa femme et deux enfants	4	0	0	0	1	0	10
17. Fabus	1	0	0	0	0	0	0
18. Timonier	1	0	0	0	0	1	20
19. Du Trou et sa femme	2	0	0	0	0	0	4
20. Bourgmont	1	0	0	0	0	0	4
21. Baptiste, nègre	0	1	0	0	0	0	6
22. Joseph L'Espagnol, sa femme et deux enfants	4	0	0	0	0	0	5
23. Ant.e l'Espagnol	1	0	0	0	0	0	5
24. Biron et un enfant	2	0	0	0	0	0	4
25. St. Jean et sa femme	2	0	0	0	0	0	0
26. La Forest	1	0	0	0	0	0	10
27. Becquet sa fe. et deux enfants	4	0	0	0	1	0	4

Census Counts

	Maîtres	Engagés ou domestiques	Esclaves nègres	Esclaves sauvages	Bet. corn.	Chev.x	Terrains défrichés
28. La jeune Lalande	1	0	0	0	0	0	0?
29. Pradel	1	0	2	0	3	1	0
30. Barselone	1	0	0	0	0	0	5
31. Du Sablon et sa femme	2	0	0	0	0	0	5
32. Des Essarts	1	0	0	0	0	0	0
33. Robillart et sa femme	2	0	0	1	1	1	10
34. Dragon	1	0	0	0	0	6	5
35. Chassin sa fe. et deux enfants	4	0	0	2	7	2	10
36. La Jeunesse dit Le Gros	1	0	0	2	1	1	8
37. La Plume et un enfant	2	0	3	0	3	2	8
38. Bellegarde et deux enfants	3	0	1	2	3	1	20
39. Langevin et sa femme	2	0	0	0	0	0	0
40. St. Pierre sa fe. et un enfant	3	0	0	1	1	0	7
41. Lantrulu et sa femme	2	0	0	0	0	0	5
42. Gardon sa fe. et un enfant	3	0	0	0	0	0	6
43. Antoine et sa femme	2	0	0	0	0	0	5
44. Canarel et un associé	2	0	0	0	0	0	8
45. Robin et un associé	2	0	0	1	0	0	8
46. Daniel	1	0	0	0	0	0	6
47. Capitaine et sa femme	2	0	0	1	0	0	4
48. St. Jacques sa fe. et un enfant	3	0	0	0	0	0	6
49. Pierre	1	0	0	0	0	0	6
50. Gouverneur et Brun	2	0	0	0	0	0	4
51. Belhumeur et sa femme	2	0	0	0	0	0	8
52. Moreau ? sa fe. et un enf	3	0	0	0	0	0	4
53. Dauphiné sa femme et deux enfants	4	0	0	0	0	0	3
54. Beausejour et son camarade	2	0	0	0	0	0	8

(continued)

Census Counts (*continued*)

	Maîtres	Engagés ou domestiques	Esclaves nègres	Esclaves sauvages	Bet. corn.	Chev.x	Terrains défrichés
55. Thomas	1	0	0	0	0	0	6
56. Bellerose	1	0	0	1	0	0	5
57. Le Normand	1	0	0	0	1	0	4
58. Texier sa fe. et un enfant	3	0	0	0	0	0	8
59. La Pointe sa fe. et 1 enfant	3	0	2	0	3	1	20
60. Ignace Hebert	1	0	0	0	3	0	10
61. Le Vieux Turpin et deux enfants	3	0	0	1	7	1	0
62. Deux P. Jesuittes et deux c urés missionnaires	4	2	9	2	15	4	100
63. Girardeau sa f. et un enfant	3	1	1	1	3	2	33
64. Melique off.er LaJeunesse sa femme et un enfant ses fermiers	4	1[a]	0	1	4	6	70
65. La Fatigue sa fe. et 2 enfants	4	1	1	0	4	1	35
66. DesVignes sa fe. et deux enfans	4	0	5	2	9	2	24
67. La Lande L'aisne sa femme et quatre enfants	6	1	1	4	13	1	50
68. Du Longpré sa fe. et deux enfants	4	3[b]	2	4	13	4	50
69. Carriere sa femme et deux enfants	4	1	11	1	14	1	80
70. Le Vieux Potier sa fe. et quatre enfants	6	0	1	2	12	2	80
71. Deslaurier sa fe. et un enfant	3	2	0	1	3	1	20
72. Le jeune Turpin sa fe. et quatre enfants	6	2[c]	2	2	9	3	30
73. Baillargeon sa femme et 2 enfants	4	3	3	2	6	3	30
74. Collet	1	0	0	0	1	1	10

Census Counts

	Maîtres	Engagés ou domestiques	Esclaves nègres	Esclaves sauvages	Bet. corn.	Chev.x	Terrains défrichés
75. De Launay sa femme et deux enfants	4	1	0	2	8	0	40
76. Lamy sa fe. 3 enfants et son neveu	6	1	3	0	9	2	150
77. Michel Philippe sa fe. et 6 enfants	8	2	5	3	15	5	100
78. St. Pierre sa fe. et deux enfants	4	0	2	0	9	3	30
79. La Sonde sa fe. et un enfant	3	2	0	1	7	3	56
80. Bourbonnois sa fe. et trois enfants	5	0	2	5	21	3	150
81. Leonard Bosseron sa fe. et quatre enfants	6	1[d]	7	2	13	4	100
82. Mercier sa femme et un enfant	3	1[e]	0	0	3	3	35
83. Ollivier et sa femme	2	0	0	0	0	0	0
84. Glinel sa fe. et deux enfants	4	1	0	1	7	3	20
85. Potier le Jeune sa fe. et un enfant	3	1	4	2	5	3	40
86. La Renaudiere sa fe. et deux enfans	4	0	0	0	0	0	0
87. Melet et sa femme	2	0	0	0	1	2	12
88. Cadouin et sa femme	2	0	1	1	10	3	20
89. Beaujoly	1	0	0	0	2	1	10
90. La Lande le jeune sa fe. et 3 enfants	5	1[f]	6	6	16	2	150
91. Franchomme off.er et sa femme	2	1[g]	3	1	7	2	20
92. La Rigueur et sa femme	2	1	0	0	0	1	10
93. Bienvenu le jeune	1	0	0	1	4	1	20
94. Adam	1	0	0	0	4	0	5
95. De Noyan	1	0	0	0	0	0	0
96. Gautier(?) et sa fe.	2	0	0	0	9	0	0
97. Hebere et sa fe.	2	0	1	0	1	2	25

(continued)

	Maîtres	Engagés ou domestiques	Esclaves nègres	Esclaves sauvages	Bet. corn.	Chev.x	Terrains défrichés
98. Boisseau sa femme et deux enfants	4	0	0	0	0	0	0
99. Liberge	1	0	0	0	0	0	0
100. St. Cernay	1	0	0	0	4	0	4
101. La Bonte Tailleur	1	1	0	0	0	0	0
102. Cailloux sa femme et deux enfants	4	0	0	0	0	0	0
103. Portié et sa femme	2	0	0	0	0	0	0
104. St. Jean sa fe. et quatre enfants	6	0	0	0	1	0	0
105. Pignet armurier	1	0	0	0	0	0	0
106. La Vigne	1	0	0	0	4	0	10
107. Du Lude	1	0	0	0	0	0	0
108. Poudret l'aine	1	0	0	1	0	0	0
109. Du Lude voyageur	1	0	1	1	5	0	0
110. Villeneuve sa fe. et un enfant	3	0	0	0	1	1	6
Totals	280	37	129	66	362	121	2210

Note: *Maîtres* = husbands, wives, and children; *Engagés ou domestiques* = contract employees/indentured servants and domestic servants; *Esclaves nègres* = African slaves, no gender or age distinctions; *Esclaves sauvages* = Native slaves, no gender or age distinctions; *Bet. corn.* = horned livestock (cattle and oxen); *Chev.x* = horses; *Terrains défrichés* = cleared agricultural plots.

[a] KM 25-2-12-1, transfer of rights for services of Jacques, engagé of Melique, to Gardon. Also KM 25-3-12-1, agreement of Jean-Baptiste André (Census, no. 21) to serve as domestic servant for one year to Lt. Pierre Melique.

[b] Perhaps one was Jean-Phillipe, a brother. See part I.

[c] These two may be the lessees of a farm in the estate of the Danis children, Pierre La Souhaite/Souhaitait (?) and his wife Marguerite Creuseau, KM 24-9-13-1.

[d] KM 24-10-16-2, there was a brother, Jacques.

[e] A brother of Marie Baret, Louis, is mentioned in the marriage contract of Magdelaine Mercier to Robert, KM 45-8-14-1.

[f] In 1730, the Texier minors had a tenant farmer, Bastien François, who brought suit against a slave belonging to the minors, Jean Baxé. Baxé was witness to a marriage of slaves in 1750, see notes in Census no. 66 above.

[g] Jean Sanguingoara. See part I for his story, and for information on Marguerite and the slaves.

GLOSSARY OF FRENCH TERMS

NOTES

ESSENTIAL ILLINOIS COUNTRY READING

INDEX

GLOSSARY OF FRENCH TERMS

ARPENT: as linear measurement, approx. 192 ft.; as surface measurement, approx. .85 acre

AUBAIN: person not assimilated into French society and therefore not legally a citizen of the French realm

BATEAU: flat-bottomed river boat

CHOPINE: unit of liquid measure, equal to approximately one-half a liter

COMMUNAUTÉ: community of possessions, both real estate and personal, held by a legitimately married couple

COMPAGNIE DES INDES: (Company of the Indies) investment company that managed French Louisiana on behalf of the French crown during the 1720s

COUTUME DE PARIS: traditional French customary laws that governed domestic life in much of northern France

CURATEUR (FEM. CURATRICE): financial guardian for married persons younger than twenty-five years of age

DIT (FEM. DITE): literally "called," used to introduce a nickname

DONNÉ: lay person dedicated to serve a religious order

EMPLACEMENT: a residential property

ENGAGÉ: hired worker under contract for a fixed period of time, often employed in the fur trade

GREFFE: depository for civil records, usually maintained by a notaire

GREFFIER: filing clerk for civil records, subordinate to a notaire

IMMEUBLES: real estate

LA MER: the Gulf Coast

LE PAYS D'EN HAUT: Upper Canada, including the Great Lakes

LE PAYS DES ILLINOIS: the Illinois Country, originally the territory of the greater Illinois Nation of Indians

MAJORITÉ: coming of age, achieved on twenty-fifth birthday

MARGUILLIER: church warden elected by parishioners

MÉTIS (FEM. MÉTISSE): person of mixed blood, for our purposes Indian and French

MEUBLES: personal property

NOTAIRE: legal official of high status in French Louisiana

PIED: unit of linear measure, equals 12.76 English inches

PIROGUE: dug-out canoe

POT: liquid unit measure, equals approximately two quarts

POTEAUX-EN-TERRE: structure erected with wooden posts set in the ground

RÉGNICOLE: legally, a native-born or naturalized citizen of France

SAUVAGE (FEM. SAUVAGESSE): Native American

TERRAIN: a residential property

TERRES: plowlands

TUTEUR (FEM. TUTRICE): guardian for unmarried minors (that is, younger than twenty-five years of age)

Introduction

1. Clarence W. Alvord, *The Illinois Country, 1673–1818*, The Centennial History of Illinois, vol. 1 (Springfield: Illinois Centennial Commission, 1920). Alvord also has the distinction of having discovered, in a forgotten niche of the Randolph County Courthouse in Chester, Illinois, the increasingly famous Kaskaskia Manuscripts. This extraordinary collection of manuscripts, now properly housed and curated in the courthouse, has been painstakingly collated and calendared by Margaret K. Brown and Lawrie C. Dean.

2. See David J. Costa, "Miami-Illinois Tribe Names," in John Nichols, ed., *Papers of the Thirty-first Algonquian Conference* (Winnipeg: University of Manitoba, 2000), 30–53. See also, Carl Masthay, ed. and comp., *Kaskaskia Illinois-to-French Dictionary* (St. Louis: privately printed, 2002), 125, no. 173. Masthay's erudite book is based on Jacques Largillier's dictionary (originally yet incorrectly attributed to Jacques Gravier—though he likely had a hand in its creation). It includes (2–5) "An Overview of the Illinois Language" by David J. Costa. The manuscript of the dictionary is located in the Watkinson Library, Trinity College, Hartford, Connecticut. See also Michael McCafferty. "Jacques Largillier: French trader, Jesuit brother, and Jesuit scribe *par excellence*." *Journal of the Illinois State Historical Society*. Vol. 104, No. 3 (Fall, 2011), 188–98. Although the word "Illinois" is of Miami-Illinois origin, David Costa, Ives Goddard, and Michael McCafferty argue that the Ottawas originally borrowed the phrase, "he/she speaks in a regular way," from the Miamis, who spoke a dialect of the same Algonquian language as that spoken by the Illinois.

3. See Reuben G. Thwaites, ed., *Jesuit Relations and Allied Documents* [hereafter *JR*], 73 vols. (Cleveland, OH: Burrow Brothers, 1896–1901), 54:166.

4. Reprint edition (Carbondale: Southern Illinois University Press, 2003).

5. For examples see Margaret Kimball Brown, *Reconstructing an Eighteen-Century Village: Chartres in Illinois* (Belleville, IL: Village Publishers, 2020); Carl J. Ekberg, *French Roots in the Illinois Country: The Mississippi Frontier in Colonial Times* (Urbana: University of Illinois Press, 1998); Carl J. Ekberg, *Stealing Indian Women: Native Slavery in the Illinois* Country (Urbana: University of Illinois Press, 2007); Sophie White, *Wild Frenchmen and Frenchified Indians: Material Culture and Race in Colonial Louisiana* (Philadelphia: University of Pennsylvania Press, 2012); Robert Michael Morrissey, *Empire by Collaboration: Indians, Colonists, and Gov-*

ernments in Colonial Illinois Country (Philadelphia: University of Pennsylvania Press, 2015); David MacDonald, *Lives of Fort de Chartres: Commandants, Soldiers, and Civilians, 1720–70* (Carbondale: Southern Illinois University Press, 2016).

6. For example, see Gilles Havard, *Histoire des coureurs de bois: Amérique du Nord, 1600–1840* (Paris: Les Indes savantes, 2016), especially chapters 14, 15, 16.

7. The most authoritative late seventeenth-century and early eighteenth-century editions of the *Coutume* were compiled and edited by Claude de Ferrière (his first edition was *Texte des Coutumes de la Prévosté et Vicomté de Paris* [Paris: Jean Cochart, 1680]), an avocat (lawyer) who had standing in the Parlement de Paris. Despite its name, this was not a legislative assembly but rather the highest law court in France until it was wiped out by the French Revolution. All seventeenth- and eighteenth-century editions of the *Coutume* are consistent in their rendering of the texts of the various Articles and in their numbering of said Articles. Therefore, our citations of various Articles will be confined simply to providing the relevant numbers of the respected articles. However, extensive commentaries on the articles vary considerably from edition to edition. When citing Ferrière's commentaries about particular articles of the *Coutume*, volume and page numbers from the following edition are provided. *Nouveau Commentaire sur La Coutume de la Prévoté et Vicomté de Paris*, 2 vols. (Paris: Libraires Associés, 1770). Morris S. Arnold has explained how the *Coutume* was introduced to French Louisiana even before the founding of New Orleans in 1718. See: Arnold, *Unequal Law Unto a Savage Race: European Legal Traditions in Arkansas, 1686–1836* (Fayetteville: University of Arkansas Press, 1985), 12.

8. William Bent, the famous trader and builder of Bent's Fort on the upper Arkansas River married a Cheyenne—Misstanta, or "Owl Woman"—in 1835, but it is not at all clear what legal protections, if any, she was afforded as his wife. She predeceased Bent. As we shall see, Illinois women had more agreeable names than Cheyennes. See: Anne F. Hyde, *Empires, Nations & Families: A History of the North American West, 1800–60* (Lincoln: University of Nebraska Press, 2011), 162–65, 354–55.

9. Edme-Gatien Salmon (*commissaire-ordonnateur*) to minister, July 17, 1732, Archives Nationales d'Outre Mer, Aix-en-Provence, Article C^{13A} volume 15: fols.166–68. Henceforth given as ANOM, C^{13A} with appropriate volume and folio numbers.

10. Burial record online at familysearch.org, Kaskaskia Parish Records (henceforth KPR), image 20.

11. Havard, *Histoire des coureurs de bois*, chapter 33.

12. Concerning widows' rights under the *Coutume* in French Canada, see Josette Brun, "Le veuvage en Nouvelle-France au XVIIIᵉ siècle: De la Coutume de Paris aux contrats de mariage de Louisbourg," in *Veufs, veuves et veuvage dans la France d'Ancien Régime: Actes du Colloque de Poitiers (11–12 juin 1998)*, ed. Colette H. Winn, collected by Nicole Pellegrin (Paris, 2003), 71–88.

13. Concerning the creation of the Illinois Provincial Council, see "Règlement pour l'establissement d'un conseil provincial aux Illinois," ANOM, series B 43:103–4; also, Brown, *Reconstructing*, 29, 66–67.

14. See John A. Dickinson, "New France: Law, Courts, and the *Coutume de Paris, 1608–1760*," in *Canada's Legal Inheritances*, ed. W. Wesley Pue and DeLloyd J. Guth (Winnipeg, MB: Canadian Legal History Project, Faculty of Law, The University of Manitoba, 2001), 32–54.

15. Fleuriau, "Exposé," December 1728, in ANOM, series F³ 242:144–45.

16. Most recently in Brett Rushforth, "Slavery, the Fox Wars, and the Limits of Alliance," *William and Mary Quarterly* 63 (2006): 53–80; also R. David Edmunds and Joseph L. Peyser, *The Fox Wars: The Mesquakie Challenge to New France* (Norman: University of Oklahoma Press, 1993).

17. There is no recorded instance in which an Illinois Indian widow of a French man took in a second marriage an Indian man for her husband.

18. Concerning Indian women's attraction to French men, see Havard, *Histoire des coureurs de bois*, 696–714; Tracy Neal Leavelle, *The Catholic Calumet: Colonial Conversions in French and Indian North America* (Philadelphia: University of Pennsylvania Press, 2012), 161–70; Linda Carol Jones, *The Shattered Cross: French Catholic Missionaries on the Mississippi Frontier, 1698–1725* (Baton Rouge, LA: Louisiana State University Press, 2020), 67–69, 183–86.

19. See especially Sahila Belmessous, "Assimilation and Racialism in Seventeenth and Eighteenth-Century French Colonial Policy," *American Historical Review*, 110, no. 2 (April 2005): 322–49; White, *Wild Frenchmen and Frenchified Indians*; also Guillaume Aubert, "The Blood of France: Race and Purity of Blood in the French Atlantic World," *The William and Mary Quarterly*, 3ʳᵈ ser., 61, no. 3 (2004): 439–78.

20. See Robert Michael Morrissey, "The Power of the Ecotone: Bison, Slavery, and the Rise and Fall of the Grand Village of the Kaskaskia," *Journal of American History* (December 2015): 267–91.

Principal Characters

1. Michael McCafferty of Indiana University renders this name "Dawn's Light Woman," which is all the more powerful because it is in the vocative case.

Chapter 1: The Illinois Country

1. Francis Jennings popularized the notion of a European "invasion" of North America during the early modern period. See Francis Jennings, *Invasion of America: Indians, Colonialism, and the Cant of Conquest* (New York: Norton, 1976). As Jennings' title intimates, he was a moralist in high dudgeon, damning Europeans for their ethnocentrism and brutalities. See H.C. Porter, "Cant, Colonialism, and Ethnohistory," *The Historical Journal* 33 (September 1990): 683–92. Curiously, Jennings, who served as director of the Indian History Center at the Newberry Library in Chicago, Illinois, ignored the French villages of the colonial Illinois Country. James

Axtell's "invasion"—in James Axtell, *The Invasion Within: The Context of Cultures in Colonial North America* (Oxford: Oxford University Press, 1985)—is much more nuanced than Jennings' work. See also James Axtell, "Ethnohistory: An Historian's Viewpoint," *Ethnohistory* 26 (Winter, 1979), especially 7–8. Axtell, although having spent much time on the Jesuits, never followed them westward to the Illinois Country and their base at Kaskaskia.

2. See Jones, *The Shattered Cross* and Leavelle, *The Catholic Calumet.*

3. *William and Mary Quarterly,* "Forum: Settler Colonialism in Early American History," 3d ser., 76 (July 2019): 361–450.

4. Allan Greer, "Settler Colonialism and Empire in Early America," in ibid., 387.

5. Morris S. Arnold, *The Rumble of a Distant Drum: The Quapaws and Old World Newcomers, 1673–1804* (Fayetteville: University of Arkansas Press, 2000). (See especially "Introduction," xv–xxi.)

6. Concerning the decline of the Illinois Nation, see Joseph Zitomersky, *French Americans— Native Americans in Eighteenth-Century French Colonial Louisiana* (Lund, Sweden: University of Lund Press, 1994), chapter 7; E.J. Blasingham, "The Depopulation of the Illinois Indians," pts. 1 and 2, *Ethnohistory* 3 (Autumn 1956): 361–412.

7. On Marquette, see Joseph P. Donnelly, *Jacques Marquette, S.J., 1637–75* (Chicago: Loyola University Press, 1968); Raphael N. Hamilton, *Marquette's Explorations: The Narratives Reexamined* (Madison: University of Wisconsin Press, 1970). It is very likely that some *coureurs de bois* had reached the Mississippi River via Green Bay and the Wisconsin River before Marquette and Jolliet used that route in 1673. See Havard, *Histoire des coureurs de bois,* 56.

8. Pierre Margry, "Lettres de Cavelier de La Salle et correspondance relative à ses entreprises (1678–85)," pt. 2 of *Découvertes et établissements des Français dans l'ouest et dans le sud de l'Amérique septentrionale,1614–98; mémoires et documents inédits recueillis et publiés par Pierre Margry* (Paris: Maisonneuve, 1879); Mark Walczynski, *Inquietus: La Salle in the Illinois Country,* Center for French Colonial Studies, no. 12 (Plano, TX: Center for French Colonial Studies, 2019); Patricia K. Galloway, ed., *La Salle and His Legacy: Frenchmen and Indians in the Lower Mississippi Valley* (Jackson: University of Mississippi Press, 1982).

9. On La Salle in the Illinois River valley, see especially Walczynski, *Inquietus.*

10. Alvord, *The Illinois Country, 1673–1818,* chapter X. Ekberg, *French Roots,* chapter 2. Mary Borgias Palm, *The Jesuit Missions of the Illinois Country 1673–1763* (Cleveland, OH: n.p., 1931), chapter 2.

11. ANOM, series B 43:103–4.

12. For recent discussions of the Grand Village of the Kaskaskias on the upper Illinois River, see Robert Michael Morrissey, "The Power of the Ecotone: Bison, Slavery, and the Rise and Fall of the Grand Village of the Kaskaskia," *Journal of American History* (December 2015): 267–91; Mark Walczynski, "La Salle's Fort St. Louis of the Illinois: Documentary and Archaeological Evidence for Its Actual Location and Specific Considerations for Why It Was Built Where It Was," *Le Journal,* 26, no. 4 (2010): 1–7; Mark Walczynski, *Inquietus: La Salle in the Illinois Country,* Center for French Colonial Studies, William L. Potter Publications Series,

no. 12, chapters 4 and 5; Robert F. Mazrim, *Protohistory at the Grand Village of the Kaskaskia, The Illinois Country on the Eve of Colony*. University of Illinois, Illinois State Archaeological Survey. *Studies in Archaeology*, no. 10 (2015). See also, James Allison Brown and Kenneth Gordon Orr, *The Zimmerman Site: A Report on Excavations at the Grand Village of Kaskaskia, La Salle County, Illinois* (Springfield, IL: Printed by authority of the State of Illinois, 1961), 55–59; Margaret Kimball Brown, *The First Kaskaskia: the Zimmerman Site* (Ottawa, IL: LaSalle County Historical Society, 1973); Mary Borgias Palm, *The Jesuit Missions of the Illinois Country 1673–1763* (Cleveland, OH: n.p., 1931), 15–26.

13. See the fascinating and informative article by Michael McCafferty, "The Illinois Place Name 'Pimitéoui.'" *Journal of the Illinois State Historical Society*, 102, no. 2 (Summer 2009): 177–92. Also, Judith A. Franke, *French Peoria and Illinois Country, 1673–1846*, graphic design by Eric Johnson (Springfield, IL: Illinois State Museum, 1995).

14. *Dictionary of Canadian Biography* (hereafter *DCB*), s.v. "Pierre-Gabriel Marest"; also, Palm, *Jesuit Missions*, 39-48 and passim.

15. *DCB*, s.v. "Jacques Gravier."

16. *Jesuit Relations*, 65: 82–83. The three Seminarians were François-Jolliet de Montigny, Jean-François Buisson de St. Cosme, and Antoine Davion. See Garraghan, "New Light on Old Cahokia," *Illinois Catholic Historical Review*, XI (1928) 104–5.

17. Garraghan, "New Light," 114.

18. Ibid., 119.

19. Jean-Paul Mercier, superior of the Seminarian mission at Cahokia, called this creek "R. de Pères" on his 1735 map of the area. The map was reproduced in Ekberg, *French Roots*, 57. See also: Bonnie Stepenoff, "The Jesuit Mission on Missouri's River Des Peres," *Missouri Historical Review*, no. 114 (July 2020): 235–48; Laurence Kenny, "Missouri's Earliest Settlement and Its Name," *St. Louis Catholic Historical Review*, no. 1 (1919): 151–56.

20. Marest to Father Germon (Germain), Nov. 9, 1712, *Jesuit Relations* 66: 244; see also Palm, *Jesuit Missions*, especially chapters II and IV.

21. Quoted in Jones, *The Shattered Cross*, 115.

22. See Stepenoff, "The Jesuit Mission," 244.

23. In July 1703, Bergier complained about Sioux depredations near Cahokia. Palm, *Jesuit Missions*, 41.

24. The best coverage of the relationship between Bergier and Marest is found in Jones, *Shattered Cross*, 198–99.

25. KPR, image 6.

26. Metchagamia is Algonquian/Illinois for "big water person." Email communication, Michael McCafferty, December 12, 2020. It was the early name for what later became the Kaskaskia River. Bernard Diron d'Artaguiette's map, with data collected in 1722, depicts Rivière des Caskaskias, and thereafter French cartographers (such as the well-known Jacques-Nicolas Bellin) continued that usage. But local residents, by nature conservative in outlook, adhered to Metchagamia. See KM 22-5-10-3 (that is, 1722, May 10, document 3), 23-9-27-1, 37-7-19-1,

48-7-8-1. Also, Michael McCafferty, "While Cleaning Up a Tribe Name," *Michigan's Habitant Heritage*, no. 41, 4 (October 2020).

27. Archives de la Guerre, Château de Vincennes, series A^1 2592: 93.

28. Bronwen McShea in *Apostles of Empire: The Jesuits and New France* (Omaha: University of Nebraska Press, 2019) argues on p. 156 that Jesuits of New France "were apostles of French empire not simply of the kingdom of Christ they strove to populate with Native American souls." McShea does not deal with the Illinois Country, but the Jesuits at Kaskaskia surely supported the French civil regime in the region.

29. Marriage contract between Thuilliers Devegnois and Dorothée Mercier, Widow Chabot, November 17, 1721; 1745 copy in Louisiana Colonial Documents (lacolonialdocs.org), # 1745-02-16-01.

30. Jesuits play a large role in James Axtell's *The Invasion Within: The Context of Cultures in Colonial North America* (Oxford: Oxford University Press, 1985). Curiously, the colonial Illinois Country, profoundly influenced by Jesuits, does not appear in Axtell's valuable study.

31. John Francis Bannon, "Black-Robe Frontiersman: Gabriel Marest, S.J." *Bulletin of the Missouri Historical* Society, 10, no. 3: 351–66; *DCB*, s.v. "Jean Mermet"; Palm, *Jesuit Missions*, 42–48.

32. Marest to German, November 9, 1712, *JR*, 66: 237, 253.

33. Mermet to the Jesuits of Canada, Mar. 2, 1706, *JR*, 66:61.

34. *DCB*, s.v. "Jacques Largillier"; Michael McCafferty, "Jacques Largillier: French trader, Jesuit brother, and Jesuit scribe *par excellence*." *Journal of the Illinois State Historical Society,* 104, no. 3 (Fall, 2011): 188–98.

35. Michael McCafferty, "Jacques Largillier: French trader, Jesuit brother, and Jesuit scribe *par excellence*." *Journal of the Illinois State Historical Society,* 104, no. 3 (Fall, 2011): 188–98. McCafferty points out (p. 192) that Father Jacques Gravier, founder of the Illinois mission (see *DCB*, s.v. "Jacques Gravier") had been the first to work out the grammar of the Miami-Illinois language and had likely supplied some of the raw data that eventually went into Largillier's completed manuscript.

36. Masthay, ed. and comp., *Kaskaskia Illinois-to-French Dictionary*, 140, 177, 181, 249, 259.

37. Concerning Montaigne, North American Indians, and cultural relativism, see especially Cornelius J. Jaenen, *Friend and Foe: Aspects of French-Amerindian Cultural Contact in the Sixteenth and Seventeenth Centuries* (New York: Columbia University Press, 1976), 27–28, 146–47.

38. "Lettre du P Gabriel Marest et de Jacques L'Argilier surnommé le castor, écrit au R P Germain superieur des missions de la Compagnie en Canada par le R Mermet du village des Cascaskias, le 25^c fevrier 1715," series Gbr0172, Archives de la Compagnie de Jésus, Vanves, France; *DCB*, s.v. "Joseph-Louis Germain."

39. A stone church was built at Kaskaskia in 1741 (KM 40-7-17-1, 40-7-17-2).

40. Bourdon's first wife, Domitile Ch8ping8eta, may well have died in this epidemic.

41. KPR, image 21.

42. Marest to Germain, Nov. 9, 1712, *JR*, 66:245–47.

43. The epidemic could conceivably have been some virulent form of malaria, striking a defenseless population. Marest died during the height of the malaria season, and by mid-eighteenth century, malaria was endemic in the Illinois Country. On malaria in the Illinois Country, see Carl J. Ekberg, *Colonial Ste. Genevieve: An Adventure on the Mississippi Frontier* (Gerald, MO: Patrice Press, 1985), 250–58.

44. See "124 Years Ago in IDPH History," online at www.idph.state/il.us.webhistory11.htm.

45. Joseph Zitomersky, *French-Americans—Native Americans in Eighteenth-Century French Colonial Louisiana* (Lund, Sweden: University of Lund Press, 1994), 222; see also E.J. Blasingham, "The Depopulation of the Illinois Indians," pts. 1 and 2, *Ethnohistory* 3 (Autumn 1956): 361–412.

46. See Carl J. Ekberg, *French Roots*, chapters 1–5.

47. Marest to Germon (that is, Germain), Nov. 9, 1712, *Jesuit Relations*, 66: 292

48. André Pénicaut observed plows at Kaskaskia in 1711. See *Fleur de Lys and Calumet: Being the Pénicaut Narrative of French Adventure in Louisiana*, trans. and ed. Richebourg Gaillard McWilliams (Tuscaloosa: University of Alabama Press, 1953), 137.

49. Ekberg, *French Roots*, 202.

50. Pierre-François-Xavier de Charlevoix, *Journal d'un voyage fait par ordre du roi dans l'Amérique Septentrionale* (Paris: Rollin fils, 1744), 6:139–40. Zebedée served for years with the Jesuits in Kaskaskia, and died in 1727 a revered figure in the community (ornamented burial record in KPR, image 21).

51. In northern France, traditional agriculture seldom produced a seed/yield ratio of as much as 1/10. See B. H. Slicher van Bath, *The Agrarian History of Western Europe, A.D. 500–1850*, trans. Olive Ordish (London: Edward Arnold Ltd., 1963), 172–77. Jane Mt. Pleasant's fascinating study (*Agricultural History* [2011, vol. 84 {4}, 460–92]), in which she compares and contrasts Iroquoian agricultural production with that of western Europe during the early modern period would have been manifestly more valuable if she had included data from the Illinois Country.

52. On the flour trade down the Mississippi to New Orleans, see Ekberg, *French Roots*, chapter 6.

53. Richard White, *The Middle Ground: Indians, Empires, and Republics in the Great Lakes Region, 1650–1815* (Cambridge: Cambridge University Press, 1991), 41–49.

54. Marest to Germon (Germain), Nov. 9, 1712, *Jesuit Relations*, 66: 231.

55. D'Artaguiette's "Journal," in Newton D. Mereness (ed.), *Travels in the American* Colonies (New York: Macmillan, 1926). Concerning Bernard d'Artaguiette and his important brothers, Pierre and Jean-Baptiste, see MacDonald, *Lives of Fort de Chartres*, 7, 29, 76, 196, 206, 243. 73. D'Artaguiette, on behalf of the French crown, conducted a tour of French Louisiana in 1722–23.

56. Christopher M. Parsons, *A Not-So-New-World: Empire and Environment in French Colonial North America*, Early American Studies (Philadelphia: University of Pennsylvania Press,

2018), 186–87. Parsons' book, based on extensive readings in printed sources is a scintillating study in early modern French intellectual history, how French minds grappled with the wonders and mysteries of the Canadian environment.

57. Concerning Indian slavery, see Marcel Trudel, *L'esclavage au Canada français; histoire et conditions de l'esclavage* (Québec: Presses universitaires Laval, 1960); and Brett Rushforth, *Bonds of Alliance: Indigenous and Atlantic Slaveries in New France* (Chapel Hill: Omohundro Institute of Early American History and Culture and the University of North Carolina Press, 2012); Carl J. Ekberg, *Stealing Indian Women: Native Slavery in the Illinois* Country (Urbana: University of Illinois Press, 2007).

58. KPR, image 10.

59. Carl Masthay, comp. and ed., *Kaskaskia-Illinois-to-French Dictionary* (St. Louis, MO: privately printed, 2002); email correspondences with Michael McCafferty, October 10, 2019. Also, William C. Sturtevant, gen. ed., Raymond J. Demaillie, ed. *Handbook of North American Indians*, vol. 13 (Washington, D.C.: Smithsonian Institution, 2001) 13:564 Ekberg, *Stealing Indian Women*, 47–48.

60. On enmity between Wichitas and Padoucas, see Mildred Mott Wedel, "Claude-Charles Dutisné: A Review of His 1719 Journeys," *Great Plains Journal* 12, no. 2 (Spring 1973): 157–58.

61. KM 20--0—0--1. This document is not available on film, and this citation is taken from the inventory of the Kaskaskia Manuscripts: Lawrie Cena Dean Margaret Kimball Brown, comps. and eds., *The Kaskaskia Manuscripts: 1708–1816. A Calendar of Civil Documents in Colonial Illinois* (2014).

62. See Jay Higginbotham, *Old Mobile: Fort Louis de la Louisiane, 1702–11* (Tuscaloosa: University of Alabama Press, 1977), 538–42.

63. Brackenridge, *Views of Louisiana: Together with a Journal of a Voyage up the Missouri River in 1811* (Pittsburgh: Cramer, Spear and Eichbaum), 127. Italics added.

64. We have no sources to inform us about how residents of early Kaskaskia viewed enslaved Africans as opposed to Indians. For an introduction to how early modern Europeans generally viewed Africans and Native Americans, see David Brian Davis, "Constructing Race: A Reflection," 54 (Jan. 1997): 13–17.

65. See Ekberg, *Stealing Indian Women*, 14, 39, 67, 184.

66. Illinois census of 1752, Huntington Library, Loudoun Collection, manuscript 426.

67. In October 1726, Franchomme appeared on a list of persons requesting enslaved Africans from the Indies Company (ANOM, G^1 464).

68. Concerning Law, see James Buchan, *John Law: A Scottish Adventurer of the Eighteenth Century* (London: MacLehose Press, 2018); A. W. Wiston-Glynn, *John Law of Lauriston: Financier and Statesman, Founder of the Bank of France, Originator of the Mississippi Scheme* (New York: Newton Page, 2010).

69. See *Lettres Patentes En Forme D'edit, Portant Établissment D'une Compagnie de Commerce: Sous le Nom de Compagnie d'Occident: Donné à Paris Au Mois D'aoust 1717* (Paris: Imprimerie royale, 1717), 9–10; Glenn R. Conrad, "Administration of the Illinois Country: The

French Debate," *Louisiana History* 36 (Winter 1995), 31–53; Marcel Giraud, *Histoire de la Louisiane française*, vol. 3, *L'époque de John Law* (1717–1720) (Paris: Presses Universitaire de France, 1966).

70. Concerning the Company's activities in Louisiana, see the fascinating volume edited by Erin M. Greenwald, *A Company Man: The Remarkable French Atlantic Voyage of a Clerk for the Company of the Indies* (New Orleans, LA: The Historic New Orleans Collection, 2013).

71. In the Illinois Country, Robert Grotton St. Ange managed Louisiana's transition back to the crown, which was not fully effected until July 1732. ANOM, C^{13B}1:139–46.

72. Ekberg, *French Roots,* 34–35. Brown, *Reconstructing*, 19–20.

73. Fittingly, given its brevity and lack of achievements, little documentation exists concerning Cadillac's trip to the Illinois Country. See Cadillac to minister, May 18, 1715, ANOM, C^{13A} 3: 855–60; Governor Claude de Ramezay to minister, November 3, 1715, ANOM, C^{11A} 35: 101–4.

74. See "Mémoire" of Father Nicolas-Ignace Beaubois, who was in residence at Kaskaskia when this move was effected. ANOM, C^{13A} 12:265. See also Ekberg, *French Roots,* 70; Jacob F. Lee, *Masters of the Middle Waters: Indian Nations and Colonial Ambitions along the Mississippi* (Cambridge: Harvard University Press, 2019), 80–81.

75. Gilles Havard, *Empire et métissages: Indiens et Français dans le Pays d'en Haut, 1660–1715* (Paris: Septentrion, 2003), chapter 10; Jaenen, *Friend and Foe*, 108–9; Ekberg, *Stealing Indian Women*, 15.

76. *Fleur de Lys and Calumet: Being the Pénicaut Narrative of French Adventure in Louisiana*, trans. and ed. Richebourg Gaillard McWilliams (Tuscaloosa: University of Alabama Press, 1953), 136.

77. "Mémoire" in ANOM, F^3 24:235.

78. See White, *Wild Frenchmen and Frenchified Indians*, 110.

79. On this point, see Zitomersky, *French-Americans—Native Americans*, 374.

80. See population figures in Zitomersky, *French Americans—Native Americans*, 317.

81. He consistently spelled his name "Peltier de Franchomme." The name was originally dit Franchomme, but as was true with many French military officers in North America, the dit was transmogrified into a *de*, lending an artificial air of aristocracy to the name.

Chapter 2: Native American Wives and French Husbands

1. Kaskaskia marriage records from this time period have not survived, but the civil marriage contract between Marguerite 8assecam8c8e and Franchomme was drafted by the notary Jacques-Nicolas Buffreau Bellegarde in September 1723, and this meant that their marriage occurred a day or two later. See deposition of the notary Michel Rossard in Records of the Superior Council, Louisiana State Museum Archives, 1725-02-26-01 (hereafter LSM followed by the document number).

2. There is good evidence that Indian-French marriages were commonplace in the early French period at Arkansas Post. See Morris S. Arnold, "The Metis People of Eighteenth- and Nineteenth-Century Arkansas," *Louisiana History* 57 (2016): 261–96.

3. The author, in Susan Sleeper-Smith, *Indian Women and French Men: Rethinking Cultural Encounter in the Western Great Lakes* (Amherst: University of Massachusetts Press, 2001), deals largely with a later time period and mostly about marriages à la façon du pays, informal marriages, although often permanent. This book is about early eighteenth-century marriages, which formalized with the rites of the Roman Catholic Church and which often included civil marriage contracts.

4. Marest to Father Germon (Germain), Nov. 9, 1712, *Jesuit Relations* 66: 231.

5. KPR online at familysearch.org. Cécile Vidal has correctly noted ("Les implantations françaises au pays des Illinois au XVIIIème siècle," Mémoire de D.E.A., Université Paris IV (Sorbonne), 1991, 112) that the incidence of French-Indian marriages declined over time (1720–49), but we are dealing largely with an earlier time frame, when French-Indian marriages made up the bulk of marriages performed at Kaskaskia. See also on this subject, White, *Wild Frenchmen and Frenchified Indians*, 25.

6. On the relationship between Jesuit priests and Illinois Indian women, see Leavelle, *The Catholic Calumet*, especially chapter 7.

7. The seminal article on Marie Rouensa is: Carl J. Ekberg (with Anton J. Pregaldin), "Marie Rouensa-8cate8a and the Foundations of French Illinois," *Illinois Historical Journal* 84 (Autumn, 1991): 146–60; also, Ekberg, *Stealing Indian Women*, 35-40 and passim; Leavelle, *The Catholic Calumet*, 122–23, 154–61, 189–90; White, *Wild Frenchmen and Frenchified Indians*, 53–40, 122–27, and passim; Robert Michael Morrissey, *Empire by Collaboration: Indians, Colonists, and Governments in Colonial Illinois Country* (Philadelphia: University of Pennsylvania Press, 2015), 80–87; Sleeper-Smith, *Indian Women and French Men*, 22–37; also Gilles Havard, *Empire et métissages*, chaps. 10 and 11.

8. KPR, image 6. 8abanakic8e likely means "medicine bundle woman." Email Michael McCafferty, July 23, 2021; see also Masthay, ed. and comp., *Kaskaskia Illinois-to-French Dictionary*, 215.

9. René Jetté, comp., *Dictionnaire généalogique des familles du Québec, des origins à 1730* (Montreal: Les Presses de l'Université de Montréal, 1983), 1067 (henceforth cited as Jetté).

10. The approximate date of Marie-Rose's birth is an inference based on her marriage in 1732.

11. KPR, images 6 and 7. On the importance of the St. Ange family in early Illinois history, see Carl J. Ekberg and Sharon K. Person, *St. Louis Rising: The French Regime of Louis St. Ange de Bellerive* (Urbana: University of Illinois Press, 2015), Pt. I.

12. Death noted in Kaskaskia, KPR, image 18. Natalia Maree Belting pointed out years ago the French Canadian Tessier/Texier family in Kaskaskia was large, complicated, and difficult to sort out. *Kaskaskia Under the French Regime* (Urbana: University of Illinois press, 1948 [reprint edition, Carbondale: Southern Illinois University Press, 2003]), 87.

13. Concerning the creation of the Illinois Provincial Council, see "Règlement pour l'establissement d'un conseil provincial aux Illinois," ANOM, series B 43: 103–4; Brown, *Reconstructing*, 70–74, 86–88; Ekberg, *French Roots*, 34–36; Morrissey, *Empire by Collaboration*, 105–9.

14. KM 21-9-13-1.

15. Concerning the appointment of *tuteurs* and *curateurs* under French customary law, see François Lange, *Nouvelle Pratique Civile, Criminelle, et Beneficiale* (Paris: François le Breton, 1719), 137–41. Claude de Ferrière, *Introduction à la Practique contenant l'Explication des principaux Termes de Practique & de Coûtume* (Lyon: Théodore Labbé, 1701), 528–30; also, Marcel Marion, *Dictionnaire des institutions de la France aux XVIIe et XVIIIe siècles* (Paris: A. & J. Picard, 1969), 543.

16. See Gwendollyn Midlo Hall, *Africans in Colonial Louisiana: The Development of Afro-Creole Culture in the Eighteenth Century* (Baton Rouge: Louisiana State University Press, 1992), chapter 3; also Daniel H. Usner, Jr., "From African Slavery to American Captivity: The Introduction of Black Laborers to Colonial Louisiana," *Louisiana History*, 20 (1979): 25–48; Cécile Vidal, *Caribbean New Orleans: Empire, Race, and the Making of a Slaves Society* (Chapel Hill: University of North Carolina Press, 2019), chapter 1.

17. KM 21-9-13-1.

18. In 1725, Lalande petitioned the Provincial Council to have friends and family members elect a new tuteur for the three Tessier children so that he could occupy himself with his own children by Catherine (KM 25-9-3-1).

19. Marriage contract in KM 21-12-11-1.

20. See copy of baptismal record in KM 23-10—1.

21. This according to Illinois Indian language specialists, Carl Masthay and Michael McCafferty. Email correspondences, March 3–4, 2015.

22. Jetté, 305.

23. KPR, image 21. This burial record states that Charles had been married three times.

24. House measurement given in KM 24-7-26-1.

25. Ibid. These *arbitres* were Guillaume Pottier, Jacques (?) Pottier, Léonard Billeron dit Lafatigue, Michel Philippe, J. Dandanau, and Jacques Lalande. An inventory of the Danis estate was done the day before (KM 24-7-25-1), but this document has gone missing.

26. See Marylynn Salmon, *Women and Propety Law in Early America* (Chapel Hill: University of North Carolina Press, 1986), 141–42.

27. KM 24-7-26-1.

28. Paul Alliot, "Historical and Political Reflections on Louisiana," in James A. Robertson (ed.), *Louisiana Under the Rule of Spain, France, and the United States, 1785–1807*, 2 vols. (Cleveland, OH: The Arthur H. Clark company, 1911), 1:133.

29. The French expression "pièce d'Inde" derived from the Spanish "pieza de India," which, referring to African slaves, meant "healthy and in the prime of life." See Philip Curtin, *The Atlantic Slave Trade* (Madison: University of Wisconsin Press, 1969), 22.

30. Burial record by Father Beaubois, KPR, image 20.

31. *Coutume*, Article CCXXIX.

32. KM 24-9-10-1.

33. François Lange, *Nouvelle Pratique* (Paris: François le Breton, 1719), 138.

34. KM 24-9-10-2. Concerning the composition of marital communautés, see Ferrière 2: Titre X, "De communauté des biens," 1–115.

35. This posts-in-the-ground type of construction has been thoroughly analyzed in Melburn D. Thurman, *Building a House in 18th Century Ste. Genevieve* (Ste. Genevieve, MO: Pendragon's Press, 1984).

36. See Ekberg (with Anton J. Pregaldin), "Marie Rouensa-8cate8a," 146–60.

37. KPR, image no. 23.

38. Documents pertaining to Lalande's selection as tuteur have not survived, but there would have been a formal process involving friends and relatives, in accordance with the *Coutume*.

39. KM 25-10-8-1; KM 25-10-8-2.

40. KM 24-9-13-1 and KM 24-9-13-2 provide particulars on everything included in the lease.

41. Manuscript census in ANOM, G^1 464. The census was compiled by Commandant Robert Grotton de St. Ange.

42. One of these children is listed as a "bâtard," but this child may have been an orphan, for the 1732 census sometimes, curiously, does not distinguish between bastards and orphans.

43. See Carl J. Ekberg, *French Roots*, chapter 6.

44. See KM 47-1-11-1 for the inventory of her communauté with Louis Turpain. Louis married for a third time, Hélène Hébert, daughter of Ignace and Hélène Danis, in March 1751 (marriage contract in KM 51-3-20-3), but he died before the year was out, at age fifty-seven years (KM 51-11-18-1).

45. Census in Huntington Library, Loudoun Collection, manuscript 426.

46. Concerning infant mortality in colonial Illinois, see Carl J. Ekberg, *Colonial Ste. Genevieve: An Adventure on the Mississippi Frontier* (Gerald, MO: Patrice Press, 1985), 245, 271.

47. Rendition of Indian name provided by Michael McCafferty in an email (July 19, 2021).

48. Baptismal records in KPR, images 11 and 14; and "Extrait des registres de baptêmes de la paroisse de ND. de Cas, depuis le mois de may 1723 jusqu'en mois de may 1724." ANOM, $G464^{12}$ 5 ff.

49. KM 28-11-11-1.

50. Under French customary law (*Coutume de Paris*), family property was usually governed by marriage contracts rather than wills—see Hans W. Baade, "Marriage Contracts in French and Spanish Louisiana: A Study in 'Notarial' Jurisprudence," *Tulane Law Review* 53 (December 1978): 1–92—which were necessary only in special circumstances, such as cases of illegitimate births. More on this below, chapter 7.

51. "Dispositif de l'arrest du Conseil Supérieur de la Louisiane," December 8, 1728. ANOM, F^3 242:146–47. De Launay was Guillaume Pottier's best friend, who, likely on a trading trip, must have brought Pottier's suit forward to the Superior Council in New Orleans.

52. *Coutume*, Art. CCCXVIII.

53. These are the words of *Commissaire-ordonnateur* Jacques de La Chaise in a letter to the Compagnie (February 15, 1729, ANOM, F³ 242:142–43).

54. KM 28-11-11-1.

55. ANOM, F³ 242: 147.

56. More on the issue of Indian women's inheritance rights below, in chapter 9.

57. Historians agree on the distinctly subordinate position of women in traditional Illinois Indian marriages. See, most recently, Tracy Neal Leavelle, *The Catholic Calumet*, 165–66; Linda Carol Jones, *The Shattered Cross,* 67–69, 183–86; Robert Michael Morrissey, "The Power of the Ecotone: Bison, Slavery and the Rise and Fall of the Grand Village of the Kaskaskia," *Journal of American History* (December 2015): 267–91.

58. Havard, *Histoire des coureurs de bois*, 696–714.

Chapter 3: Jacques Bourdon in Life and in Death

1. See Leslie Choquette, *Frenchmen into Peasants: Modernity and Tradition in the Peopling of French Canada* (Cambridge: Harvard University Press, 1997), 27–54.

2. It is frustratingly unclear just what qualified a person to serve as a notaire in the Illinois Country, as some men who served as notaires in the region were only marginally literate.

3. A Bourdon family website (www.malonedirectory. tripod.com/jacques_bourdon.htm) is now available. See also Jetté, 150; Cyprien Tanguay, *Dictionnaire généalogique des familles canadiennes depuis la fondation de la colonie jusqu'à nos jours*, 7 vols. (Montreal: Senécal, 1871–90), 2:416; *DCB, s.v.* "Jacques Bourdon."

4. Finiels, *An Account of Upper Louisiana*, ed. Carl J. Ekberg and William E. Foley and trans. Carl J. Ekberg (Columbia: University of Missouri Press, 1989), 113.

5. It is worth noting, though, that even after having settled down in Kaskaskia Bourdon remained engaged in trading activities, and that in 1708 he was down on the Gulf Coast. See Jay Higginbotham, *Old Mobile: Fort Louis de la Louisiane, 1702–11* (Tuscaloosa: University of Alabama Press, 1977), 396.

6. KPR, image 6.

7. See Carl J. Ekberg, *Stealing Indian Women: Native Slavery in the Illinois* Country (Urbana: University of Illinois Press, 2007), 30–37. The Bourdon, whom Claude de Ramezay, acting governor of Canada, described in 1714 as incorrigibly lawless, was clearly another member of the large and extended Bourdon family, very likely Jacques's younger brother Pierre. See Ramezay to the Minister, September 18, 1714, in ANOM, C¹¹ᴬ vol. 34, fol. 356; *Wisconsin Historical Collections*, 16:302–3; Jetté, *Dictionnaire*, 150. Suzanne Sommerville has identified the outlaw Bourdon of Ramezay's letter as Pierre, not Jacques in *Michigan's Habitant Heritage* 40 (January 2019), 23–24.

8. Natalia Maree Belting, in her *Kaskaskia Under the French Regime*, Reprint edition (Carbondale: Southern Illinois University Press, 2003), 15, especially n. 27, was the first scholar to

attempt to sort out Bourdon's complicated life. Belting made numerous mistakes when discussing Bourdon, but she deserves much credit for being the first scholar to understand and convey Bourdon's importance to the early history of the Illinois Country.

9. See Masthay, ed., *Kaskaskia-Illinois-to-French Dictionary*, 102.

10. Pierre was baptized April 17, 1701. KPR, image 6, Bourdon appears in 1717 as a godfather with his second wife Marguerite 8assecam8c8e, meaning that Domitile Ch8ping8eta was deceased. Ibid., image 7.

11. KPR, image 7 for both baptismal records.

12. In Illinois Country manuscripts, Marguerite's Indian name appears in a variety of forms. The correct form, based on reliable Kaskaskia Manuscripts and Kaskaskia parish records is 8assecam8c8e. To avoid further confusion, it must be noted that the Indian name sometimes attributed to Marguerite—Ouaquamo Quoana—is incorrect. See White, *Wild Frenchmen and Frenchified Indians*, 43, 45–46, 48, 63, 64, 133–34.

Michael McCafferty and Carl Masthay have provided much help with Indian names, which are exceedingly difficult to sort out. No written records, either sacramental or civil, have survived for either of Bourdon's two marriages to Indian women.

13. KM 23-6-25-1.

14. The full name of the parish was Notre Dame de l'Immaculate Conception de Kaskaskia, which was usually shortened to l'Immaculate Conception de Kaskaskia.

15. Article CCLXXXIX. Nicolas-Michael Chassin, an original member of the Illinois Provincial Council, noted that Jesuits at Kaskaskia had served as stand-in notaires. Chassin to unknown, July 1, 1722, ANOM, C^{13A} 6:299.

16. *Coutume*, Art. CCC.

17. Beaubois's use of the plural, "Cascakias," referred to the Kaskaskia Indians.

18. "Saguingora" is the form that Father Nicolas-Ignace used in Bourdon's will of 1723, and, unless in a direct quote where it appears differently, we will adhere to Beaubois's form. Master genealogist Gail F. Moreau has traced the name in Canadian records back to 1669 and can find no evidence that the name was Native American; the origin of the name remains obscure. Email communication, December 9, 2020.

19. KPR, image 6.

20. Jetté, 475.

21. Curiously, Natalia Maree Belting did not take notice of this family in her ground-breaking book, *Kaskaskia Under the French Regime*, reprint edition (Carbondale: Southern Illinois University Press, 2003).

22. KPR, image 6.

23. Sophie White has done a penetrating analysis of Saguingora as a case study concerning the position and status of Métis persons in Illinois Country society. White, *Wild Frenchmen and Frenchified Indians*, chapter 5.

24. KPR, image 5. See also the excellent and informative article concerning Antoine Baillargeon's family, Gail. F. Moreau, *Michigan's Habitant Heritage*, 35, October 2014, 181–87.

Jetté, 40–41, includes some contradictory and confusing information on the Baillargeon-Ch8ping8eta couple, including the suggestion (with no documenttion) that they were married at Kaskaskia in 1697. Kaskaskia was settled only beginning in 1703.

25. KM 23-7-1-1.

26. KPR, image 20.

27. *Coutume*, Article CCXLI; Ferrière, *Nouveau Commentaire sur La Coutume de la Prévoté et Vicomté de Paris* (Paris: Libraires Associés, 1770) 2:94–97.

28. KM 23-7-1-1. Marie Rouensa, who died in Kaskaskia two years after Bourdon, was a close second in the overall amount of wealth. Concerning Rouensa and Bourdon, see Ekberg, "Marie Rouensa-8cate8a," 155–60; Ekberg, *Stealing Indian Women*, 35–41.

29. Inventory in KM 23-7-1-1.

30. *Histoire de l'Amérique française* (Paris: Editions Flammarion, 2003), 253.

31. See Edward B. Jelks, Carl J. Ekberg, and Terrance J. Martin, *Excavations at the Lauren's Site*, Studies in Illinois Archaeology, no. 5 (Springfield: Illinois Preservation Agency, 1989), 78, 104.

32. This usage was ubiquitous during the 1720s. See, for examples, KM 23-7-1-1; KM 23-9-10-1; KM 23-9-19-1; KM 24-5-20-2; KM 24-9-2-2; KM 25-2-12-1; KM 25-3-15-1; KM 28-3-6-1.

33. See Jay Higginbotham, *Old Mobile: Fort Louis de la Louisiane, 1702–11* (Tuscaloosa: University of Alabama Press, 1977), 220.

34. KM 23-7-12-1.

35. Born March 4, baptized March 5, 1724, ANC G[1] 412:5 ff. godfather was Pierre Collet, godmother Dorothée Mechiper8taa, after whom the child was named.

36. See Michael McCafferty, "About Jean-Antoine Robert Le Boullenger," at http://ilaatawa akani.org/about_document.php?name=LeBoullenger. On the same website, David J. Costa discusses the French-to-Illinois dictionary compiled by Le Boullenger.

37. Bourdon estate inventory, KM 23-7-1-1.

38. Franchomme's first documented appearance in Kaskaskia occurred on July 1, 1723 (KM 23-7-1-1), although he had surely been present in town for some months before that date.

39. Baptismal record now deposited in the Archives Départementales des Ardennes in Charleville-Mézières.

40. This description is in Franchomme's final will and testament (KM 28-3-6-1). More about this important document in chapter 8.

41. The *Duc de Noailles* made several trips across the Atlantic to Louisiana during the 1720s. Converted into a slaver, it arrived in New Orleans in April 1728 with 262 African slaves, many of whom were seriously ill with scurvy and dysentery. Seventy of the original cargo had perished on the trans-Atlantic voyage. Perier and La Chaise to the Company of the Indies, April 9, 1728, ANOM, C[13A] 11:27. See also Gwendolyn Midlo Hall, *Africans in Colonial Louisiana: The Development of Afro-Creole Culture in the Eighteenth Century* (Baton Rouge, LA: Louisiana State University Press, 1992), 77–80.

42. Beauchamp's career in French Louisiana is well documented in ANOM, C[13A] series. See index in Marie-Antoinette Menier, Étienne Taillemite, and Gilberte de Forges, comps. and

eds., 2 vols., *Inventaire des Archives Coloniales: Correspondance à l'arrivée en provenance de la Louisiane* (Paris: Archives Nationales, 1983) 2:723.

43. Letter from Jean Jadard dit Beauchamp to his brother Pierre Jadard, March 15, 1720, courtesy of Raphaël Lacaille of Montmeillant.

44. Ekberg, *French Roots*, chapter 6.

45. Franchomme may have come up the Mississippi River with the famous explorer, Étienne Véniard de Bourgmont, in the spring of 1723. Bourgmont mentioned Franchomme in a letter written from Fort d'Orléans on the Missouri on January 2, 1724 (ANOM, C¹³ᴬ 8, 213).

46. Franchomme first appears in local Kaskaskia records in early July 1723 (KM 23-7-1-1).

47. See White, *Wild Frenchmen and Frenchified Indians*, 121–22.

48. Natalia Maree Belting was the first scholar to take notice of this fact about social life in early Kaskaskia. *Kaskaskia Under the French Regime* (Urbana, IL: University of Illinois press, 1948 [reprint edition, Carbondale: Southern Illinois University Press, 2003]), 74.

49. D'Artaguiette "Journal," in Newton D. Mereness, ed., *Travels in the American* Colonies (New York: Macmillan, 1926), 68. D'Artaguiette's comments notwithstanding, it must be noted that Kaskaskia's parish church at this time was still a vertical-log structure.

50. These facts were reported when Franchomme was at New Orleans in February 1725, arranging to have Michel Rossard, notaire and clerk to the Superior Council, draft what amounted to a duplicate marriage contract. See LSM, 1725-02-15-01 and 1725-02-26-01. The Provincial Council in Illinois did not officially recognize Bellegarde as notaire until April 1724, but the validity of his notarial work was never challenged. See his official appointment by Boisbriant and des Ursins in KM 24-4-11-3.

Chapter 4: Marguerite 8assecam8c8e is Attacked

1. Either Commandant Boisbriant, or town commandant Jean-Baptiste Girardot, would have made this appointment. Appointment of militia officers in the Illinois Country remains an important but elusive subject.

2. See Belting, *Kaskaskia Under the French Regime*, 15.

3. See Jetté, 410.

4. Baptism at age 3, June 3, 1713, KPR, image 7. January 11, 1724, Mariane Fafart married Nicolas François Marie Quadrin ANC G¹ 412:5 ff. Civil marriage contract of Fafard and Cadrin, KM 24-1-8-1.

5. KM 23-6-2-1. The Council's final judgment was handed down in September 1723.

6. KM 23-9-11-1.

7. François Lange, *La Nouvelle Practique Civile, Criminelle et Bénéficiale* (Paris: François le Breton, 1719), 139; Ferrière, *Commentaire sur la Coutume*, 2:78. Indeed, although married children under the age of twenty-five were free to sell their personal possessions (*biens propres*), they could not sell or mortgage family real estate (*immeubles*) without the consent of a guardian

(tuteur or curateur). See *Coutume*, Article CCXXXIX, and, especially, Ferrière, *Commentaire sur la Coutume* 2:77.

8. Pierre's child was baptised "Dorothée," namesake of his revered mother, on March 4, 1724. "Extrait des registres de baptêmes de la paroisse de ND. de Cas, depuis le mois de may 1723 jusqu'en mois de may 1724." ANOM, G464[12] 5 ff.

9. KM 23-9-11-1.

10. Majority was not achieved under the *Coutume* until age twenty-five, but as children matured, arrived at puberty, and married before that age, they were considered "emancipated," which gave them certain control (but not absolute) over their personal property, but not their real estate. See above, chapter 2.

11. Historical studies of the *Coutume* have generally focused on issues involving estate inventories rather than on cases where the marital communauté continued. See François Olivier-Martin, *Histoire de la Coutume de la Prévôté et Vicomté de Paris* (Paris: Éditions Ernest Leroux, 1926), 2:263–64.

12. See *Coutume*, Art. XIII; and Ferrière, *Nouveau Commentaire*, 1:49–50.

13. KM 23-9-11-1.

14. KM 23-9-11-1.

Chapter 5: Franchomme Prevails

1. According to final will and testament (KM 28-3-6-1).

2. See, for example, a marriage contract drafted in January 1723. KM 23-1-16-1.

3. See Louis Le Grand, *Coutume du Bailliage de Troyes* (Paris: Montalant, 1737).

4. *Coutume*, Article CCXX.

5. Ferrière, *Commentaire sur la Coutume*, 2:3–4.

6. Ignace Broutin's map of 1734, "Carte d'une partie des Illinois," shows a well-established road between Kaskaskia and Fort de Chartres (Division of Cartes et Plans, Archives du Ministre de la Marine, Château de Vincennes).

7. KM 23-9-11-1.

8. This is in KM 23-9-11-1, although the date on Pierre's final appeal seems to be September 25, 1723.

9. See Hans W. Baade, "Marriage Contracts in French and Spanish Louisiana: A Study in 'Notarial' Jurisprudence," *Tulane Law Review* 53 (December, 1978): 9–10.

10. Concerning the qualifications necessary to be a notaire, see Claude de Ferrière, *La science parfaite des notaires ou le moyen de faire un parfait notaire* (Paris: Charles Osmont, 1715), especially chapter 3; Marcel Marion, *Dictionnaire des institutions de la France aux XVIIᵉ et XVIIIᵉ siècles* (Paris: A. & J. Picard, 1969), 400; also Morris S. Arnold, *Unequal Laws unto a Savage Race: European Legal Traditions in Arkansas, 1686–1836* (Fayetteville: University of Arkansas Press, 1985), 19–21.

11. If Protestants were excluded from notarial positions, it went without saying that Jews were as well. And, of course, Jews were officially banned in French Louisiana, as affirmed in Article I of the Louisiana Black Code of 1724. "Édit concernant les Nègres à la Louisiane," *Publications of the Louisiana Historical Society* 4 (1908), 76.

12. See Ferrière, *La science parfaite des notaires*, 1:9–10.

13. Chassin to unknown, July 1, 1722, ANOM, C¹³ᴬ 6:299–300.

14. KM 23-10-22-2.

15. For an interesting discussion of how French identity could be constructed in the eighteenth century, see Saliha Belmessous, "Être française en Nouvelle-France: Identité française et identité coloniale aux dix-septième et dix-huitième siècles," *French Historical Studies* 27 (Summer 2004): 507–40.

16. He died in August 1724. Jetté, 150.

17. Ibid.

18. Under certain conditions, with approval from a *curateur*, married minors could alienate property. See discussion in Lange, *Nouvelle Pratique*, 140, 476; and Ferrière, *Nouveau Commentaire*, 2:76–77.

19. KM 23-10-22-2.

20. KM 23-10-22-2. Included within this rubric is Noyon's undated claim and the Council's decree (dated October 29, 1723) addressing Noyon's issues.

21. KM 23-10-22-1, Provincial Council's contemporary copy in KM 23-10-22-2. Because the claims of both Noyon and Franchomme were filed the same day (October 22, 1723), it is not possible to determine who was reacting to whom.

22. KM 23-10-26-2.

23. KM 23-11-6-1. Inventory of effects conveyed to Noyon with no values attached to the respective items.

24. Noyon's undated request is in KM 23-10-22-2.

Chapter 6: Textures of Life

1. Two reference books are indispensable for understanding the domestic material environment of French Canadians in the eighteenth century: Michel Lessard and Huguette Marquis, *Encyclopé des Antiquités du Québec* (Montréal: Éditions de l'Homme, 1971); Nicole Genêt, Luce Vermette, and Louise Décarie-Audet, *Les Objects Familiers de nos Ancêtres* (Montréal: Éditions de l'Homme, 1974).

2. Concerning Early Modern French living spaces, see Jean-Louis Flandrin, *Familles: parenté, maison, sexualité dans l'ancienne société* (Paris: Hachette, 1976), 94–95; Robert Mandrou, *Introduction à la France moderne: Essai de psychologie historique, 1500–1640* (Paris: Albin Michel, 1961), 39–41.

3. The most complete description of the house is in the preliminary inventory of the Bourdon estate done in July 1723 (KM 23-7-1-1); that done in October (KM 23-10-26-2) is less detailed.

A comprehensive study of Illinois Country architecture cries out to be done. See, however, Charles E. Peterson, *Colonial St. Louis: Building a Creole Capital* (St. Louis, MO: Missouri Historical Society, 1949); Peterson, "Early Ste. Genevieve and Its Architecture," *Missouri Historical Review* 35 (1941): 207–32; Melburn D. Thurman, *Building a House*; also Ekberg and Person, *St. Louis Rising*, chapter 6; Ekberg, *Colonial Ste. Genevieve*, 285–96.

4. See Ekberg, *Colonial Ste. Genevieve*, 301. The Ménard House was later altered when the rear portions of the surrounding *galerie* were enclosed and incorporated into the main house.

5. In 1725, Joseph Catherine, carpenter, contracted with the Compagnie des Indes to build a single, front gallery on the Company's warehouse at Fort de Chartres (KM 25-X-X 1). This is an unusual case.

6. Carl J. Ekberg, *Louis Bolduc: His Family and His House* (Tucson, AZ: The Patrice Press, 2002), 22–24.

7. KM 21-9-13-1; KM 25-8-16-1.

8. KM 23-10-26-2. Concerning vertical-log construction, see Melburn D. Thurman, *Building a House*.

9. At the seminarian mission complex in Cahokia, there were separate quarters for African and Indian slaves. See Ekberg, *Stealing Indian Women*, 35.

10. Concerning "patates anglaises" in the Illinois Country, see Pierre-Charles Delassus de Luzières to Governor Carondelet, March 6, 1797, Archivo General de Indies (Seville), Papeles de Cuba, 35.

11. Concerning bake ovens in French North America, see Lise Boily and Jean-François Blanchette, *Les fours à pain au Québec* (Ottawa: Musée national de l'homme, 1976); Jay Dearborn Edwards and Nicolas Kariouk Pecquet du Bellay de Verton, comp., *A Creole Lexicon: Architecture, Landscape, People* (Baton Rouge: Louisiana State University Press, 2004), 103. The best study of bake ovens in the Illinois Country is: Robert Mueller, "Baking Their Daily Bread Ovens and Bread Making in Colonial Ste. Genevieve," unpublished ms.

12. William Bennett Munro, *The Seignorial System in Canada: A Study in French Colonial Policy* (Cambridge, MA: Harvard University Press, 1907), 121.

13. On Illinois Country domestic material culture, see Robert F. Mazrim, *At Home in the Illinois Country: French Colonial Domestic Site Archaeology in the Midwest 1730–1800*, Studies in Archaeology No. 9 (Urbana: Illinois State Archaeological Survey, 2011).

14. KM 23-7-1-1.

15. On Canadian butter molds, see Michel Lessard and Huguette Marquis, *Encyclopédie des Antiquités du Québec* (Montreal: Les Éditions de l'Homme, 1971), 250–51.

16. Masthay, *Kaskaskia Illinois-to-French Dictionary*, 529.

17. The catalog of the Bibliothèque Nationale in Paris contains four editions of Belloste's book: 1696, 1705, 1715, and 1734. The book appears in the preliminary inventory of Bourdon's estate done on July 1, 1723, just two days after his death (KM 23-7-7-1).

18. KM 22-9-23-1.

19. See Carl J. Ekberg, *A French Aristocrat in the American West: The Shattered Dreams of Delassus de Luzières* (Columbia: University of Missouri Press, 2010), source document no. 16.

20. Masthay, ed., *Kaskaskia-Illinois-to-French Dictionary*, 250.

21. Ibid. 90.

22. This according to Franchomme's will (KM 28-3-6-1). This oddly named hôtel must have been associated somehow with Cardinal Jules Mazarin, who served as chief minister to the young Louis XIV. 1643–61.

23. KM 23-10-26-1 and KM 23-10-26-1.

24. Census in ANOM, G^1, 464.

25. KM 23-11-4-1.

26. KM 23-11-8-3. Total debts amounted to less than 200 livres.

27. KM 23-11-8-4.

28. KM 23-11-8-4.

29. See John Francis McDermott, *A Glossary of Mississippi Valley French, 1673–1850*, Washington University Studies—New Series. No. 12 (St. Louis, 1941), 120.

30. We are indebted to three exceptional linguists—Michael McCafferty, David Costa, and Carl Masthay—for sorting out this curious and important document.

31. KM 23-11-8-4.

32. Carl J. Ekberg, "Terrisse de Ternan: Epistoler and Soldier," *Louisiana History* 23 (Fall 1982), 400–408.

33. KM 23-1-21-1.

34. *DCB*, s.v. "Charles-Henri-Jospeh de Tonty de Liette."

35. KM 23-11-8-4.

36. After the Foxes were crushed on the Illinois prairie in 1730, the Chicago portage was again sometimes used for communication between the Illinois Country and Canada, especially via Michilimackinac. See, for example, KM 43-8-9-1.

37. See Jetté, 150.

38. Ibid.

39. KM 25-1-1-1.

40. Jacques Mathieu, *Nouvelle-France*: *Les français en Amérique du Nord XVIᵉ-XVIIIᵉ siècle* (Quebec: Presses de l'Université Laval, 1981), 147.

41. KM 25-2-1-1. Marie-Claire, born and raised in Paris, led an extraordinary life in the Illinois County. See Carl J. Ekberg, "Marie-Claire Catoire: A Parisian Woman in Colonial Ste. Genevieve," *Missouri Historical Review*, 114 (January 2020): 105–20.

42. KM 25-1-24-1.

43. Jay Dearborn Edwards and Nicolas Kariouk Pecquet du Bellay de Verton, comp., *A Creole Lexicon: Architecture, Landscape, People* (Baton Rouge: Louisiana State University Press, 2004), 153; Ekberg, *Colonial Ste. Genevieve*, 216. "Piece d'Inde" was usually reserved for African male slaves, but in this instance both males and females are thus designated.

44. See inventory, KM 23-7-1-1.

45. Census in ANOM, G^1 464.

46. However, as late as 1728, Franchomme still owed Pierre Bourdon 200 livres, see KM 28-3-6-1.

47. KM 24-5-20-1.

48. KPR, image 23.

49. KPR, images 25 and 26.

Chapter 7: The Marriage Contract

1. The Superior Council reported the arrival in New Orleans of Boisbriant and Étienne de Bourgmont in the same dispatch (Superior Council to the Indies Company, Jan. 20, 1725, ANOM, C^{13A} 9:13–20).

2. The Chickasaws, usually allied with the British, were inveterate enemies of the French. Concerning the threat that Chickasaws posed to French sojourners on the Mississippi. See D'Artaguiette "Journal," in Newton D. Mereness, ed.), *Travels in the American* Colonies (New York: Macmillan, 1926), 31, 33, 62–63. See also the March 1722 death records of two Kaskaskia men "killed on the Mississippi by Chickasaws," KPR, image 18.

3. LSM 1725-2-15-1

4. Ibid. Rossard penned in the Superior Council's orders to Bellegarde at the end of Franchomme's petition.

5. LSM 1725-2-16-2.

6. Concerning communautés, see Ferrière 2: Titre X, "De communauté des biens," 1–115.

7. See Claude de Ferrière, *Introduction à la Pratique, contenant l'Explication des principaux Termes de Pratique & de Coûtume* (Lyon: Guilliment et Labré, 1701), 385.

8. Although seldom exercised, a widow's right of renunciation was clearly explained in Article CCXXXVII of the *Coutume*.

9. Concerning *entre-vifs* donations see Ferrière 2:188–95, "Titre des Donations and Article CCLXXII." See also François Olivier-Martin, *Histoire de la Coutume de la Prévôté et Vicomté de Paris* (Paris: Éditions Ernest Leroux, 1926), 2:483–91.

10. LSM 1725-2-16-3

11. LSM 1725-2-16-4.

12. LSM 1725-02-26-01.

13. As seen above, Commandant Boisbriant had effected the separation of the Kaskaskia Indian mission from the French village of Kaskaskia.

14. See Gilles Havard, *Empire et métissages: Indiens et Français dans le Pays d'en Haut, 1660–1715* (Paris: Septentrion, 2003), 633–34.

15. Concerning du Tisné as commandant, see David MacDonald, *Lives of Fort de Chartres: Commandants, Soldiers, and Civilians, 1720–1770* (Carbondale: Southern Illinois University University Press, 2016), 39–47, 200; Brown, *Reconstructing*, 89–93.

16. KM 25-3-15-1.

17. The 1726 Illinois census lists four African slaves and one Native American in the Franchomme household (Part II).

18. Richard N. Ellis and Charlie R. Steen, "An Indian Delegation in France, 1725," *Journal of the Illinois State Historical Society*, 67, no. 4 (September 1974), 385–405; White, *Wild Frenchmen and Frenchified Indians*, 28, 110.

19. KM 25-6-28-1.

20. Poudret was active in the Mississippi and Missouri River valleys during the 1720s, trading in, among other things, Native American slaves. See Ekberg, *Stealing Indian Women*, 18–22. Census, no. 108.

21. Sophie White speculates that Saguingora accompanied Franchomme on his 1725 trip to New Orleans (White, *Wild Frenchmen and Frenchified Indians*, 183). This is possible but unlikely, for this was a fast, dedicated trip for Franchomme—in and out of New Orleans for the specific purpose of getting his marriage contract validated.

22. This is known because on September 28, the notary from Fort de Chartres, Perillau, used the Franchomme-Marguerite residence as a temporary office in Kaskaskia. KM 25-9-28-3.

23. After Étienne died, the *Métisse* Élisabeth married well a second time, taking for her husband in 1735 Alexandre De Celle Duclos, a marine officer at the fort. KM 35-11-21-1 marriage contract of the widow of Estienne Hébert and DuClos. Census, no. 77.

Chapter 8: The Fox Scourge

1. Document dated April 11, 1694, ANOM, C^{13A} 1:27.

2. The most thorough study of the Fox-French wars is R. David Edmunds and Joseph L. Peyser, *The Fox Wars: The Mesquakie Challenge to New France* (Norman: University of Oklahoma Press, 1993). This book, as the title suggests, deals most thoroughly with the Canadian side of the French involvement and scants the involvement of the Illinois Country villages. A recent summary of this enmity between the Foxes and the French is found in Morrissey, *Empire by Collaboration*, chap. 5. See also Joseph L. Peyser, "The Fate of the Fox Survivors: A Dark Chapter in the History of the French in the Upper Country," *Wisconsin Magazine of History* 73 (Winter 1989–90), 83–85; Brett Rushforth, "Slavery, the Fox Wars, and the Limits of Alliance," *William and Mary Quarterly* 63 (2006), 53–80.

3. Gaspard Chausasegros de Léry quoted in 1712, Collections of the State Historical Society of Wisconsin, vol. 16, *The French Regime in Wisconsin* I, 1634–1727, ed. Reuben G. Thwaites (Madison: State Historical Society of Wisconsin, 1902), 293.

4. See Robert Michael Morrissey, "The Power of the Ecotone: Bison, Slavery and the Rise and Fall of the Grand Village of the Kaskaskia," *Journal of American History* (December 2015), 678–79.

5. Bourgmont's comments are in a memoir that he may have written at Fort de Chartres toward the end of 1724 (ANOM C^{13A} 8:447–50). Concerning Bourgmont as an Indian diplomat, see Frank Norall, *Bourgmont: Explorer of the Missouri, 1698–1725* (Lincoln: University of Nebraska Press, 1988); Carl J. Ekberg and Sharon K. Person, *St. Louis Rising: The French Regime of Louis St. Ange de Bellerive* (Urbana: University of Illinois Press, 2005), chap. 1.

6. Edmunds and Peyser, *Fox Wars*, 23–26.

7. D'Artaguiette "Journal," in Newton D. Mereness (ed.), *Travels in the American Colonies* (New York: Macmillan, 1926), 32.

8. See ANOM, C13A, vols. 6–12.

9. Chassin to unknown, July 1, 1722, ANOM, C^{13A} 6:298.

10. Pierre-François-Xavier de Charlevoix, *Journal d'un voyage fait par ordre du roi dans l'Amérique Septentrionale* (Paris: Rollin fils, 1744), 6:122.

11. D'Artaguiette "Journal," in Newton D. Mereness (ed.), *Travels in the American* Colonies (New York: Macmillan, 1926), 72.

12. *Proceedings of The American Philosophical Society*, Vol. 82, No. 2, 1940. Reprint edition by Literary Licensing, 2013.

13. Jaenen, *Friend and Foe*, 137–39.

14. Gilles Havard, *Empire et métissages: Indiens et Français dans le Pays d'en Haut, 1660–1715* (Paris: Septentrion, 2003), 158.

15. Adam Stueck, "A Place Under Heaven: Amerindian Torture and Cultural Violence in Colonial New France, 1609–1729," PhD dissertation, Marquette University, 2012, 4.

16. See Richard White's description of Simon Kenton's experiences with the Shawnees (*Middle Ground*, 392–94).

17. See description in Ekberg and Person, *St. Louis Rising*, 29–30.

18. Concerning the symbolic significance of capital punishment in Old Regime France, see Michel Foucault, *Discipline and Punish: The Birth of The Prison,* trans. Alan Sheridan, 2nd ed. (New York: Vintage Books, 1995), chap. 1. Damiens' drawing-and-quartering provoked a backlash, and this method of execution was never again employed in France.

19. KPR, image 20.

20. KPR, image 21.

21. Description of Melique's background provided in KM 25-3-2-1.

22. Census, no. 64 (Part II) lists one enslaved Native American in Melique's household.

23. KM 26-11-13-1 and 2; KM 26-11-24-1.

24. Perier to minister, May 2, 1727, ANOM, C^{13A}10:226–27.

25. See Carl A. Brasseaux, *France's Forgotten Legion: Service Records of French Military and Administrative Personnel Stationed in the Mississippi Valley and Gulf Coast Region, 1699–1769.* Baton Rouge: Louisiana State University Press, 2000, CD-Rom, s.v. "Desliettes." Also, David J, MacDonald, *Lives of Fort de Chartres: Commandants, Soldiers, and Civilians in French Illinois, 1720–70* (Carbondale: Southern Illinois University Press, 2016), 49–53.

26. Beauharnois to Deliette, Aug. 20, 1727 in *Wisconsin Historical Collections*, 3: 163.

27. Extract of Mercier's letter, Jan. 31, 1727, ANOM, C^{11A} 1728, fol, 308.

28. Perier and La Chaise to minister, Nov. 1, 1728, ANOM, C^{13A} 11:111. Perier's independent report (if he ever wrote one) has not survived.

29. KPR, image 26. Franchomme also witnessed the signing of the couple's marriage contract the same day (KM 28-6-7-2).

30. See *DCB*, s.v. "Le Marchand de Lignery."

31. See R. David Edmunds and Joseph L. Peyser, *The Fox Wars: The Mesquakie Challenge to New France* (Norman: University of Oklahoma Press, 1993), 114–15, regarding Lignery's frustration with DesLiette and the Illinois detachment. Also, MacDonald, *Lives of Fort de Chartres*, 52–53.

32. ANOM, C^{11A} 1728, fol. 307.

33. Edmunds and Peyser, *Fox Wars*, chap. 6, "Genocide." *DCB*, s.v. "Charles de la Boische de Beauharnois.".

34. Edmunds and Peyser, *Fox Wars*, chap. 6, "Genocide."

35. Brett Rushforth, *Bonds of Alliance: Indigenous and Atlantic Slaveries in New France* (Chapel Hill: Omohundro Institute of Early American History and Culture and the University of North Carolina Press, 2012), 207.

36. Rushforth, *Bonds of Alliance*, 217. Suzanne Boivin Sommerville ("'Detroit never saw such a collection of people.' The Start of the 'Fox Wars' 300 Years Ago," *Michigan's Habitant Heritage*, 33 [April 2012], 1–5) provides a fresh and nuanced account of the Fox-French conflict at Detroit in 1712.

37. See Beauharnois to naval minister Jean-Frédéric Phélypeaux de Maurepas (October 4, 1733, ANOM, C^{11A} 59:111–12), in which Beauharnois complains about many Indian slaves being freed without notarial due process.

38. In days of yesteryear, historians generally sought to avoid making moral judgments. Ethnohistorians have led the way in diminishing this avoidance. See "Berhard W. Sheehan, "Indian-White Relations in Early America: A Review Essay," *William and Mary Quarterly* 26 (April 1969): 267–86; also James Axtell, "A Moral History of Indian-White Relations Revisited," *The History Teacher* 16 (February 1983): 169–190; Axtell, "Ethnohistory: An Historian's Viewpoint," *Ethnohistory* 26 (Winter, 1979): 1–13.

39. See Ekberg, *Stealing Indian Women*, 48.

40. Boisbriant to directors of the Compagnie des Indes, 1725, ANOM, C^{13A} 8: 447–48.

41. The threat posed by "Renards" was a ubiquitous topic for years in Louisiana correspondance. See ANOM, C^{13A}, esp. vols. 9–13.

42. Melique was killed by Foxes early in 1727, and his death was reported soon after in New Orleans. Governor Étienne Perier and Commissaire ordonnateur Jacques de La Chaise to Compagnie des Indes, Apr. 22, 1727, ANOM, C^{13A} 10:174–76. Melique left behind a major estate, including farmland, a new *poteaux-sur-solle* house, a large stable, and a huge barn, measuring twenty-six by fifty-one pieds (see KM 26-11-24-1).

43. KM 28-3-6-1.

44. Other options under the same Article of the *Coutume* included the presence of two notairess or one notaire plus the curate of the testator's home parish.

45. It is odd that Marguerite would not have had relatives among the Illinois Indians at the village mission site.

46. This was François-Marie de Vincennes who would soon establish the post of Vincennes on the lower Wabash River. See Ekberg and Person, *St. Louis Rising*, 34, 41. Vincennes married Marie-Philippe Du Longpré in 1730. See Census, no. 68, for his wife's family.

47. Ekberg (with Anton J. Pregaldin), "Marie Rouensa-8cate8a," 179.

48. Census in ANOM, G^1 464.

49. KM 23-7-1-1.

50. Concerning the meaning of skin colors in French Louisiana, see White, *Wild Frenchmen and Frenchified Indians:* 121–22, 201–4.

51. See Sue Peabody, *There Are No Slaves in France: The Political Culture of Race and Slavery in the Ancien Régime:* (New York: Oxford University Press, 1996).

52. KM 28-8-6-1.

53. Concerning Ternan's career in the Illinois Country, see Carl J. Ekberg, "Terrisse de Ternan: Epistoler and Soldier," *Louisiana History* 23 (Fall 1982): 400–408; David MacDonald, *Lives of Fort de Chartres: Commandants, Soldiers, and Civilians, 1720–70* (Carbondale: Southern Illinois University Press, 2016), 138–43, 221–25, 243–44.

54. This was Pierre St. Ange, eldest son of Robert Grotton St. Ange and older brother to Louis St. Ange de Bellerive. Pierre was killed in the disastrous Chickasaw campaign of 1735. See Ekberg and Person, *St. Louis Rising,* 22–31, passim.

Chapter 9: Aubains and Régnicoles

1. Commissaire-ordonnateur Jean-Baptiste Dubois-Duclos and seminarian priest Henri Rouleaux de La Vente hotly debated *métissage,* the priest being in favor it and the administrator opposed. See Ekberg, *Stealing Indian Women,* 25–26; White, *Wild Frenchmen and Frenchified Indians,* 30–32, 116–17.

2. KM 28-11-3-1 records Le Boullenger's last appearance in Kaskaskia until he returned to town in early 1731. He died at Mobile in 1741 (Beauchamp to minister, Apr. 4, 1741, ANOM, C13^A 26:208).

3. See Emily Clark, *Masterless Mistresses: The New Orleans Ursulines and the Development of a New World Society, 1727–1834* (Chapel Hill: University of North Carolina Press, 2007), 85.

4. Pottier's awkward situation is described in a Superior Council record (ANOM, F^3 242:146).

5. The estate of Franchomme and Marguerite was inventoried in 1728 (KM 28 -- -- 11) but the original document has not survived.

6. Fleuriau (1679–1752) was born and raised in France and educated there as a jurist. He enjoyed an astonishingly long run as Procureur Général (1722–52) and was perhaps the most important administrator ever tp serve in French Louisiana He certainly deserves a dedicated biography.

7. Fleuriau's "Questions" and the "Exposé" are found in ANOM, F^3 242:144–45. This document is not dated, but Fleuriau seems to have drafted it during the first week of December 1728.

8. Ibid., 146–47.

9. December 18, 1728, ANOM, series A, vol. 23: 102–3. Both the draft and the final version of the Council's decree were based largely on Fleuriau's "Exposé," although they differ in some

details. For example, the Pottier bastardy case appears only in the draft decree (for this case, see above, chap. 2), not in the final version, for it was not directly relevant to the fundamental issue that the Council was addressing—that is, problems arising when Indian wives with no children became widows. White, *Wild Frenchmen and Frenchified Indians*, 130–32, has briefly examined this interesting case, coming to somewhat different conclusions than ours.

10. Prohibition of White-Black marriages in Louisiana was inscribed in Article VI of the Code Noir. "Édit concernant les Nègres à la Louisiane," *Publications of the Louisiana Historical Society* 4 (1908), 77.

11. See Carl J. Ekberg (with Anton J. Pregaldin), "Marie Rouensa-8cate8a and the Foundations of French Illinois," *Illinois Historical Journal* 84 (Autumn, 1991), 146–60, esp. 156–57.

12. Linguist Carl Masthay suggests that "Aubain" may derive from the twelfth-century Frankish *alibanus*, 'belonging to another ban,' that is, another military band, another tribe.

13. Concerning the *Aubain-Régnicole* issue in French Canada, see Gilles Havard, "'Les forcer à devenir Cytoyens': État, Sauvages et citoyenneté en Nouvelle-France (XVIIᵉ-XVIIIᵉ siècle), *Annales, Histoire, Sciences Sociale* (May 2009), esp. 990–92.

14. Concerning the plight of Louisiana during the 1720s, See Marcel Giraud, *Histoire de la Louisiane française*, vol. 5, *La Compagnie des Indes, 1723–31* (Paris: l'Harmattan, 2012).

15. *Lettres Patentes En Forme D'edit, Portant Etablissment D'une Compagnie de Commerce: Sous le Nom de Compagnie d'Occident: Donné à Paris Au Mois D'aoust 1717* (Paris: Imprimerie royale, 1717), 9–10. See also, Marcel Giraud, *Histoire de la Louisiane française*, vol. 3, *L'époque de John Law* (1717–20) (Paris: Presses Universitaire de France, 1966).

16. Article I of the Code Noir was pro-active on the issue of Jews in Louisiana, decreeing that they should be chased ("chassé) from the colony and must all be gone within three months from the date the decree was promulgated (March 1724). "Édit concernant les Nègres à la Louisiane," Publications of the Louisiana Historical Society 4 (1908), 76. Louis XIV's Edict of Fontainebleau of 1685 revoked Henri IV's Edict of Nantes of 1598, thereby outlawing the Protestant church "in our realm and in all countries and territories under our rule." See http://huguenotsweb .free.fr/histoire/edit1685.htm

17. Aubert—"The Blood of France," 439–78—chastises fellow historians (471, n. 63) for refusing to see the "racial implications" of the decree, but these "implications" strike one as more imputed than real. Race and racialism are now *consumingly* popular topics in French colonial studies. Saliha Belmessous has examined how racialism developed in Canada as attempts at assimilation foundered ("Assimilation and Racialism in Seventeenth and Eighteenth-Century French Colonial Policy," *American Historical Review*, vol. 110, no. 2 [April 2005] 322–49). Belmessous does not deal with colonial Louisiana (or the Illinois Country) whatsoever; Aubert provides some offhand remarks about the colony. But see White, *Wild Frenchmen and Frenchified Indians*, 1–8, 14–20, 115–22, 135–37, 169–70, 201–7, 230–32.

18. Ferrière, *Nouveau Commentaire sur La Coutume*, II: 350–51. See also the extended discussion about *Aubains* and the limitations on their rights within France in Lange, *La Nouvelle Practique Civile*, 127–31.

19. Saliha Belmessous has argued that "*francisation* [assimilation] was more a political program than a religious one." Saliha Belmessous "Assimilation and Racialism in Seventeenth and Eighteenth-Century French Colonial Policy," *American Historical Review*, 110, no. 2 (April 2005): 323. The Superior Council's actions in 1728 do not diminish that argument.

20. See "Projet du mémoire du roi. . . ," ANOM, C^{13A} 4:977-78. See also Ekberg, *Stealing Indian Women*, 26.

21. Jennifer M. Spear, "Colonial Intimacies: Legislating Sex in French Louisiana," *William and Mary Quarterly* 60 (January 2003): 75–98. Spear's investigations did not include the Illinois Country.

22. Concerning Tartarin and his attitudes toward mixed marriages, see ibid., 27–30; White, *Wild Frenchmen and Frenchified Indians*, 139.

Chapter 10: Marguerite 8assecam8c8e's Last Dance

1. Marriage contract in KM 29-8-24-1.

2. KM 22-9-23-1.

3. KM 24-10-24-1.

4. As explained earlier, the *Coutume* (Art. CCLXXXIX) provided curates with authority to draft last wills and testaments, but it is not clear by what authority Tartarin drafted the Blot-Marguerite marriage contract. A Jesuit missionary at Arkansas Post claimed that the king had authorized curates to make "all kinds of contracts," but the priest adduced no source for this claim. See Morris S. Arnold, *Unequal Laws unto a Savage Race: European Legal Traditions in Arkansas, 1686–1836* (Fayetteville: University of Arkansas Press, 1985), 28.

5. See Ekberg and Person, *St. Louis Rising*, 128–36.

6. KM 29-8-4-1. "Presbytère" suggests that the Jesuit missionary priest who was serving as curate of the parish (Tartarin at this time) had an independent residence within the Jesuit compound that lay along the right bank of the Kaskaskia River at the eastern edge of the town.

7. KM 29-28-4-1.

8. Ibid.

9. See Lange, *La Nouvelle Practique Civile*, 331.

10. Marie-Philippe du Longpré, daughter of Étienne-Philippe and of Marie Ma8enkikoue.

11. Concerning mutual donations among spouses, see Coutume, Art. CCLXXX; also, Lange, *La Nouvelle Practique Civile*, chapter XXIV.

12. Coutume, Art. CCXXIX.

13. Concerning Dutisné's career in Louisiana, see MacDonald, *Lives of Fort de Chartres*, 41–47. 143–45 and passim; Brown, *Reconstructing*, 89–93; Mildred Mott Wedel, "Claude-Charles Dutisné: A Review of His 1719 Journeys," *Great Plains Journal* 12, no. 1 (Fall 1972): 4–25, and ibid., no. 2 (Spring 1973): 146–73.

14. Census in ANOM, G^1 464.

15. See KM 39-2-27-1; 39-5-14-1. See also White, *Wild Frenchmen and Frenchified Indians*, chapter 5.

16. Census in ANOM, G¹ 464. Marguerite received three African slaves and two Indians in the 1723 division of Bourdon's estate (KM 23-7-1-1; 23-10-26-1). On the 1726 census (see Part II), the Franchomme-Marguerite household owned three African slaves and one Indian, suggesting that one of their Native American slaves had died in the two-year interim between the division of the estate and the enumeration of the census.

17. This parcel was two arpents "de face," meaning that the longer dimension was the usual, forty arpents, within the Kaskaskia's common field. See Ekberg, *French Roots*, 47, 67, 114, 246.

18. Nevertheless, as Sophie White has demonstrated, it is very difficult to find much "Indian-ness" in Illinois Country material culture as seen in estate inventories. (White, *Wild Frenchmen and Frenchified Indians*, 35.)

19. Concerning billiard parlors in the Illinois Country, see Ekberg, *Stealing Indian Women*, 105, 107, 115, 133, 154–56.

20. KM 37-4-15-4.

21. After Marguerite's death. Blot leased a billiard parlor (very likely the same one) from Pierre Lacourse (KM 46-10-11-1).

22. See Jean-Louis Flandrin, *Familles: parenté, maison, sexualité dans l'ancienne société* (Paris: Hachette, 1976), 117–22.

23. KM 40-3-22-2.

24. KM 23-7-1-1.

25. ANOM, G¹ 464.

26. KM 48-12-20-1.

Conclusion: The Critical Decade

1. *Lettres Patentes En Forme D'édit, Portant Établissment D'une Compagnie de Commerce: Sous le Nom de Compagnie d'Occident: Donné à Paris Au Mois D'aoust 1717* (Paris: Imprimerie royale, 1717), 9–10. See also Glenn R. Conrad, "Administration of the Illinois Country: The French Debate," *Louisiana History* 36 (Winter 1995): 31–53.

2. Clarence W. Alvord, *The Illinois Country, 1673–1818*, The Centennial History of Illinois, 1 (Springfield: Illinois Centennial Commission, 1920). Alvord's greatness is due to his achieve-ment in presenting the first coherent (though incomplete) picture of the colonial Illinois Coun-try, *and* that his work is still worth citing.

3. KM 23-6-14-1.

4. Renault does appear on the 1726 census as the owner of 20 African slaves (Census, no. 2), but it is not entirely clear how many of these were working as miners and how many at assorted other tasks, such as building out Renault's ambitious *habitation* (estate) at St. Philippe, just north of Fort de Chartres. See Brown, *Reconstructing*, 30.

5. The best study of lead mining in eighteenth-century Missouri remains Lucy E. Handley's remarkable "Lead Mining in the Mississippi Valley During the Colonial Period," MA thesis, St. Louis University, 1942.

6. ANOM, C^{13A} 26:11–12. Native Americans in the American Midwest had been surface mining galena ore since pre-Columbian times. See Broxton W. Bird, Jeremy J. Wilson, Jaime Escobar, George D. Kamenov, Harvie J. Pollard, G. William Monaghn. "Pre-Columbian lead pollution from Native American galena processing and land use in the midcontinental United States." *Geology* 47, 12 (2019): 1193–97.

7. KM 23-10-26-2. The unusual quantity of oats (seventy minots) included in Marguerite's allotment eludes easy explanation. Bourdon, always the trader, was perhaps marketing it to Illinois Indians for their horses.

8. ANOM, G^1 464. Measurement of arable lands (*terres*) in the Illinois Country was almost always accomplished in linear arpents, with widths varying greatly, while the standard length of forty arpents was understood. The use of "terrains" in the 1726 census to describe agricultural, as opposed to residential, land was highly unusual, suggesting that whoever enumerated the census was unfamiliar with traditional agricultural nomenclature.

9. Ekberg, *French Roots*, 216.

10. Ibid., 215.

11. ANOM, G^1 464.

12. Ekberg, *French Roots*, 173–74, 216–38.

13. Havard, *Histoire des coureurs de bois.*

14. Lieutenant Jean-Baptiste Girardot had removed himself from the pool of eligible bachelors in Kaskaskia by marrying Thérèse Neveu in November 1722 (Census, no. 63).

15. Susan Sleeper-Smith, *Indian Women and French Men*; Jacqueline Peterson and Jennifer S.H. Brown, eds., *The New People: Being and Becoming Métis in North America* (University of Manitoba Press, 1985).

16. Peabody, *There Are No Slaves in France,* 60, 68.

17. Aubert, "The Blood of France," 439–78.

18. *Caribbean New Orleans: Empire, Race, and the Making of a Slave Society* (Chapel Hill: University of North Carolina Press, 2019). It is instructive to compare Vidal's work with Gwendolyn Midlo Hall's award-winning *Africans in Colonial Louisiana: The Development of Afro-Creole Culture in the Eighteenth Century*, was published in 1992 (Baton Rouge: Louisiana State University Press). Hall's four-hundred-page book, which now seems timid and quaint compared to Vidal's, contains only a score of references to "race relations."

19. White, *Wild Frenchmen and Frenchified Indians*, 2.

20. *Red, White, and Black: The Peoples of Early America* (Englewood Cliffs: Prentice-Hall, 3rd ed., 1992), 280.

21. Aubert "The Blood of France."

22. Concerning Arkansas Post, see especially Morris S. Arnold, *The Rumble of a Distant Drum: The Quapaws and Old World Newcomers, 1673–1804* (Fayetteville: University of Arkansas Press, 2000), 10–14.

23. This facility is now a major component in the French national health care system.

24. See Carl J. Ekberg, "Marie-Claire Catoire: A Parisian Woman in Colonial Ste. Genevieve." *Missouri Historical Review*, 114 (January 2020): 105–20.

25. Ste. Genevieve Civil Records, Estates no. 30 (microfilm Missouri History Museum library, St. Louis).

26. Concerning the issue of Indians adopting French identities, see Saliha Belmessous, "Être français en Nouvelle France: Identité française et identité coloniale aux dix-septième et dix-huitième siècles," *French Historical Studies* 27 (Summer 2004): 507–40. Gilles Havard has argued that in French colonies Catholicism was a "determing element in French identity." Gilles Havard, "'Les forcer à devenir Cytoyens': État, Sauvages et citoyenneté en Nouvelle-France (XVIIᵉ-XVIIIᵉ siècle), *Annales, Histoire, Sciences Sociale* (May 2009): 990.

27. Jaenen, *Friend and Foe*, 153–85; Sahila Belmessous, "Assimilation and Racialism in Seventeenth and Eighteenth-Century French Colonial Policy," *American Historical Review*, 110, no. 2 (April 2005): 322–49.

28. Beauharnois to Ministre de la Marine, Jean-Frédéric Phélypeaux de Maurepas, Oct. 4, 1733, ANOM, C¹¹ᴬ 59:111–12.

29. Significantly, neither Trudel nor Rushford discuss racialization or racism in their studies of Native American slavery in Canada. Marcel Trudel, *L'esclavage au Canada français; histoire et conditions de l'esclavage* (Quebec: Presses universitaires Laval, 1960); and Brett Rushforth, *Bonds of Alliance: Indigenous and Atlantic Slaveries in New France* (Chapel Hill: Omohundro Institute of Early American History and Culture and the University of North Carolina Press, 2012).

Part II

1. ANOM, G¹ 464. Though the census document carries the date 1726, internal evidence makes clear that it was compiled in late 1724 or very early 1725 in the Illinois Country. For consistency with its labeling in the archives, the date 1726 is retained.

2. "French" and "Frenchmen" in the essay and following census and notes encompasses both those born in France and French Canadians. Marie La Boissière was described as a "natural daughter" in notarial manuscripts. KM 23-4-12-1, marriage contract with Joseph Baron. The question of when her mother was manumitted is not answered in the records. After the death of her first husband, Marie married, in 1759, a militia officer of Ste. Genevieve and moved to the west bank of the Mississippi, where she remained until her death in 1768.

3. On the significance of notaires in the Illinois Country, see Part I.

4. At least one couple, La Violette and his wife Catherine Ekipakin8a, migrated to Mobile. Jay Higginbotham, *Old Mobile: Fort Louis de la Louisiane, 1702–1711* (Mobile, AL: Museum of the City of Mobile, 1977), 282. Their names do not re-appear in the Kaskaskia Parish Records (hereafter KPR): references to Kaskaskia Parish Records online at http:www.familysearch .org>Search>Records>Research by Location>Illinois, Diocese of Belleville, Catholic Parish Rec-

ords, 1729–1956>Browse>Randolph>Kaskaskia Island>Immaculate Conception>1695-1833 Baptisms, Marriages, and Deaths (62 images); 1741–1834 Marriages, (118 images). All references are to the first register unless noted.

5. The counting gets tricky—here, men who reported wives that could not be identified were not counted as married, and "identifiable" couples includes men whose living and easily identified wives were inexplicably not enumerated.

6. 1701 marriage record, http://www.ancestry.com, Québec, Canada, Vital and Church Records (Drouin Collection), 1621-1968, M, Montréal, Basilique Notre-Dame 1701–1704, image 85 of 314. Forestier (Fortier) signed her name in the register. The Kaskaskia sacramental record where she was noted as godmother is an extract, with no signatures. Beaudreau and Forestier both died by 1714, Gail Moreau-DesHarnais and Diane Wolford Sheppard, *Le Détroit du Lac Érié, 1701–1710,* vol. 1 (Royal Oak, MI: French-Canadian Heritage Society of Michigan, 2016), 130-32.

7. See KPR, images 6 and 7 for the records in this paragraph. Deshayes (Census, no. 80) arrived at Mobile on August 1, 1704, having crossed the Atlantic on the *Pelican*. The origins of Marie Tetio (Census, no. 67), and Françoise La Brise (Census, no.70), remain unconfirmed. At least one historian concluded, without citing any source, that Tetio was a Native woman, though similar French names are found in Canadian records. The earliest notarial records in Kaskaskia that mention French women are from the notaires' registers only; the documents themselves are no longer in the collection.

8. The journey of the Lacroix family (Census, no. 5) was successful; the Neveu family (Census, no. 63) suffered tragedy and death.

9. The numbers in this and the following paragraphs should all be considered tentative, based on sometimes incomplete information in sources.

10. See, for example, Census, no. 71, Deslauriers; and Census, no. 98, Thérèse Boisseau, whose mother was never named. Thérèse married and remained in the community.

11. In Kaskaskia baptismal records, godmother Marie-Magdelaine Quesnel signed "MM." KPR, images 12, 13, and 14.

12. *First Families of Louisiana*, Glenn R. Conrad, trans. and comp. (Baton Rouge, LA: Provincial Press, 1970), 1: 26-30. Gail Moreau-DesHarnais, "Morbihan, Paris, New Orleans, Natchez, Kaskaskia, Fort de Chartres: Baleine Women," unpublished manuscript.

13. Known sacramental marriage records exist only for the women from the *Baleine* and several others.

14. 8abanakic8e likely means "Medicine Bundle Woman," but could possibly mean "Delaware Woman." See Part 1. Apechic8rata, "she who has a little nose." Email, Michael McCafferty, July 21, 2021.

15. Joseph Zitomersky, in *French Americans-Native Americans in Eighteenth-Century Colonial Louisiana: The Population Geography of the Illinois Indians 1670s–1760s* (Lund, Sweden: Lund University Press, 1994), 261, used d'Artaguiette's numbers for some of his estimates. Anthropologists commonly multiply the reported counts of warriors by five to estimate the total population.

16. One of the illegitimate children did not survive (Pivert, Census, no.86), and two others do not appear again in records (Bechet, Census, no. 38, and St. Jacques, Census, no. 48). Guillaume Pottier (Census, no. 85), who accused his wife of adultery, was unsuccessful in excluding the child (and his wife) from inheritance. See Part I.

17. KPR, image 15.

18. Cécile Vidal, *Caribbean New Orleans: Empire, Race, and the Making of a Slave Society* (Williamsburg, VA and Chapel Hill, NC: Omohundro Institute of Early American History and Culture and the University of North Carolina Press, 2019), 53–58. Vidal describes the beginnings of slavery in Louisiana in detail.

19. Among the thirty-some locations included on the 1726 Louisiana census, 1,540 African slaves were counted, so the number in the Illinois Country was less than ten percent of the total. See complete census referenced in note 1.

20. Boisbriant arrived in New Orleans December 20, 1725. In the full census, dated January 1, 1726, he is enumerated in New Orleans on rue de Condé. The Jesuit Beaubois (Census, no. 62) likely arrived there with him; Bourgmont arrived in New Orleans January 9, 1725. ANOM, C^{13A}, 9:13ff.

21. Census, nos. 3, 15, 24, 66, 72, 78, 81, 83, 84, 87, 90, 91, and 103 note widows who remarried.

22. For example, in the 1787 Spanish censuses of St. Louis and Ste. Geneviève, Missouri Historical Society Archives, census collections.

23. Above all, the Kaskaskia Manuscripts (KM), Kaskaskia and Fort de Chartres parish records online at http://www.familysearch.org, Archives Nationales d'Outre Mer (ANOM), and Louisiana Superior Council records online, http://www.lacolonialdocs.org (hereafter LSM followed by the document number). In addition, René Jetté, comp., *Dictionnaire généalogique des familles du Québec, des origins à 1730* (Montréal: Presses de l'Université de Montréal, 1983), hereafter Jetté, provided guidance in locating original baptismal records among the Canadian sacramental registers in the Drouin Collection online at http://www.ancestry.com. Jetté and the indexing of Massicotte assisted in finding online *contrats d'engagement*, located at www.familysearch.org.

24. Marthe Faribault-Beauregard, ed. *La Population des forts français d'Amérique (XVIIIe siècle): répertoire des baptêmes, mariages et sépultures célébrés dans les forts et les établissements français en Amérique du Nord au XVIII siècle,* 2 vols (Montréal: Bergeron, 1982), hereafter F-B; *The Census Tables for the French Colony of Louisiana from 1699 Through 1732,* Charles R. Maduell, Jr., comp. and trans. (Baltimore, MD: Genealogical Publishing Company, 1972).

25. Pierre Dugué de Boisbriant, born Ile de Ste. Thérèse, Canada, baptized Montreal, died 1736 in France, W. Stanford Reid, "DUGUÉ DE BOISBRIAND, PIERRE," in *Dictionary of Canadian Biography*, vol. 2, University of Toronto/Université Laval, 2003–, accessed August 30, 2018, http://www.biographi.ca/en/bio/dugue_de_boisbriand_pierre_2E.html. Boisbriant held titles of Knight of the Military Order of St. Louis, First Lieutenant of the King in the province of Louisiana, and Commandant of the Illinois. Titles for both men in *VC*, 809–10.

26. He died in the 1729 uprising of the Native Americans at Natchez post.

27. *VC*, 366–68.

28. Reproduced in Sara Jones Tucker, ed., *Indian Villages of the Illinois Country Part I, Atlas* (Springfield, IL: Illinois State Museum, 1942), plate 22.

29. *VC*, 853–63. Pierre Perico gave his age as seventeen, and his birthplace, but that particular word was written over for the aim of correction, and the result is illegible. Perico first appears in 1725, leased to La Plume for three years to work at his pit-sawing enterprise. Perico received a death sentence for stealing merchandise, mostly clothing, from the company storehouse. Perico first named the other two as accomplices and then dropped the claim.

30. "Extrait des registres de baptêmes de la paroisse de ND. de Cas, depuis le mois de may 1723 jusqu'en mois de may 1724." ANOM, G464[12] 5ff. (Hereafter "Extrait des registres.") Parents not named. The godfather Buisseret is unknown. Moulé was the wife of Jacques-Joseph Catherine, master carpenter, KM 28:-:5-3. The couple does not appear by name in this census.

31. "Extrait des registres."

32. Ibid. On the St. Ange family, see Carl J. Ekberg and Sharon K. Person, *St. Louis Rising: The French Regime of Louis St. Ange de Bellerive* (Urbana: University of Illinois Press, 2015).

33. KM 23-6-14-1.

34. Kaskaskia Land Books B, 11.

35. Map reproduced in Sarah Jones Tucker, *Indian Villages of the Illinois Country*, Atlas, plate 22.

36. KM 23-8-22-1, contract with André Chabernon, born in St. André, diocese of Limoges, France, to work on the farm and care for the horses. He would receive 400 francs of goods from the Company's warehouse.

37. Contract with Martin, KM 23-8-21-1.

38. Conrad, *First Families*, 1:30.

39. Winston De Ville, *The New Orleans French, 1720–1733* (Baltimore, MD: Genealogical Publishing Co., 1973), 35, transcription of marriage record. De Ville transcribed Martin's name as "Jean Martin Doruilliers."

40. When the widow Martin remarried in 1726, she had two children, KM 26-12-13-1.

41. The first mention of François La Croix in Kaskaskia in a notarial record was in 1726, KM 26-2-14-1, the marriage contract of his daughter Agnès. Lacroix later stated that he had his land grant from Boisbriant, which would have predated the commandant's departure in 1724, see KM 55-2-23-1.

42. Baptism at http://www.ancestry.com Québec, Canada, Vital and Church Records (Drouin Collection), 1621–1968, S, Sainte, Sainte Anne de Beaupré, image 48 of 877, son of François and Anne Ganier (Jetté, 625, Gagné, with a different month). KM 55-6-16-3, François Lacroix of Kaskaskia donation to St. Gemme (his son-in-law) for old age care. Burial, KPR, image 32, age ninety-three at death.

43. First marriage at http://www.ancestry.com Québec, Canada, Vital and Church Records (Drouin Collection), 1621–1968, Sainte, Ste-Anne-de-Beaupré, 1691, image 3 of 6, noted her

age as seventeen. Jetté, 826, the bride's mother, Marguerite Auollée, never came to New France, meaning that Barbe was born in France.

44. The "died by" date indicates that no burial record was found. Such estimates derive from estate documents or a surviving spouse's remarriage. Two children from Monmainier's marriage with Mercier, Julien and Marianne, remained in Canada, noted in inventory after her death, KM 33-6-25-1. Son Jean-Baptiste Mercier, Census, no. 82, and daughter Dorothée Mercier, Census, no. 66, were in Kaskaskia.

45. KM 26-2-14-1, marriage contract of Agnès and Boisset, one of the very few extant manuscripts written by the Jesuit Joseph-François de Kereben at the St. François Xavier Mission of the Metchagamia village.

46. KM 37-9-29-2, marriage contract to Jean Chauvin, son of Jacques and Marie Couchon of Québec.

47. KM 32-11-8-1, note of marriage contract of "Socie" and Barbe Lacroix; KM 33-2-16-3, Saucier named as their son-in-law. Saucier resided in St. Philippe and died by September 17, 1758, KM 58-9-17-1.

48. KM 33-2-16-1, statement of François's goods to be excluded from his parents' communauté.

49. Burial record April 8, Ste. Genevieve Parish records, image 754 at http://www.familysearch.org/search/catalog/SteGenevieve roll#008133964.

50. KM 33-7-13-1, sale of land in prairie St. Philippe, Jean-Baptiste Ste. Gemme Beauvais and wife Marie-Louise Lacroix. KM 48-7-15-1, testimony in infant slave murder; Louise Lacroix was 44 years old.

51. KM 33-2-14-1, marriage contract with Gouin noted her birthplace.

52. See also Ekberg and Person, *St. Louis Rising*, 240. Langlois was a fur trader in early St. Louis.

53. KM 33-2-14-1, marriage contract executed at St. Philippe; (KM 52-4-7-1), registration of the marriage contract.

54. *Collet's Index of Cahokia Marriages*; KM 56-2-28-1, note of marriage contract.

55. KM 39-11-8-2, note of marriage contract, (KM 41-10-25-1) registration. See Census, no. 51.

56. "Montréal. Enregistrement d'une permission accordée par Philippe Rigaud de Vaudreuil gouverneur de la Nouvelle-France, à François Lacroix, ci-devant de la Côte de Beaupré, de deux canots et sept hommes, lui compris, pour aller avec sa femme et leurs cinq enfants s'établir aux Illinois dans la mission des prêtres du séminaire de Québec, 4 juin 1723, BAnQ Vieux-Montréal, Fonds Juridiction royale de Montréal, (06M,TL4,S34,P92)."

57. KM 22-12-4-1, note of partnership, first appearance of name of Rollet. KM 45-7-27-1, he was established at Cahokia by 1745.

58. KM 30-11-7-1, declaration by François-Xavier Ripaux Rollet, concerning the sale during his minority on January 17, 1717, of land at Grondines which he had inherited from his father Richard Ripaux. Baptism at http://www.ancestry.com Québec, Vital and Church Records (Drouin Collection), 1621–1968, G, Grondines, 1680–1745, image 10 of 88. Also Jetté, 987, parents Richard Ripault de Rolet and Marie Aubert. Jetté erroneously says François-Xavier was

also called Jacques, noting that Jacques married Françoise Delomay in 1716, with children born in Grondines.

59. KM 52-10-12-1, note of a lease by the widow Rollet to Jean-Baptiste Desgagnes.

60. KM 29-11-28-1, she was authorized by her husband to sell a house and its lot "in the prairie" in November 1729, to Louis St. Ange de Bellerive, and again the next year she carried out a sales contract on behalf of the couple, KM 30-6-23-1. These authorizations suggest that the property was deemed to be hers. Her Native name and origin "Peoria" appear only in one record, after her death, KM 48-8-18-1, the marriage of her daughter Domitille. The 1732 census enumerated both parents and two children, ANOM, G¹, 464.

61. *Collet's Index of Cahokia Marriages*, Louis Gaut of Tours, France, son of Michel Gaud and Helene Prou.

62. Baron's birthplace was Boucherville, Canada, KM 48-8-18-1, marriage contract. The contract was drafted at the *maison* of *Ste. Famille des Kaokias*.

63. KM 45-7-27-1, marriage contract, mentioned a daughter by Rollet's first wife. Marie was the daughter of Jean-Baptiste and Marie Barreau.

64. KM 47-6-12-2, marriage contract, sacramental record, KPR, image 12 of 118.

65. KM 24-4-4-1, sale of lot and house in the Indian village by the couple. Suzanne Pimitsinon was authorized by Nault to make the transaction; the land was sold to (Antoine?) Giard.

66. KM 40:1:-:1, placing of seals after his death. KM 37-3-12-1, power of attorney, indicated birthplace. KM 36-1-8-1, parents François and Thérèse Chartier, named in marriage contract to Françoise Becquet. Jetté, 845, contract to travel west. http://www.familysearch.org, Catalog, Author, Jean-Baptiste Adhémar, film #008328666, images 2842 and 2843, dated April 3, 1715.

67. Birth and death dates unknown. The name "Ch8perikinga" appeared in the baptismal record of Marie-Jeanne, and "Pimitsinon" in the sale of the lot on April 24.

68. In the 1732 census, Nault's household was enumerated with one legitimate child but no wife.

69. "Extrait des registres." Godfather was Étienne Hébert, godmother Hélène Dany. The names of children alive but omitted in the counts appear, as do children born earlier and later than the census, to give a more complete insight into the course of lives of each family.

70. KM 36-1-8-1, Françoise Becquet, daughter of Jean-Baptiste and Catherine Barreau.

71. Antoine Giart, parents Charles Geart and Claude Prat, http://www.ancestry.com Québec, Canada, Vital and Church Records (Drouin Collection), 1621-1968, M, Montréal, Basilique Notre-Dame, 1682, image 10 of 229. Also Jetté, 493, contract to travel west, June 5, 1707. KM 24-4-4-1, recipient of land and house sold by Nault and wife Suzanne Pimitsinon. KM 34-11-12-1, marriage contract of Antoine Giard and Marie-Anne LaFontaine, Widow Martin. Their daughter Catherine married Gabriel Cerré in 1764. KPR, image 33 of 118. KM 40-3-17-1, mentioned as churchwarden in 1740. Jean-Baptiste Giard, possibly his nephew, appeared by name first in 1737, KM 37:-:-:1.

72. KM 47-4-18-2, mentioned as deceased.

73. Baptism http://www.ancestry.com Québec, Canada, Vital and Church Records (Drouin Collection), 1621–1968, Q, Québec, Notre-Dame, 1667–1677 transcript, 1669, image 47 of 527, parents Antoine and Marie-Jeanne Guerin/Brunet. KM 23-9-10-4, Du Pré's testimony in the Baillargeon complaint. KM 28-1-12-1, date of death in the renunciation of the estate.

74. Marriage at http://www.ancestry.com Québec, Canada, Vital and Church Records (Drouin Collection), 1621–1968, Q, Québec, Notre-Dame, 1691–1703, image 223 of 287. Jean-Baptiste, son of Antoine and Marie Guerin/Gerein; maître forgeron (blacksmith). Françoise Marchand, daughter of François and Madeleine Groleau/Grosleau; born at the parish of St. Joseph at the Pointe Lévy. The governor of Trois Rivières was a witness at their marriage.

75. KM 26-1-29-1, inventory of community property of Du Pré and the deceased Marchand.

76. Baptism at http://www.ancestry.com Québec, Canada, Vital and Church Records (Drouin Collection), 1621–1968, Q, Québec, Notre-Dame, 1691–1703, image 246 of 287. Also, Jetté, 390.

77. Baptism at http://www.ancestry.com Québec, Canada, Vital and Church Records (Drouin Collection), 1621-1968, L, Lachine, Sts-Anges-Gardiens, 1676-1756, image 98 of 362. The 1732 census listed the widow Pré and two legitimate children. Marie Saka8ie was the only widow on that census, and she remarried the same year.

78. KM 28-5-3-2, note of marriage contract. In other records her name was spelled Saka8ie and Seco8kiaha. The May 5, 1728, sacramental record by the Jesuit Tartarin spelled her name Marie Chekaokia, KPR, image 26. See Bontems below, Census, no. 9.

79. Jetté, 390.

80. (KM 41-8-9-2) Registration and inscription of marriage donation. The couple moved to St. Louis in time to appear on the 1766 census by commandant St. Ange de Bellerive. See Ekberg and Person, *St. Louis Rising*, 239.

81. A 1721 baptismal record was signed by a Jean Ricard, Fort de Chartres, St. Anne Parish Register (hereafter SAPR: references to St. Anne Parish Records online at http://www.family search.org>Search>Records>Research by Location > Illinois, Diocese of Belleville, Catholic Parish Records, 1729–1956>Browse>Randolph>Fort de Chartres>St. Anne (transferred to St. Joseph)>1721–-1840 Baptisms, Marriages, Deaths, First Communion, Confirmations (603 images)), image 3. In March 1723, Ricard was owed forty-eight livres for wine he supplied during the illness of one La France at Cahokia, KM-23-3-30-1. Letter in Pierre Hurtubise, "Relations inédites des missions de l'Illinois" *Eglise et Théologie* 8 (1977): 281. An inventory was noted in 1727, KM 27:-:-:3, for Jean Richard, inhabitant of St. Philippe, perhaps the same man.

82. Baptism at http://www.ancestry.com Québec, Canada, Vital and Church Records (Drouin Collection), 1621-1968, L, Lachine, Sts-Anges-Gardiens 1676–1707, image 5 of 235, parents Claude and Marie Leger. First appearance of Cécire in notarial records in note of partnership KM 22:-:-:6. KM 25-4-2-2, grant of two arpents of land.

83. *VC*, 833, named his birthplace and parents, Claude and Marie Leclerc. Also Jetté, 212. Cécire was a royal interpreter.

84. KM 28-2-15-1, adjudication of land belonging to the deceased Bontems.

85. Jetté, 212. Jetté's marriage estimations seem to be based on the birth date of the first known child. She was called Marie "Illinoise" in the baptism of a daughter with Pineau in 1743, SAPR, image 12, and in her burial record several weeks later, image 13. Her burial record noted her age as about forty.

86. See Census, no. 7, Du Pré.

87. KM 32-9-9-1, fragment of marriage contract.

88. KM 39-4-27-1, marriage contract of Marie-Josèphe Cécire and Antoine Cheneau.

89. SAPR, image 7, birth and baptism. KM 28-7-12-1, mentions just one unnamed minor child of Bontems, whose guardian was discharged by Pierre Du Pré several months after Du Pré's marriage to the widow Cécire.

90. Name spelled variously. Several mentions of a Pierre Neuport appear in Canadian records, for example, http://www.ancestry.com Québec, Canada, Actes Notariés (Notarial Records), Montréal, Pierre Raimbault, (1697–1727), in 1712 a Pierre Neuport sold his habitation on the Grande Isle Bouchard. In 1713, a Sr. Neufport signed a contract in Montreal to travel to Detroit, http://www.familysearch.org, Catalog, Author, Adhémar, Antoine, 1668-1714, image 1159. KM 21-:-:-1, first appearance in Kaskaskia records in 1721. The 1732 census showed a wife and son. KM 37-10-1-1, the son, Jean-Baptiste, is mentioned in 1737. KM 45-6-27-2, noted in a sale of land that Neuport died in 1743.

91. KM 24-5-2-4, land grant to Joseph Baron.

92. KM 23-4-12-1, marriage contract, son of Pierre Baron and Marianne Baudon; parents' names and birthplace. Baptism at http://www.ancestry.com Québec, Canada, Vital and Church Records (Drouin Collection), 1621–1968, B, Boucherville, 1669–1783, image 125 of 199. His godmother was the wife of Joseph Huet dit Dulude (father of the Dulude brothers, see Census, nos. 107 and 109). Jetté, 51, father's name Léger.

93. KM 58-1-21-1 mentions the widow. KM 48-11-11-2, agreement of Baron with François Coulon de Villiers. KM 59-4-20-1, inventory of the marital estate before the widow's remarriage.

94. Baptismal record for Marie, KPR, image 6. Her mother's name appeared in the baptismal record as Atchica Panic8e, but in later records, Marthe Accica. KM 23-4-12-1, Marie was the natural daughter of François Labossière and Marthe Accica; i.e., they were not married.

95. Burial record, died February 19, interred February 20, at http://www.familysearch.org Ste. Genevieve Church Records, 1759-1993, roll#008133964, image 709.

96. Ste. Genevieve (Missouri) Archives, hereafter SGA, Marriage Contracts, # 44.

97. KM 45-6-8-1, marriage contract. SAPR, image 48, burial of Suzanne Baron wife of Joseph Metot, age eighteen.

98. KM 60-6-9-1, sale of house at Fort de Chartres, gave her age as twenty-three. The 1732 census enumerated four legitimate children for Baron and his wife (no names). Another daughter, perhaps, Agnès, was born in 1745, *VC*, 56 and died in 1748, *VC*, 139. Records also show a Joseph Baron who died in 1745, *VC*, 56-57.

99. Marriage record at Ste. Genevieve, February 5, 1760, http://www.familysearch.org Ste. Genevieve Church Records, 1759-1993, roll #008119539, image 539.

100. KM 25-7-25-1, signed as a witness, in a strong, legible, and flowing signature. No record of a wife or child found. KM 24-9-2-2, mentioned in the will of Gouin at Fort d'Orléans, suggesting that d'Arbonne was there. The name "Darbonne" appears in Conrad, *First Families*, 1: 46, with birthplace and age, noted as a cadet of the troops, departing France in 1720 on the *Union*. In March 1721, a d'Arbonne signed a legal document in New Orleans, LSM 1721-03-01-01. Possibly his first name was Gabriel—the handwriting is difficult to read.

101. Baptism, http://www.ancestry.com Québec, Canada, Vital and Church Records (Drouin Collection), 1621–1968, P, Pointe-Aux-Trembles, St-Enfant-Jésus-de-la-Pointe-aux-Trembles, 1674–1700, image 186 of 470, parents Nicolas and Angélique Gautier. Marriage contract KM 24-1-24-1 for Chaput's parents, Nicolas and Angélique Landreville (adit name for some Gautier families), and birthplace. Contract to travel west August 20, 1718, image online at www.familysearch.org, Catalog, Author, Adhémar, Jean-Baptiste, film #008274280, image 869. Death date refers to the date of his widow's remarriage to Ignace Hébert, see below.

102. Marriage with Chaput, extract, "Extrait des registres" and marriage contract, see above. KM 28-11-27-1 marriage contract of Hélène Danis with Hébert. Danis's mother was likely a Native woman, though no record confirms it. With her second husband, Danis had nine children. Danis was first identified as Widow Hébert in KM 51-03-20-02. She did not remarry after Hébert's death. Danis was one of several widows integral to the establishment of St. Louis, see Ekberg and Person, *St. Louis Rising*, 301.

103. Baptism at http://www.ancestry.com Québec, Canada, Vital and Church Records (Drouin Collection), 1621–1968, P, Pointe-aux-Trembles, St-Enfant-de-Jésus-de-la-Pointe-aux-Trembles, 1674–1700, image 165 of 470, parents Joseph and Jeanne Langlois. Also, Jetté, 740.

104. Date of the widow's remarriage, see below.

105. Baptism, KPR, image 6. KM 24-2-8-1 marriage contract; sacramental marriage January 11, 1724, KPR, image 25. She died the day before at 10 in the evening, burial, SAPR, image 13.

106. KM 39-3-11-1 marriage contract. Also spelled Heneaux, Hunau, Huneau, and several other variants.

107. SAPR, image 8 and *VC*, 14.

108. SAPR, image 46, age about twenty-one.

109. KM 44-1-3-1, a minor at his mother's death. Only one child was enumerated in the 1732 census.

110. "Hébert et sa femme" appear two times; both probably refer to Étienne Hébert, Census, no. 97. With the date of the census uncertain, the wife enumerated could be either Françoise or Marie-Louise. KM 25-4-30-1, Hébert was captain of the militia at Fort de Chartres, "residing at Kaskaskia." His younger brother was Ignace, Census, no. 60.

111. Baptism at http://www.ancestry.com Québec, Canada, Vital and Church Records (Drouin Collection), 1621–1968, B, Boucherville, 1669–1783, image 78 of 199. KM 27-2-11-2, marriage contract with Philippe, named his parents, Ignace and Marguerite St. Michel, and his birthplace.

112. KM 35-11-21-1, remarriage of the widow Hébert.

113. KM 21-1-15-1, note of marriage contract. KM 23-10-26-3, Hébert made an agreement for exchange of property.

114. KM 25-2-5-1, power of attorney by Estienne Hébert of Fort de Chartres and wife Marie Louise Coignon, widow of François Chesne. In 1722 Chesne and Coignon buried a child, image 19, KPR.

115. KM 27-2-11-2 marriage contract, daughter of Michel Philippe and Marie 8canic8e Rouensa (see Census, no. 77). KPR sacramental marriage the next day, image 25.

116. "Extrait des registres." Tabouret was the wife of Joseph Gardon dit La Jeunesse, tenants of Melique, Census, no. 64.

117. Sans Chagrin was a dit name of more than one man. Antoine Chesneau, also Sanschagrin, first appeared in notarial records in 1739. KM 20-8-18-1, a Sanschagrin was a purchaser in an auction.

118. SAPR, image 48. The word "cemetery" was written over with "church." He and his son appear to have been church officials, signing many sacramental records.

119. KM 21-3-28-1, note of marriage contract of François Hennet. Charpin was named in the children's marriage contracts.

120. Conrad, *First Families*, 1: 27, Jeanne Charpin arrived in Louisiana in 1719 aboard the *Mutine*.

121. KM 34-4-15-1, inventory of the deceased Charpin. KM 34-4-15-2 named the six children that were minors upon her death.

122. KM 36-12-17-1, named a different wife for Chabot.

123. KM 34-10-18-3, marriage contract of Chabot and Marie Hennet named the first husband.

124. KM 46-6-26-1, marriage contract.

125. "Extrait des registres." Godfather was Étienne Hebert, godmother Madeleine Cordier.

126. KM 40-4-23-1, Le Jeune was born in Salzburg (present-day Austria).

127. SAPR, image 78. She was the daughter of Pierre Roi and Agnès Philippe, see Census no. 36 Chassin.

128. KM 48-11-11-1, sale of property by Cadron, part of the inheritance of his late wife.

129. KM 47-6-18-1, marriage contract. The groom was a voyageur.

130. Record noted as torn where the family name should appear, *VC*, 183-4.

131. KM 57-2-7-1, marriage contract.

132. Named as a minor child in the estate inventory, KM 34-4-15-1.

133. KM 22-4-22-1, note of partnership with Olivier. KM 24-5-6-1, estate appraiser, May 6, 1724, named Jean Fabut dit La Jeunesse. A slave of Jean Faber named Marie-Jeanne was baptized October 31, 1723, age four. Jeanne L'Enfant was the godmother, "Extrait des registres."

134. *VC*, 15-16 baptism of Marie Joseph, daughter of Jean Fabert and Denise Manisure at Ft de Chartres, 1726. KM 28-5-29-1 and 28-7-31-1, the widow's remarriage mentioned a child. Sacramental record of remarriage of the widow of Faber(*sic*) to François Dionet, August 1, 1728, KPR, image 27.

135. KM 25-8-22-1, lease of house and lands.

136. KM 34-4-15-2, inventory of community property of Hennet and his deceased wife.

137. KM 26-6:-:1, signature, rough and unpracticed, but in his own hand; KM 30:-:-:2, the marks of villagers' pigs; KM 32-1-14-1, sale of his house.

138. De Ville, *New Orleans French*, 40, transcription of marriage record of Du Trou and Grace.

139. KM 31:-:-:9, inventory.

140. These names—Grace, and Larmeau/Larmuseau—are perhaps too different to be considered the same woman. Beginning with a document in 1730, only the name Marie-Josèphe Larmuseau in its variant spellings appears. Larmuseau survived Du Trou and remarried Hubert Finet by 1741, KM 41-12-4-1.

141. SAPR, image 121, burial of Finet, age eighty, in St. Philippe, 1760. The widow married Antoine Chesneau dit Sanschagrin in January 1762, SAPR, image 105.

142. Suzanne Boivin Sommerville and Gail Moreau-DesHarnais, "Étienne de Veniard, *Escuyer, sieur* de Bourgmont: From France to Québec to Détroit to 'Missouri' to Fort d'Orléans, and his return to France: Documentary Evidence" CD-ROM n.d. Also Ekberg and Person, *St. Louis Rising*, chapter 1.

143. KM 25-3-12-1, contract. He made his mark, a cross, on the contract, with Melique and Antoine Girard signing.

144. For presence in 1724, see baptism of Mathurin below. KM 45-2-26-1, parents named in the marriage contract of their daughter Marie-Josèphe to Pineau.

145. Their daughter was born in Paris, so this is a reasonable conclusion, see below.

146. SAPR, image 22, for her birthplace. Pineau was the widower of Marie Saka8ie, Census, no. 9.

147. SAPR, image 63. He was born in Paris, France.

148. French and Spanish Archives (hereafter FSA), Missouri Historical Society Archives, instrument 2295, inventory of Quebedeau and LaVille, 1764. SAPR, image 111, sacramental marriage.

149. "Extrait des registres," godfather was de la Loëre de St. Gilles, godmother Marie Maurice Medar(d), wife of Etevenard, see below.

150. KM 45-7-20-1, marriage contract. Her mother and her godmother, Marie Baret (Census, no. 82) stood with her at the contract ceremony.

151. Frank Norall, *Bourgmont, Explorer of the Missouri, 1698–1725* (Lincoln: University of Nebraska Press, 1988), 125. The beginning of La Renaudière's journal mentions an Antoine as an employee of La Renaudière.

152. Pierre de Charlevoix, *Journal of a Voyage to North-America* (London: R. and J. Dodsley, 1761), 2:220.

153. Notes of Antoine L'Espagnol in KM 39-5-31-2, 40-2-9-1, and 40-11-20-1.

154. This is one of several entries where no wife was enumerated though records confirm her presence. Marie Maurice Medard brought a slander suit against Blanche Vigneron in 1725, KM 25-5-17-1.

155. Baptism at http://www.ancestry.com Québec, Canada, Vital and Church Records (Drouin Collection), 1621-1968, M, Montréal, Basilique Notre-Dame, Montréal, 1705–1712,

image 20 of 377, gives his father's name Pierre. Parents named in *VC*, 939 as (Henry) Biron and Jeanne Desmouchelles and birthplace identified as Ville-Marie. Also Jetté, 105. KM 24-4-11-2 Henry Biron and Jean-Baptiste Lalande made an exchange which included an African slave couple and a Native slave woman that came into the possession of Biron. Lalande seems to have been on his way to Canada, where he would receive the inheritance of Biron from the hands of Biron's brother.

156. KM 26-8-18-1, "deceased Henry Biron."

157. Burial of Pierre Thevenard, April 2, 1724, "Extrait des registres." KM 24-4-24-1 marriage contract Biron and Widow Etevenard. Extract of sacramental marriage record, "Extrait des registres." Gail Moreau-DesHarnais has deduced that this is the Marie Morisse who arrived on the *Mutine* with her sister Anne in 1719, "The Other Bienvenu Family of Kaskaskia in present-day Illinois: Philippe Bienvenu and Françoise Allaire Part 5A Françoise Rabut, wife of (1) Pierre Durand; (2) Pierre Desené dit Melet" *Michigan's Habitant Heritage*, 36:3 (July 2015): 143–149.

158. KM 24-5-6-1, inventory of Widow Etevenard and daughter Agnès. A son, Pierre Etevenard, was baptized June 5, 1721, KPR, image 15.

159. KM 20-8-18-1, a St. Jean participated in an auction in 1720. KM 24-5-20-1, he separated from his housemate with an inventory of his goods. KM 38-4-29-1, date of the remarriage of Bailly to Le Comte.

160. KM 38-4-20-1, remarriage contract named her parents, Guillaume Bailly and Helene Plat, and birthplace. KM 26-6-4-1, sale of house to the couple. They cared for the orphaned daughter of Claude Illeret and Marie Simone Martin (KM 35-8-20-1). KM 31-10-30-1, she signed in her own hand a mutual donation with her husband, which stated they had no children and no hope of having any.

161. KM 38-4-20-1, marriage contract. See Census, no. 104.

162. KM 24-11-19-1, purchaser in the sale of the effects of Le Gras.

163. Son of Jean-Baptiste Becquet and Françoise Masse, Paris, France; daughter of Léger Bareax and Marie Nabare. KM 36-1-8-1, parents named in the Neau marriage contract. Conrad, *First Families,* 1:92, married in France, they arrived in Louisiana in 1720 on *La Gironde.*

164. SAPR, image 119, burial of Widow Becquet, no further identification.

165. "Extrait des registres." KPR, image 21, death date seems to read November 19, and the child's age, 21 months.

166. KM 36-1-8-1, marriage contract. See Neau, Census, no. 5.

167. SAPR, image 7, *VC*, 9. The month and day are from Dean and Brown; the register appears to say November 6.

168. KM 57-1-24-1, note of marriage contract. Ekberg and Person, *St. Louis Rising*, 238.

169. KM 46-6-26-1, marriage contract.

170. Ekberg and Person, *St. Louis Rising*, 304, n. 150, age eighty-five at burial.

171. KM 47-6-12-2, her widower, François-Xavier Rollet, remarried on this date.

172. Margaret Kimball Brown, "Who's Who in Illinois in 1726," unpublished paper for the French Colonial Historical Society, 1990. *VC*, 358–59, Lalande sold a house and lot at Kaskaskia

in August 1726. *VC*, 518, a document was signed at the house of Jean-Baptiste Lalande at Fort de Chartres in 1745.

173. See Ekberg and Person, *St. Louis Rising*, Chapter 1 for his time at Fort d'Orléans. KM 24-10-2-1, signature. Pradel likely left the Illinois Country on or before May 27, 1727, when he granted power of attorney to Terisse de Ternan, LSM 1728-11-28-1. Pradel is a major figure in Vidal, *Caribbean New Orleans*.

174. KM 26-2-19-1, sealing of the forge of Levé (Leveillé). KM 30:-:-:2, pigs.

175. KM 23-4-5-1 and KM 26-6-7-2; KM 30:-:-:2.

176. KM 28-11-13-1, estate distribution.

177. KM 26-5-:-1, Onesime Fortunay ecuyer Sieur de Lessard, purchased a slave from La Plume. KM 27-11-27-1, marriage contract with Catherine Bechet for his birthplace. Her previous husband was Bellegarde. See KM 37-1-17-1 and Bellegarde, Census, no. 38. SAPR, image 29, marriage of daughter Catherine de Lessart to Toussaint Pothier, son of Jean-Baptiste and Françoise La Brise on October 11, 1745. De Lessart was noted as an officer of the militia.

178. "Extrait des registres." Cordier, wife of Robillard, see next entry.

179. A Louis Robillard is listed in the manifest of the *Loire*, departing Lorient, France, in August 1720. Conrad, *First Families*, 1:112. This Robillard was accompanied by a wife, who may not have survived the voyage. In the Illinois Country, KM 25-1-1-2, signature of Robillard. *VC*, 349, October 1725 purchase of house, Robillard was identified as sergeant of the troops and neighbor to Delessart, also sergeant. By 1733, Robillard and his wife lived in St. Philippe, *VC*, 407, and in Cahokia by 1739, KM 39-5-16-1. LSM 1746-05-12-01 and 1746-05-12-03, he was traveling between the Illinois Country and Pointe Coupée.

180. In the marriage transcription by De Ville, *New Orleans French*, 89, Louis's parents were Charle and Marie Ougeunarde; Marie-Magdelaine's were Louis and Magdelaine Marreine. Cordier was one of the girls from La Saltpetrière in Paris, arriving on the *Baleine* at Biloxi in the Louisiana Colony in (probably) January 1721. Moreau-DesHarnais, "Baleine Women," 16–17.

181. Randall Ladnier, *The Brides of La Baleine*, revised edition edited by Dale Ladnier (Sarasota, FL: RDL Press, 2017), 57. An excellent family genealogy site is http://www.louisianalineage.com/Guillaumelemoinepage.htm. It includes an image of the original burial record for Cordier.

182. LSM 1762-05-01-01, remarriage of Cordier in Pointe Coupée. Likely Louis Robillard died there rather than in the Illinois Country.

183. None of the children has a baptismal record in the Illinois Country. Marie-Magdelaine, age fourteen, married Antoine Rivière dit Baccané, KM 43-7-9-1, and after his death, René Kiercereau. Kiercereau served many years as *chantre* of the churches in St. Louis and St. Ferdinand, Missouri. He and Marie-Magdelaine were an important couple in the first years of St. Louis. Ekberg and Person, *St. Louis Rising*, 242.

184. Marriage record, *Sacramental Records of the Archdiocese of New Orleans vol. 1, 1718–1750* (New Orleans: Archdiocese of New Orleans, 1987), 224.

185. Married at Pointe Coupée, marriage contract, LSM 1762-09-02-01.

186. KM 24-7-8-1.

187. KM 30:-:-:2.

188. KM 26-12-13-1, marriage contract.

189. Departed France for Louisiana in October, 1717, Conrad, *First Families*, 1:1.

190. KM 30-10-28-1, request for inventory by his widow. Belting, *Kaskaskia Under the French Regime*, 19, he was recalled in 1725, and arrived in New Orleans in 1729.

191. KM 22-11-2-1, note of marriage contract.

192. KPR, image 6.

193. Daughter of Michel Philippe and Marie 8canic8e Rouensa. KM 45-10-10-1, land sale mentions the date of inheritance of the land from Charlotte's late mother.

194. KM 37-7-6-1, marriage contract.

195. KM 37-2-11-1, marriage contract. SAPR, image 92, May 10, 1758, marriage of their daughter Élisabeth.

196. KM 41-7-16-1, marriage contract.

197. KM 45-6-8-2, marriage contract. The couple moved to Ste. Genevieve. See estate of Antoine Huneau, SGA, Estates # 127.

198. KM 25-8-16-1, inventory of Marie 8canic8e Rouensa. On August 18, Pierre Ako and Agnès Philippe renounced their share in ownership of Bibianne, perhaps in order to manumit her, noting her service to their mother. KM 25-8-18-6.

199. KM 26-8-3-2.

200. KM 24-5-6-1 and KM 25-10-1-1.

201. KM 23-6-22-1, contract with Melique. KM 25-7-25-1, partnership.

202. SAPR, image 20, the record has no month or day. It appears to say he was about 60. Conrad, *First Families* 1:22 he arrived in Louisiana in 1719 as a corporal in the brigade of miners. The list of passengers says that four wives and three children of miners accompanied them, but did not name them. KM (42-8-27-1), in 1742 he gave his house, land, slave, and possessions to Louis Marin and his wife Magdelaine Barrois in return for care until his death.

203. KM 25-1-29-1, contract to Deveignets in January 1725. Because of the uncertain date of this census, he is counted in the entry for Devignets, Census, no. 66.

204. The name Bellegarde was associated with two men in the mid-1720s. The first, Nicolas Buffreau de Bellegarde, was a notaire. LSM 1725-02-16-02, he was twenty-four years old in 1725, unlikely to have a wife and children, and none are found in the records. A witness signature of Bellegarde, clear but unrefined, appears in KM 25-8-22-1, and this must be Bougnolle/Boulougne. KM 26-6-5-1, "Bellegarde" was noted as in New Orleans in June, 1726 (as thenotaire Bellegarde was?). The baptism for a daughter of Catherine Bechet, father unknown, was performed by Le Boullenger in November 1719. The child was named Françoise after her godmother, Françoise La Brise. KPR, image 10.

205. KM 27-11-26-1, election of Catherine Bechet as guardian to daughters Jeanne and Marie/Marie-Anne. See notes for Beausejour below. Bellegarde may not have returned from New Orleans; the cause of his death was not given.

206. KM 37-1-14-1 noted Bougnolle, Bechet, and Delessart were all deceased. Bechet had a daughter in the marriage with Delessart.

207. KM 27-11-27-1, marriage contract, also *VC*, 914-916. Most of her property was noted as livestock and slaves.

208. KM 37-1-17-1 for his full name.

209. KM 37-:-:-46 note of marriage contract. KM 41-7-16-1 distinguishes Jacques Philippe from Jacques Phillipe Du Long Pré.

210. Jeanne Boulogne de Louvière signed as godmother to her niece, SAPR, image 55. Division of estate of Marie Anne Boulougne, requested by widower Charles Phlibot, LSM 1773-02-08-01, contains the inventory of Boulougne and Philippe. Her name is consistently misspelled in the Spanish manuscript records (as Bonhomme) in the file but is given as Marie Anne Bellegarde in the French portions.

211. The name Langevin is associated with four men, first, Jacques Martin, KM 22-11-18-1, note of sale. Also Brunsard Langevin and his brother Laurent, possibly deceased in 1722, KM 22-6-18-1, inventory of Laurent. No wife located for either Brunsard brother. René Grude dit Langevin was not yet married to de Blée if this census was compiled in late 1724, but perhaps he was engaged. Grude is mentioned in one of the Bourdon inventories, KM 23-7-1-1.

212. His age in the unusually detailed sacramental marriage record is thirty-four, and parents, François and Mathurine Fretau, and birthplace were named, KPR, image 23. The sacramental marriage was witnessed by the chief of the Tamaroa and Le Chevreuil Blanc "chef français." Thanks to Gail Moreau-DesHarnais for sharing the image of his baptismal record in France.

213. KM 39-4-6-2, note of marriage contract of the widow Langevin.

214. KM 25-4-11-1, marriage contract. The last name Colleret is found in SAPR, image 72. Marie-Barbe Colleret de Blée's name appears in variously jumbled versions. See also SAPR, image 96, marriage of Paul La Brosse and Marie Grude.

215. KM 39-4-6-2, marriage contract Le Vasseur and Widow Langevin.

216. KM (61-6-17-2), registration of marriage contract.

217. The three children are named in KM 39-3-3-3.

218. SAPR, image 72.

219. There are several men with the dit name St. Pierre, but the family numbers and timeline fit Dirousse best. Dirousse was called an innkeeper, *hobergiste*, KM 41-9-25-2. See also Census, no. 78.

220. His name in the transcribed marriage record is Pierre Dirouche and no dit name appears, De Ville, *New Orleans French*, 34. DesHarnais, "Baleine," 3, suggests she may have come from France. Named together in property transactions KM 25-5-7-1 and KM 26-6-19-1.

221. KM 26-6-19-1, the child "Derouches" received a gift from his godfather. Burial KPR, image 45, October 4, 1792, named François's wife with a marginal note "three children."

222. KPR, image 17 of 118.

223. Conrad, *First Families*, 1:212. KM 30-:-:-2, pigs.

224. Joseph Gardon was godfather to a child of Jacques Robar (?) and Marie Conte, baptized in March 1724, "Extrait des registres." KM 25-1-12-1, Gardon was a tenant farmer of Melique in 1725 and 1726. KM 25-2-12-2, transfer of contract for Melique's engagé named Jacques. A Marie Tabouret arrived in Louisiana on the *Mutine* as one of a group of young women sent "by order of the king," in 1719, Conrad, *First Families*, 1: 27. See also Melique, Census, no. 64. No reference found to a child.

225. Camus and Vigneron departed La Rochelle in May 1719 on the *Deux Frères*. Camus was on the list of illicit salt dealers, and Blanche Vigneron's name appeared in a list of women exiled for fraud, Conrad, *First Families*, 1:63, 65. Both Antoine Camus and "Blanche" are named, separately, in the 1721 census of New Orleans, Maduell, *Census Tables*, 20–21. KM 36 -:-:95 as the wife of Louis Thomas. There was a mutual donation in the second marriage.

226. *VC*, 848-50, Camus and Blanche were named in a slander suit brought by Biron's wife in 1725, see Census, no. 24. Blanche received a bequest in the will of Gouin at Fort d'Orléans in gratitude for her care during his illness. This suggests she was also at the fort out on the Missouri, KM 24-9-9-2. Her husband was noted as the drummer in Pradel's company in 1725, *VC*, 850.

227. See Thomas, Census, no. 55. KM 40-8-3-1, seals were placed on the possessions of the communauté at her death.

228. KM 25-9-2-1, Caignarel signed the document, the sale of a sow, with a strong and flowing signature. Full name given in KM 25-3-23-1, mutual donation and power of attorney granted to Caignarel by Poupart dit Rencontre. Conrad, *First Families*, 1:23, listed a soldier Cagnarel who arrived in Louisiana in 1719 on the *Comte de Toulouse* with Renaudière and a number of miners. In 1719, on the ship *St. Louis*, was a deserter or exile named François Poupart dit Rencontre from Beaumont, Maine, France, age thirty-seven, Conrad, *First Families*, 1: 43.

229. KM 24-11-19-1, sale.

230. KM 25-11-19-1, agreement. A Daniel Ollivier, like Cagnarel, was a soldier who arrived in Louisiana on the same ship as Renaudière and the miners, Conrad, *First Families*, 1: 23.

231. KM 22-11-1-1, Capitaine was a purchaser of a blue limbourg capote in an auction. KM 24-6-19-1 a "Capitenne" signed as witness. KM 25-9-12-2 purchase, KM 1722-32:-:-:10 note of a debt for the barn.

232. Parents' names in De Ville, *New Orleans French*, 8, Jacques Bernard and Françoise Plonzard/Plonzin and Jacques Aleaume and Jeanne Segure.

233. One of the *Baleine* women; her age on the ship roster was 18. Moreau-Desharnais, "Baleine Women," 6. Their marriage was witnessed by other Illinois habitants, Pierre Dirouche and Raimond Brosse. KM 26-5-23-1, *VC*, 881, Bernard's wife bore a child out of wedlock during his absence in New Orleans, but whether the child enumerated here is that child cannot be determined. De Ville, *New Orleans French*, 8, noted the marriage of Jacques Bernard called St. Jacques and Denise "Alio" on June 22, 1721. She signed her name "Alihome." Bernard remarried in June 1730 in New Orleans. His deceased wife's name was given in that record as "Lorine Eliaume." De Ville, *New Orleans French*, 5, the widow in his second marriage remarried in 1732.

234. There is no surname Pierre in Kaskaskia manuscripts from this time, and St. Pierre appears just above. KM 26-5-23-1, Pierre Hullin was the alleged father of the child with the wife of Bernard dit St. Jacques. KM 26-2-4-1, Hullin was granted land by Boisbriant in 1724. KM 26-11-24-1, he became a tenant of Melique. Another Pierre was Marguerite's third husband (see text).

235. KM 31-4-7-1 names both men in a transaction, a mutual donation, in 1731. Their names also appear together as owners of pigs, KM 30:-:-:2. Le Brun could sign his name, roughly; Gouverneur could not.

236. KM 25-11-25-1, first appearance of his name was at an auction in 1725.

237. Conrad, *First Families*, 1:64, Jeanne L'Enfant was a passenger on the *Deux Frères*, departing France on August 16, 1719. She was listed as "exiled for fraud." Antoine Camus and Blanche Vigneron (Census, no. 43) were on the same ship.

238. KM 38-11-24-1, marriage contract with the soldier Pajot names her parents Jean and Jeanne Fansfort, and her first husband, Poujart dit Bellehumeur.

239. See Lacroix, Census, no.3. L'Enfant's two previous husbands were named in her marriage contract to Pajot.

240. Assigning this entry to Louis Marin de la Malgue (as others have done) is problematic. Marin's first known wife in the Illinois Country, Françoise "Missouri," was still married to her first husband DuBois in 1724 and 1725. Moreover, Françoise had two children with DuBois, and both survived into her second marriage with Marin, so enumerating just one child would be an error. Louis Marin's first appearance in local notarial records was in 1730, a signature on the inventory of the deceased du Tisné, KM 30-5-17-1.

241. KM 26-2-16-1.

242. Conrad, *First Families*, 1:53.

243. KM 33-1-2-1 and 33-4-21-1, a sale by the couple and its annulment.

244. SAPR, image 119, Ambroise, died April 3, int. April 5; image 121, Madame Sansregret, day of December is unclear, funeral at 10 a.m.

245. SAPR, image 49. He was about sixty years old at death. KM 33-11-1-1, declaration from his deathbed about active and passive debts. Apparently, he recovered.

246. Moreau-DesHarnais, "Baleine Women," 40, marriage recorded in New Orleans, also De Ville, *New Orleans French*, 95. Her name in the marriage record was Anne Rolais (groom Antoine Sorel). Rolais's name was not on the list of *Baleine* passengers. KM 33-12-8-1, the minor daughters of Sorel and his deceased wife are named.

247. KM 35-11-14-1, marriage contract.

248. KM 40-7-30-1, marriage contract. Groom was born in France.

249. SAPR, image 5.

250. SAPR, image 71. The couple moved to St. Louis, Ekberg and Person, *St. Louis Rising*, 243.

251. SAPR, image 42, baptism of their son Martin.

252. KM 20-8-18-1 and KM 22-9-23-1, a Le Conte purchased items in estate auctions. KM 25-6-6-1, in June 1725 Catherine Bechet, wife of Bellegarde, who was at New Orleans, sold land she had acquired from Beausejour. She declared that she could not sign her name. KM 26-6-5-1,

the next year Beausejour sold her his house and lot, and four young pigs for 700 livres of farine. Her husband was noted as still at New Orleans.

253. KM 24-11-19-1, a Thomas was identified as a soldier in 1724, and Louis Thomas appears in records through 1749. Conrad, *First Families*,1:31, notes a soldier, Louis Thomas, who left France in 1719 on the *Mutine*, the same ship that carried some of the young women from La Rochelle who married and settled in the Illinois Country. By 1736 he was married to Blanche Vigneron (Census, no. 43) (KM 36-:-:95), whom he was accused—and, it seems, acquitted—of beating to death in 1740. He signed a statement of fees and debts after the death of his wife, KM 40-9-24-1, and was a witness to a marriage contract in 1749 (KM 49-4-28-1).

254. KM 24-7-8-1 identifies his name and dit name. Bellerose did not marry, and he made several old-age agreements and wills. KM 40-9-24-1, his last signature appeared in September 1740.

255. There were two men with the dit name Normand, but Guillaume is present in pre-1726 records. KM 33-4-11-1, Denis Fosse, dit Normand, could sign his name, which also distinguishes the two men. Louis Normand dit La Brière first appeared in records beginning in the 1730s and should not be considered for this entry.

256. KM 24-7-8-1, identified by his mark, also *VC*, 344-45. KM 26-9-27-1, Le Normand occupied the lot next to Gossiau. KM 26-9-30-1, deposition provides his birthplace and parents. Havre de Grace was an early name for the French city of Le Havre.

257. Ladnier, *The Brides of La Baleine*, 57. See http://www.louisianalineage.com/Guillaumelemoinepage.htm for an image of the original burial record.

258. KM 22-4-28-1, note of marriage contract. A family, LeDoux dit La Treille, in Charlesbourg, near Quebec, had a daughter Marie-Thérèse, born June 11, 1694, parents Nicolas and Marie-Anne Renard. Baptism at http://www.ancestry.com Québec, Canada, Vital and Church Records (Drouin Collection), 1621-1968, C, Charlesbourg, ALL, 1679–1794, image 94 of 1120. Le Doux must have been a widow with a son when Lemoine married her, but no record could be found to discover the name of her first husband, François's father to confirm this baptism as Lemoine's wife. KM 23-5-17-1, Thérèse died before May 17, 1723. About to depart for New Orleans (à la mer), Lemoine donated his property to her son François should he not return to the Illinois Country. He was counted in New Orleans on the 1726 census, with a wife and child, on rue Royale.

259. De Ville, *New Orleans French*, 63, marriage record transcription.

260. Winston De Ville, *First Settlers of Point Coupée* (New Orleans: Polyanthos, 1974), 27–28, recorded the marriage of Guillaume Lemoine called le Normand, parish of Notre Dame, diocese of Rouen, widower of Marie L'este (Saumerine), son of Jacques Lemoine and Jeanne Madre, August 21, 1742, to Marie (torn) native of St. Erbilon in Bretagne daughter of Jean Gaynard and Françoise(?).

261. Marriage contract, LSM 1762-05-01-01.

262. Jetté, 1067, son of Pierre and Catherine Varin. Jetté noted Pierre as the brother of Louis Tessier, whose widow Catherine 8abanakic8e married Jean-Baptiste Lalande (Census, no. 90). Contract to the west, 1693 and 1694.

263. KM 22-12-27-1, Pierre Texier is first identifiable in an association agreement with Antoine Coussot, dissolved after Texier's death, KM 31-4-6-1, in a request by the widow for an inventory. There were several Texier dit Lavigne men, and Belting, *Kaskaskia Under the French Regime*, laid out the possibilities in her presentation of the 1752 census. Jean-Baptiste Texier dit Lavigne married, possibly for the first time, in 1726, KM 26-5-18-1. Pierre seemed more likely for this entry.

264. KM 41-1-4-1, death date in inventory; KM 39-6-20-1, marriage contract with Benetôt.

265. KM 75-3-6-1, his widow and her new husband purchased a property from Antoine Tessier dit Lavigne, son of Jean-Baptiste and Marianne Milleret.

266. KM 51-1-11-1, note of marriage contract.

267. KM 41-1-4-1, these three minor children were named in the inventory after Gaudié died.

268. Baptism at http://www.ancestry.com Québec, Canada, Vital and Church Records (Drouin Collection), 1621–1968, Q, Québec, Notre-Dame (baptêmes 1621–1679), 1667–1679, image 122 of 148, parents Hubert and Marie Vié. Also Jetté, 1051. KM 23-11-25-1, first mentioned promising to build a house.

269. KPR, image 7. 1720 was the date of La Pointe's remarriage.

270. Baptismal record, KPR, image 7.

271. SAPR, image 41.

272. KM 31-4-3-1, marriage contract. Her father was identified as an officer of the militia.

273. KPR, image 10.

274. KPR, image 19, buried near the church.

275. KM 25-9-10-2, named in a September 1725 lease of a farm, buildings, crops, and livestock, plus Ladrieu, by La Pointe to Pichard.

276. Baptism at http://www.ancestry.com Québec, Canada, Vital and Church Records (Drouin Collection), 1621–1968, V, Varennes, 1693–1696, image 7 of 28. KM 24-5-2-3, grant to Hébert the younger 3 x 50 at Fort de Chartres. KM 28-11-27-1, marriage contract with the Widow Chaput (Census, no. 13), named his parents, Ignace and Marguerite St. Michel, and birthplace. Ignace Hébert was for several decades militia captain at Fort de Chartres. His son-in-law Jean-Baptiste Martigny was militia captain at St. Louis. Ekberg and Person, *St. Louis Rising*, especially 59–61.

277. Marguerite Fafard dite Couc, Turpin's wife, whom he was accused of abusing, did not live in the Illinois Country. See Moreau-DesHarnais and Wolford Sheppard, *Détroit* 1: 267.

278. Baptism at http://www.ancestry.com Québec, Canada, Vital and Church Records (Drouin Collection), 1621–1968, M, Montréal, Basilique Notre–Dame, 1681–1694, image 56 of 229.

279. KM 24-9-10-1, present in 1724, election of guardian for child of Louis Turpin and deceased wife Marie Colon. Jean-Baptiste the father was interred August 16, 1731, in New Orleans, Suzanne Boivin Sommerville, *Le Détroit du Lac Érié*, 1701–1710, 2:168 n 14. A Jacques Turpain was interred in Kaskaskia in 1723, KPR, image 20. Jetté, 1101-02, Jean-Baptiste, Louis (Census, no. 72), and Jacques (deceased before this census) were brothers, all sons of Alexandre Turpin and Marie-Charlotte Beauvais.

280. Marriage record, see Moreau-DesHarnais and Wolford Sheppard, *Détroit* 1:119. Marguerite's parents were Jean Fafard and Marguerite Couc.

281. Moreau-DesHarnais and Wolford Sheppard, *Détroit* 1: 267-68. An excellent account of the family.

282. KM 37-2-3-1, died in the Chickasaw campaign that killed Pierre St. Ange and Vincennes.

283. KM 35-1-15-1, marriage of Marie, natural daughter of Jean-Baptiste Turpin and Marie-Jeanne, of Mobile.

284. ANOM, D² D, 10, contains the timeline by Beaubois, "Noms des Pères Jesuites qui sont à la Louizianee depuis 1718 jusqu'en 1725," written in Paris in 1725, and "État des Prêtres Missionaires," dated 1724. These two records, plus the local sacramental records, provided the information for this entry. Also useful is Mary Borgias Palm, *The Jesuit Missions of the Illinois Country, 1673–1763* (Cleveland, OH: n.p., 1931), 48–59. Kereben was present at Fort de Chartres, KM 23-7-20-1. See Sharon K. Person, "A Jesuit Priest in Eighteenth-Century Illinois: Encounters with Illinois Chiefs, Native Lands, and French Customs," unpublished manuscript.

285. KM 25-5-15-1, absent for several months at the Native village of Pimitéoui (present-day Peoria, IL).

286. *VC*, 5 and SAPR, image 3, in September 1721 he performed the baptism of Marie Metivier, daughter of Henri and Marguerite Clerjon (Census, no. 78). He noted himself as Superior of the Illinois Missions.

287. "État des Prêtres;" SAPR, image 4, September 1721, baptism, Beaubois identified himself as curé of the parish. In 1720 he referred to himself as *aumonier* (chaplain) of the troops (KPR, image 11) and "curé de la paroisse de la Conception," image 12. His last (legible) parish record at Kaskaskia in this time period was a burial in July 1724, KPR, image 21. By Christmas Le Boullenger was officiating at burials.

288. KPR, image 21, November 10, buried in the church under the second bench *du milieu* (in the middle).

289. Thuillier Devegnois, Census, no. 66.

290. Ekberg and Person, *St. Louis Rising*, 16, 25; "État des Prêtres."

291. "État des Prêtres." In January 1725, Thaumur signed on to a letter written by Le Boullenger and Kereben to protest the recent peace made by de Lignery at La Baye (Green Bay) between the Foxes and the northern lake Nations. *Wisconsin Historical Collections*, XVI, 450-464. A Reverend (Antoine) Chabot, mentioned in KM 25-1-1-2, was curate of a parish Ste. Anne in Canada, not in Illinois. His 1728 will is at https://numerique.banq.qc.ca/patrimoine/details/52327/3354272.

292. KPR, image 22, marriage May 2, 1724.

293. SAPR, image 6, July 9, 1726, Angélique, daughter of Louis and Thérèse, slaves of the Jesuits.

294. "Extrait des registres."

295. KPR, image 17 of 118, witness at marriage of slaves in 1730.

296. Birthplace and birth date confirmed by Girardot family biographer Charlotte Slinkard, personal correspondence, October 9, 2018.

297. KM 23-2-23-3 notes Girardot as commandant. KM 30-7-17-1, inventory of du Tisné, Girardot was deceased.

298. KM 22-11-9-1, note of marriage contract. LSM 1747-05-16-02, copy of the original contract. Jetté, 501, for her parents, Jacques and Michelle Chauvin. While traveling to the Illinois Country in 1722, her mother, two sisters, and brother perished in an Indian attack near the juncture of the Ohio and Mississippi; her father, another brother and a slave were taken captive. KPR, image 18. LSM 1744-02-17-02, procuration in New Orleans of Marie-Catherine Neveu (wife of Jacques Hubert de Bellair), related to parents' estate in Canada. Her parents, Jacques Neveu and Michelle Chauvin, died "en montant aux Illinois."

299. Baptism at http://www.ancestry.com Québec, Canada, Vital and Church Records (Drouin Collection), 1621–1968, R, Repentigny, 1679-1746 (transcript), image 44 of 205.

300. KM 45-7-28-2 refers to her as deceased.

301. Louis du Tisné was baptized April 29, 1733, KPR, image 8. Du Tisné, officer, his wife and three children appear in the 1732 census. Du Tisné was killed alongside Pierre St. Ange and François Bissot de Vincennes, husband of Marie Du Long Pré, in 1736, at the hands of Chickasaw warriors.

302. KM 41-6-5-1, marriage contract of de la Gautrais and Neveu identifies her as the widow of Louis du Tisné and Girardot.

303. KPR, image 21. The original record is very faded, and it is possible that it does not say age five years, as given in F-B 2:189.

304. "Extrait des registres."

305. SAPR, image 6, baptismal record. Perhaps Pierre was the Girardot who reported on the Illinois Country losses at Belle Famille to Macarty at Fort de Chartres (Macarty to Kerlérec, August 30, 1759, ANOM C^{13A} 41:103). Girardeau became Justice of the Peace in St. Philippe under the British. SAPR, image 99, marriage of Pierre Girardot and Marie-Madeleine Loisel, 1761. In the marriage record Girardot was noted as ensign of the troops.

306. "Extrait des registres."

307. Melique arrived in Louisiana in 1718, Conrad, *First Families*, 1:19. KM 21-6-29-1, inventory of Pierre Roi, Melique owed him a pig; KM 40-3-24-1 refers to the inventory at his death in 1727. The child is likely Melique's natural daughter, Françoise, also KM 40-3-24-1.

308. *VC*, 831 testimony for names of parents, Pierre and Anne de Matigny, age, and birthplace. Thanks to Helen Valle Crist, descendant of Melique, for sharing her file on her ancestor.

309. Belting, *Kaskaskia Under the French Regime*, 33, Census, no. 30. ANOM, C^{13A}10:168, 226–27.

310. Françoise gave this as her mother's name in her marriage contract, see below.

311. Conrad, *First Families*, 2:154, Françoise Melique was one of the orphans at the Ursuline convent in New Orleans in 1731, age ten. KM 40-3-24-1, Sionneau managed the plantation after Melique's death. Her marriage contract to Siono (Sionneau) LSM 1736-06-04-01. In 1736, the Provincial council ruled that she should receive the goods left by Melique, KM 36-7-30-1.

312. KM 22-12-8-1, a relationship between Gardon and Melique began in 1722, note of debt. KM 25-1-13-1, inventory of farm implements lent to Gardon.

313. Baptism at http://www.ancestry.com Québec, Canada, Vital and Church Records (Drouin Collection), 1621–1968, M, Montréal, Basilique Notre-Dame 1695–1699, image 5 of 263. Record notes he was born at 7 p.m., and his baptismal date fell on a Sunday. His father Pierre was a tailor, mother Marie Forestier. Jetté, 102, mother's name Marie-Marthe Forcier.

314. KM 38-2-11-1, for approximate death date, inventory of the papers of the late Billeron. Parents in De Ville, *New Orleans French*, 9. An early signature, KM 23-6-2-2 Leonard Lafatigue, witness, signed L. Billeron.

315. Marie-Claire Catoire was one of the women of the *Baleine*. Moreau-DesHarnais, "Baleine Women," 16. Also De Ville, *New Orleans French*, 9, for names of parents of Marie-Claire, Pierre and Anne Potin.

316. On her life and death, see Carl J. Ekberg, "A Parisian Woman in Colonial Ste. Genevieve." *Missouri Historical Review* 144:2 (January 2020): 105-120; SGA, Estates #30.

317. KPR, image 25 of 118, sacramental marriage January 12. KM 58-3-29-1, husband and wife in land sale.

318. KM 51-1-11-2, note of marriage contract. KPR, image 17 of 118, marriage January 12. She was the daughter of Pierre Aubuchon and Marie Brunet.

319. KM 48-1-6-1, marriage contract. For the lives of Marie-Claire Catoire and the Billeron children, especially Marianne, see Carl J. Ekberg, *François Vallé and His World* (Columbia: University of Missouri Press, 2002).:

320. All birth years calculated from ages in KM 40-5-12-1, nomination of guardians after Billeron's death.

321. There was a Jean-Baptiste Devignes dit Provencal, *VC*, 355, dated February 16, 1726, who seems to have been a single man.

322. KM 40-12-3-1 for his full name. Their marriage contract, noted KM 21-11-17-1, places them in the Illinois Country. Baptism at http://www.ancestry.com Québec, Canada, Vital and Church Records (Drouin Collection) 1621–1968, M, Montréal, Basilique Notre-Dame, 1680–1689 (copie textuelle), image 258 of 286, parents Jacques and Jeanne Bernard. Also, Jetté, 1081. Contract signed in Montreal to travel to Lake Superior, July 1, 1719, image online at www.familysearch.org, Search, Catalog, Author, Pierre Raimbault, 1697–1727, image 165.

323. KM 48-1-4-1, division of estate of Nicolas Thuilliers Devegnois.

324. LSM 1745-02-16-01 is a copy of the original 1721 marriage contract to Devegnois. He was thirty, she was twenty-two. Her first husband Pierre Chabot (to whom Dorothée was the second wife) was interred August 7, 1721, age sixty, KPR, image 18. In 1770 Dorothée was still alive, noted in marriage contract of her daughter Marie-Rose, KM 70-5-26-1.

325. Married July 15, 1756, KPR, image 24 of 118. Dorothée was noted as the widow of Nicolas "Desvignets." Rotisseur was buried June 27, 1762, SAPR, image 125. His burial record noted in the margin "bonhomme" and that he was royal interpreter.

326. Baptism, KPR, image 14. LSM 1745-02-16-01, marriage contract mentions Pierre Chabot as the son of Chabot and Mercier, as do several additional documents. Pierre Chabot was named as a half-brother (*frère uterin*) in the marriage contract of Françoise (see below). In 1739, Pierre Chabot, voyageur of the Illinois, living with Devegnois, purchased a Black slave

from the Company of the Indies. An earlier child of the elder Chabot, also named Pierre, was born in 1709 to a Native wife, KPR, image 6.

327. Marie-Claire Catoire was his godmother. "Extrait des registres."

328. Husband's birthplace of Detroit and siblings' names in the marriage contract, KM 47-1-7-1.

329. KPR, image 16 of 118, 1750 marriage of Jacques Seguin and Marie-Rose "Tuillier."

330. KM 70-5-26-1.

331. *VC*,12 and SAPR, image 7.

332. KPR, marriage, image 30 of 118, January 17, 1761.

333. KM 64-1-17-1, note of marriage contract. Seguin's mother, Françoise, was a Native woman. Sacramental marriage, KPR, image 33 of 118.

334. F-B 2:22 marriage to Legras, militia colonel and commandant of Vincennes post, July 18, 1779.

335. KPR, image 36 of 118, Antoine Bienvenu, widower of Élisabeth Des Vignets (Thuillier/Devegnois) married Marie-Louise Danis, February 2, 1766, at Kaskaskia.

336. Mercier brought two enslaved persons, possibly a mother and female child (une grande et une petite), from the property of Chabot into her new marriage with Devegnois. LSM 1745-02-16-01.

337. Sold to Nicolas Desvignets by Antoine "Bled" dit La Plume (Census, no. 37), KM 25-1-29-1

338. Slaves of Devegnois married in March 1728, KPR, image 26.

339. KPR, image 26, double marriage with Jean-Baptiste and Marie. Double marriages were not unusual among all the population.

340. KM 25-1-24-1.

341. KM 25-1-1-2 and 25-1-24-1. KPR, image 17 of 118, marriage of Pierre dit Senegal and Charlotte dite Manon in 1750, slaves of the widow and children of Desvignets. Interesting record, with marriage witnessed by slaves including Baxé, who made his mark in the register, and Michel, slave of the Jesuits.

342. KM 22-5-10-4, land grant to Jacques Lalande.

343. http://www.ancestry.com Québec, Canada, Vital and Church Records (Drouin Collection), 1621–1968, M, Montréal, Basilique-Notre-Dame 1681–1694, image 124 of 229, son of François Guillemot and Magdelaine Du Pont. See also Census, nos. 90 and 28 for other Lalande entries.

344. KM 37-3-6-1, receipt by the Widow Lalande.

345. KM 44-1-9-1, inventory. A branch of the Cardinal family present in mid-eighteenth-century Detroit used the dit name Testio. Gail Moreau-DesHarnais, "Edward Cicotte Ledger 1749-1752 Containing Accounts of French Settlers at Detroit." *Michigan's Habitant Heritage* 23, no. 3 (July 2008): 152. Tetio was entrusted to be the co-guardian of her children with Lalande when she remarried to Duchouquette. The 1740 estate division makes clear that there was no marriage contract between Tetio and Lalande, KM 40-1-19-1.

346. KM 39-1-27-4, inscription of donation, marriage date January 19, 1739.

347. KPR, image 7.

348. KPR, image 7.

349. KPR, image 7.

350. KPR, image 16. The priest Beaubois noted that Étienne was older (*l'aisne*) than his twin.

351. KPR, image 9 of 118, June 1, 1744.

352. KPR, image 16.

353. KM 40-1-19-1, division of the estate of Jacques Lalande among the widow and children included the deceased Gabriel.

354. KM 40-1-19-1, inventory and partition.

355. KM 25-4-30-1, Étienne Philippe Du Long Pré bought land at Kaskaskia from Étienne Hébert.

356. Jetté, 408, used a 1681 census for the approximate birthdates of this person he called Joseph Étienne dit Philippe, and his brother Michel (see Census, no. 77. KM 34-9-17-1), election of guardian for Jacques; KM 34-9-17-2, note of inventory of the community of Étienne Philippe.

357. "Little Wolf Woman" Michael McCafferty, email May 6, 2018.

358. KM 40-1-22-2, division of estate of Marie Ma8e8ensic8e.

359. KM 35-5-23-1, marriage contract. The marriage contract with Dulude was witnessed by Charles-Daniel Richard and his wife, Caterine Jouachine, who was the daughter of an Illinois chief. (See Richard, Census, no. 8.)

360. KPR, image 7.

361. KM 30-1-23-1, marriage contract. Vinsenne's signature appears on KM 27-10-20-1, marriage contract of Joseph Lorrain and Marie-Josèphe Philippe, daughter of Michel Philippe and Marie 8canic8e Rouensa, relatives of the Du Long Pré family. Vinsenne, Pierre St. Ange, husband of Marie-Rose Texier, Census, no. 90, and Louis du Tisné, see Census, no. 63, died together at the hands of Chickasaw warriors in 1736. Ekberg and Person, *St. Louis Rising*, 30-31.

362. KPR, image 7. Father Steph (Étienne) Philippe, mother Marie Ch8pirechinga. An unnamed son, six days old, was buried July 6, 1721, KPR, image 17.

363. KM 38:-:-:21, reference to the Widow Carrière.

364. Marriage record at http://www.ancestry.com Québec, Canada, Vital and Church Records (Drouin Collection), 1621–1968, L, Lachine, Sts-Anges-Gardiens, 1676–1756, image 128 of 362, gives age of Carrière as about thirty-two, voyageur of Ville-Marie, parents André and Cécile Janot; of Quesnel, age about eighteen, Olivier and Catherine Prudonne. Also Jetté, 204. On June 10, 1718, Antoine Carrière signed a contract to trade with the Ottawas, the merchandise guaranteed with his widowed mother's house on rue St. Paul in Montreal. The debt was paid. The couple was in Kaskaskia in April 1719, when Madelaine stood as the godmother to Paul Texier, son of Catherine 8abanakic8e (Census, no. 90).

365. KM (41-2-20-1), registration and inscription of donation to her second husband.

366. SAPR, image 4. His godfather was Dominique Quesnel, his mother's brother (see marriage record above). Dominique Quesnel was not enumerated elsewhere in this census; perhaps he was counted as an engagé here.

367. A twin, "Extrait des registres." The second child was Marie-Madeleine, interred the 19th of ? 1723. Burial seems to say end of November, age eight days. KPR, image 20. Celeste-Thérèse was enfranchised at age fifteen, KM 39-8-11-2.

368. KM 40-3-19-1, marriage contract.

369. KPR, image 20.

370. KPR, image 15.

371. SAPR, image 8 and *VC*, 15. In 1729, three married slave couples were noted as owned by Carrière: Jacques and Marguerite, married April 19, 1729; Joseph and Marie, married same date; and Pierre and Hélène married June 7, 1729, all three marriages KPR, image 27.

372. See also Census nos. 83 and 103.

373. No original record in Lachine to match this date of Jetté, 937, could be found. Though the two Pottiers were locally referred to as "the older" and "the younger," it seems Jean-Baptiste and Guillaume (Census, no. 85), were not brothers. Guillaume's parents married in 1688, and this might be the reason.

374. Both Pottier and La Brise were deceased by 1735. KM 35-4-27-1, petition of Jean-Baptiste to be declared of age.

375. KPR, image 7.

376. SAPR, image 43, age around thirty-one.

377. KPR, image 7.

378. KM 37-8-13-1, note of marriage contract.

379. Baptism, KPR, image 7 and 9.

380. KM 40-11-26-1, Moreau petitioned to sell property of his late wife.

381. KM 36-3-19-1, marriage contract.

382. KPR, image 14. Godfather was Jacques Bourdon.

383. KPR, image 20, age 2½ years.

384. SAPR, image 45.

385. ibid. Catherine died the day after her husband died in 1746. She was the daughter of de Lessart and Catherine Bechet.

386. KM 40-10-2-1.

387. KM 47-9-16-1, petition by guardian Millet for a new guardian for Louis. See also KM 47-9-24-1, statement of accounts.

388. SAPR, image 80.

389. SAPR, image 45, age about twenty. Three family members died within three days.

390. More than one man used the dit name de Laurie/Deslauriers. The one suggested by the records is Pierre Du Roy dit Deslauriers.

391. Jetté, 343, the 1681 census of Beaupré showed an 18-year-old Pierre Deslauriers, perhaps too old to be the same man. KM 22-9-23-1 a Deslauriers participated in an auction. KM 26-6-7-2, guarantee of payment for one Fouillard. KM 37-:-1, Pierre Du Roi was witness at the marriage of Jean-Baptiste Giard (whose mother was a Deslauriers) and Marianne Fouillard, his god-daughter. Marianne was the daughter of Jacques Fouilliard and Marianne Natchitoches, a

Native woman, married in 1724, KPR, image 23. KM 28-2-22-1, Deslauriers made a donation to his goddaughter Marianne Fouilliard.

392. Thomas was mentioned in several documents, beginning with 37-5-4-1, in which Deslauriers made a donation of 600 livres and promised to pay him 200 livres a year for good service. The agreement was annulled, KM 42-1-28-2. KM 43-4-30-1 suggests Thomas's mother may have been a Native woman—Deslauriers sold a lot in Kaskaskia which he acquired without title from the Natives who had lived there. A Thomas born to an Indian slave woman named Françoise Chonicoue (father unknown) was baptized in December 1720, KPR, image 13. Thomas was not a common name in early Kaskaskia, but no convincing connection was found between this baptismal record and Deslauriers's son.

393. See also Census, no. 61. There were several brothers Turpin: Joseph, Jean-Baptiste, Louis, and Jacques, estate inventory noted in KM 23-7-4-1.

394. http://www.ancestry.com Québec, Canada, Vital and Church Records (Drouin Collection), 1621–1968, M, Montréal, Basilique Notre-Dame, 1681–1694, image 198 of 229, son of Alexandre and Charlotte Beauvais.

395. KM 51-8-27-1, will. KM 51-10-13-1, placing of seals after his death.

396. KPR, image 20, age 22. KM 24-9-10-1 election of guardian for child of late Marie Colon and husband Louis Turpin. The father was elected guardian and Jean-Baptiste Turpin, uncle of the child, was deputy guardian.

397. Baptism, KPR, image 12; burial, image 19.

398. "Extrait des registres."

399. KPR, image 21.

400. KPR, image 23, sacramental marriage.

401. KM 47-1-11-1, inventory of community property, includes names and ages of her children with Turpin. Turpin married once more, KM 51-3-20-3.

402. KPR, image 7.

403. KM 34-4-28-1, note of marriage contract; a copy of the contract can be found in her estate papers, online at LSM 1747-06-10-01.

404. KPR, image 10.

405. "Extrait des registres."

406. KM 45-6-28-4, marriage contract.

407. KPR, image 8.

408. KPR, image 31 of 118.

409. SAPR, image 8, also *VC*, 13. KM 24-9-21-1 sale of effects of the (Charles) Danis estate.

410. SAPR, image 8, also *VC*, 14.

411. KPR, image 6.

412. Spelling from "Extrait des registres."

413. KPR, image 21, page torn and date faded.

414. "Extrait des registres." Godfather was Pierre Collet, godmother Dorothée Michiper8e.

415. KPR, burial, image 43.

416. KM 39-5-25-2, both named in a property sale.

417. "Extrait des registres."

418. See text Part I.

419. Jetté, 265, a Pierre Collet was born ca. 1676 per the census of 1681, and traveled west on a contract, June 15, 1706. Additional contract dated May 20, 1708, to Fort Pontchartrain on Lake Erie, image at http://www.familysearch.org, Catalog, Author, Adhémar, Antoine, 1668–1714, image 315 of 3055. KM 45-5-13-2. In 1722, Collet received a land grant of two arpents in the Kaskaskia prairie from Boisbriant. Collet was the godfather of Marie-Louise Lacourse, KM 44-10-31-1.

420. Baptism at http://www.ancestry.com Québec, Canada, Vital and Church Records (Drouin Collection), 1621–1968, Q, Québec, Notre-Dame, 1679–1690, image 256 of 298, son of Henry and Françoise Crêste. Jetté, 320, mother's name Crête, contract to the west, September 25, 1710, online image at http://www.familysearch.org, Catalog, Author, Adhémar, Antoine, 1668–1714, image 2214, contract Montreal to Fort Pontchartrain.

421. KM 23-10-25-1 indicates origin in Canada. KM 29-6-11-1, Widow Delaunay remarried.

422. KM 23-1-16-1, marriage contract gives parents and birthplaces; groom's parents were Henry and Françoise Crespe; bride's were Jean Brunet dit Bourbonnois and Élisabeth Deshayes.

423. KM 29-6-11-1, marriage contract.

424. SGA, Estates #79.

425. "Extrait des registres."

426. SGA, Estates #4. Belting, *Kaskaskia Under the French Regime*, 119, the couple was one of the earliest to settle in Ste. Genevieve, appearing on the 1752 census.

427. *VC*, 11. Eight days old at his death, KPR, image 21.

428. KM 29-6-11-1, Élisabeth Brunet's marriage contract with Deguire gives names and ages of children, including a two-year-old Joseph.

429. Noted as six months old in KM 29-6-11-1.

430. The nephew or engagés could have been a Lamy (François or Pierre, see KM 26-2-26-1), or a Rivard, see KM 43-1-6-1.

431. De Ville, *New Orleans French*, 57. The parents' names, Joseph Lamy and Madeleine Marie are from the sacramental marriage record. Name in baptismal index, http://www.ancestry.com Québec, Canada, Vital and Church Records (Drouin Collection), 1621–1968, S, Sorel, Not Stated, image 5 of 94. Jetté, 642, identified Lamy's parents as Joseph-Isaac and Marie-Madelaine Chevrainville, and noted a contract to travel west dated September 6, 1708, image at http://www.familysearch.org, Catalog, Author, Adhémar, Antoine, 1668–1714, image 588 of 3055. The contract to Fort Pontchartrain gave his name and birthplace.

432. KPR, image 21. F-B transcribed this record in error—there was no Lavigne killed with Lamy—the priest instead recorded the wife's name, Rivard Lavigne. Death date also stated, along with children's (Joseph and Marie-Françoise Charlotte) ages, in guardian election, KM 26-2-26-1.

433. The sacramental marriage record named her father, Antoine Rivart dit Lavigne. St. Louis Cathedral marriages 1720–1730, transcription, record no. 123. A number of women signed the original marriage record as witnesses.

434. Marriage contract of Rivart and La Source KM 26-2-26-2, and KPR, image 24. The marriage record was signed by Pierre and François Lamy.

435. "Extrait des registres."

436. KM 43-2-10-1, marriage contract.

437. "Extrait des registres." A slave of Paul Lamy, given the name Joseph, was baptized December 18, 1719, son of Paniasic8e, a Native slave woman, KPR, image 10.

438. Philippe and Rouensa had six children together, and her two sons by her first marriage to Aco were possibly included here. By the time of this census Agnès had already married.

439. First appearance in the Illinois Country in 1704, KPR, image 6. See the note above on baptismal information for his brother, Census, no. 68. Birth year estimate for Michel based on the 1681 census, Jetté, 408. A Michel Philippe signed a contract in Montreal to travel to Michilimackinac in September, 1693, online image at http://www.familysearch.org, Catalog, Author, Adhémar, Antoine, 1668–1714, 3065, and 66.

440. KM 46-1-6-1, placing of seals, usually done the day of or very soon after a person's death. Philippe was one of the most prominent men of early Kaskaskia. An early mark (he could not write) on a document was added in September 1721 (the inventory of Louis Texier and Catherine 8abanakic8e). Philippe did not remarry after Marie's death.

441. See Carl J. Ekberg and Anton J. Pregaldin, "Marie Rouensa-8cate8a and the Foundations of French Illinois." *Illinois Historical Journal* 84, no. 3 (Autumn 1991): 146-60. Burial record, KPR, image 21. She was buried in the church, under her bench.

442. KPR, image 5. His godmother was his grandmother, Marie-Jeanne. In 1739, Pierre Ako was noted as living in the Kaskaskia Indian village (*dem! ordnairement au village sauvage des Cas*), KM 39-2-7-1.

443. KPR, image 6.

444. KM 39-2-7-1, sale of land from the estate of Michel Ako.

445. KPR, image 6.

446. Not to be confused with Jacques Philippe Du Long Pré, son of Étienne and brother to the wife of Vincennes. Jacques Du Long Pré's uncle, Michel Philippe, was his guardian. KM 25-8-18-1, Joseph Delaunay was deputy guardian to all the minor children of Philippe and Rouensa. KM 47-2-6-2, election of curateur for Marie Boulougne, widow of Jacques Philippe.

447. Note of marriage contract, KM 37:-:-:46. See Census, no. 38, Bellegarde.

448. KPR, image 6.

449. KM 22-11-2-1, note of marriage contract. See Census, no. 35, Chassin.

450. KM 44-5-29-1, remarriage of her widower, René Roy.

451. KPR, image 6.

452. SAPR, image 48.

453. KM 27-2-11-2, marriage contract. KPR, image 25, sacramental marriage the next day.

454. KM 35-11-21-1, marriage contract of the widow of Estienne Hébert and Duclos.

455. KPR, image 7.

456. KM 27-10-20-1, translated in *VC*, 911–914. KPR, image 25, same day as contract.

457. KPR, image 7. Mentioned as a voyageur as late as 1748, see KM 48-1-22-1.

458. KPR, image 9. Ignace appeared among many relatives mentioned in the marriage contract of Madeleine Chassin, daughter of Agnès, KM 41-7-16-1.

459. "Extrait des registres."

460. "Extrait des registres."

461. Named in the inventory of the estate after Rouensa's death, KM 25-8-16-1.

462. This may be the same Native slave whose age was fourteen or fifteen (see Census, no. 35).

463. "Extrait des registres" for origins of Chauveau. Henri Metivier was interred February 13, 1723, age ca. thirty-five, KPR, image 19. Marguerite Clerjon was interred after January 18, 1726 (the date of the record just above, though the date on her record is obscured, possibly January 25). KPR, image 21. KM 24-1-24-1, La Chauvetot was a witness at the marriage of Mathurin Chaput and Hélène Danis. KM 24-6-18-1 sale by St. Pierre La Chauveau to Caillou.

464. KPR, image 12. Henri was born and provisionally baptized along the way from the Gulf to Kaskaskia, and brought to the priest when they arrived.

465. SAPR, image 3, and *VC*, 5.

466. Others with the dit name La Sonde/Lasonde were Nicolas Pierrot, and in the 1730s, Cadron. In 1722, a land grant to La "Branche" was located next to La Sonde. KM 22-5-10-8, Kaskaskia Land Book B, 26.

467. KM 68-9-29-1, mentions his estate.

468. KM 24-11-7-1, a 1724 record shows the wife of Pierre Pillet as Magdelaine "Boisron." A Madeleine "Boiron" (and a Marie-Anne Boiron) arrived in Louisiana in 1719 on the *Mutine*, sent by order of the king. Conrad, *First Families*, 1: 22. SAPR, image 90, parents named in marriage record for Antoine Pillet and Marie-Louise Graveline, 1758.

469. Baptism, KPR, image 17; burial image 18. He was buried near the church, a phrase repeated in the burial of young Genevieve Roi (Census, no. 84).

470. KPR, image 19.

471. "Extrait des registres."

472. KM (58-2-15-1), registration of marriage contract. Marie-Louise Beaudreau Graveline was the daughter of Gabriel Beaudreau and Catherine Forestier, see introductory paragraphs. Marie-Louise was baptized at Fort Pontchartrain (Detroit) in 1708.

473. KM 43-1-20-2, note of marriage contract. Sacramental marriage KPR, image 7 of 118, January 30, 1743, gives the groom's name as Paul.

474. KPR, image 17 of 118.

475. KPR, image 11 of 118.

476. KM 47-1-17-1, marriage contract. KPR, image 11 of 118, sacramental marriage January 23, 1747.

477. KPR, image 36, burial of Angélique Pillet dit Lasonde, wife of Gabriel Aubuchon, age forty-three, died suddenly.

478. Belting, *Kaskaskia Under the French Regime*, 97. KPR, image 23 of 118, September 2, 1755.

479. KM 68-5-28-1, marriage of Marie-Louise's daughter mentions an uncle Louis Pillet dit Lasonde.

480. KM 67-9-2-1, marriage contract.

481. SAPR, image 210, marriage in 1778.

482. KPR, image 29.

483. KPR, image 27 of 118, 1759 marriage of Jean-Baptiste Olivier and Dorothée Pillet, no parents named. SGA, Estates #191 and 199-½, 1768, show the intertwined families after Olivier's death.

484. KM 25-11-5-1. Also SGA, Estates #224.

485. KPR, image 6, early appearance of Bourbonnois. KM 24-1-18-1, first notarial record for Bourbonnois, the lease of farm for three years to Toussaint Loisel, who became his son-in-law the next month. Baptismal record at http://www.ancestry.com Québec, Canada, Vital and Church Records (Drouin Collection), 1621–1968, M, Montréal, Basilique Notre-Dame, copie textuelle, 1669-1680, 1673, image 35 of 424, son of François and Barbe Beauvais. Jetté, 180, travel contract to the west, June 7 and 14, 1694, image online at http://www.familysearch.org, Catalog, Author, Adhémar, Antoine, 1668–1714, film#008328752, image 1638, contract to Michilimackinac or Sault Ste. Marie.

486. Higginbotham, *Old Mobile*, 186 and 222, Deshayes arrived from France in 1704 on the *Pélican*, and she and Brunet were married in Mobile. De Ville, see below, noted that she signed the marriage register when daughter Marie married Cardinal. In 1751 the elderly couple made an old-age care agreement with son-in-law Pierre Aubuchon, KM 51-11-18-2.

487. Noted as born at 4 p.m., *Sacramental Records of the Roman Catholic Church of the Archdiocese of Mobile, Vol. 1, sec. 1, 1704–1739* (Mobile, AL: Archdiocese of Mobile, 2002), 10. In 1721 she signed her name in the baptismal register as the godmother of Thérèse La Violette, KPR, image 15.

488. SGA, Estates #4 daughter Élisabeth Delaunay, Estates #79, André Deguire.

489. KM 23-1-16-1, marriage contract. See Census, no. 75.

490. KM 29-6-11-1, marriage contract. Settlement of estate, SGA, Estates, # 80, 1757.

491. KPR, image 6; Cécile and Marie (below) were baptized together.

492. SAPR, image 13, interment of Cécile Bourbonnois, wife of Antoine Heneaux.

493. KM 24-2-8-1, note of marriage contract, see Census, no. 14.

494. KM 39-3-11-1, marriage contract.

495. KM 23-9-12-1, Cardinal wrote an interesting will prior to a trip to New Orleans, leaving his house to the church and livestock to his godchildren.

496. Marriages in De Ville, *New Orleans*, 4, 19. Her death date in estate papers, SGA, Estates #8. Members of the Aubuchon families were among the first to settle in Ste. Genevieve.

497. KM 46-10-8-1.

498. KM 24-10-21-1 indicates origin in Canada. KM 26-2-5-1, inventory of the late Antoine Bosseron dit Léonard.

499. Names from the inventory of Bosseron, and KPR, image 10.

500. Kerami is the name that appears most often in later documents. KM 26-2-5-1 names all four children.

501. KM 28-6-7-2, marriage contract. Sacramental marriage the same day, KPR, image 25.

502. KM 47-10-31-3, inventory of the estate of the late Suzanne Kerami. An expansive discussion of her apparel appears in Sophie White, *Wild Frenchmen and Frenchified Indians* (Philadelphia: University of Pennsylvania Press, 2012).

503. KPR, image 6.

504. KPR, image 24, marriage May 20, 1726. KM 26-6-29-1, Texier Lavigne took over guardianship of Pierre Milleret, after he married Marianne Milleret. She died in 1766, KPR, image 30.

505. KPR, image 7.

506. KPR, image 7.

507. KPR, image 10.

508. "Extrait des registres."

509. Unnamed female Black slave interred July 12, 1726 in Kaskaskia, F-B 2:202.

510. KM 25-2-6-1, there was a François Mercier at Fort de Chartres—sale and transfer by Simon dit La Pointe to François Mercier of all his rights and pretentions to the estates of his parents in Canada for 1,000 livres. KM 25-2-7-1, power of attorney by François Mercier to La Pointe. KM 23-11-8-4, a note in the Bourdon estate by Mercier the younger. No wife and child for this François were found, so Jean-Baptiste was selected.

511. KM 40-3-7-1, election of new guardian to replace the deceased guardian Mercier.

512. Marriage record at http://www.ancestry.com Québec, Canada, Vital and Church Records (Drouin Collection), 1621–1968, Sainte, Ste-Anne-de-Beaupré, 1668–1808, image 187 of 877. Jean-Baptiste Mercier, son of Jean Mercier and Barbe Monmaigny (Census, no. 3), and Marie Baret, daughter of Pierre Baret and Marie-Madeleine Belanger. Witnesses included Julien Mercier and Dorothée Mercier (Census, no. 66), brother and sister of the groom. In October 1722 a young daughter, age 11 months and 5 days, of Mercier and Baret, was buried in Kaskaskia, KPR, image 19. Jean-Baptiste came to Kaskaskia first, and his mother and sister followed.

513. KM 42-2-26-1, by this date they were spouses. KM 44-11-13-1, estate division of Jean-Baptiste Mercier, named heirs Jean-Baptiste, Magdelaine, Jacques, Étienne, Marie, and Marie-Jeanne.

514. KPR, image 73, died at St. Philippe.

515. KPR, image 9.

516. KPR, image 19.

517. "Extrait des registres." The first Jean-Baptiste must not have survived. Baptism of a daughter at St. Philippe in 1764, *VC*, 325.

518. *VC*, 18. Godfather was Leonard Billeron, godmother Élisabeth Brunet.

519. KM 44-5-29-1, marriage contract. Mentions her parents and two brothers and aunt Agnès La Croix, wife of Jean-Baptiste Chauvin, see Census, no. 3 above.

520. KM 45-8-14-1, marriage contract.

521. *VC*, 323, baptism of daughter of Bellecour at St. Philippe.

522. Mentioned in the estate division, KM 44-11-13-1, and a land adjudication, KM 59-1-28-3.

523. Mentioned in the estate division, KM 44-11-13-1.

524. *VC*, 322, baptism of son Pierre-Charles in 1762, Cadron was militia captain at St. Philippe. SAPR, image 203, marriage of daughter of Marie-Jeanne Mercier and Charles Cadron, 1774.

525. This is fairly certainly Jean Olivier and his wife. The fact that there are no children in the census is puzzling.

526. A somewhat illegible note on a random page of the KPR, image 8, may be a record of Olivier's burial in 1757.

527. KM 23-9-16-1, interrogation of witnesses regarding La Boissière's estate.

528. KPR, image 7.

529. The names of the mother(s) as deciphered in the sacramental register. Belting, *Kaskaskia Under the French Regime*, 58, mentions the marriage of Marie and Guevremont. KM 44-10-22-1, inventory of the late Guevremont; Jean Olivier is Étienne Jr.'s maternal grandfather.

530. KPR, image 7.

531. KPR, image 11.

532. KPR, image 27 of 118, 1759, marriage of Jean-Baptiste Olivier and Dorothée Pillet. She died at age 25, KPR, image 29.

533. KPR, image 16.

534. KM 48-5-12-1. In 1749, Olivier and Marthe made an agreement for old-age care with daughter and son-in-law Boyer, KM 49-4-21-1.

535. F-B transcribed this name "Clivet." No such surname is found among the records.

536. KM 48-2-9-1 mentioned a 1722 land grant. In 1731 Glinel made an agreement with the Jesuit priests to do general work, especially to farm their land, KM 31-2-1-1. The contract included a monthly payment from the stores and, on successful completion of the contract, a *pièce d'Inde* slave.

537. Baptism at http://www.ancestry.com Québec, Canada, Vital and Church Records, Q, Québec, Notre-Dame, 1690–1695, image 252 of 449, transcript, parents Jacques and Marie Pivin. Jetté, 505, KM 54-11-5-1 note of inventory of Glinel and his wife's estate, and division among their heirs.

538. Note of marriage contract KM 21-6-27-1. Spelling from KPR, image 7, baptism of Genevieve Roi, October 2, 1719.

539. Inventory KM 21-6-29-1 names the two daughters she had with Roi. A slave is mentioned but not named. This Roi was distinct from Pierre du Roy dit Deslauriers, Census, no. 71. Pierre Roi was interred June 1, 1721, KPR, image 17.

540. KM 54-11-5-1, inventory and division among heirs.

541. KPR, image 7.

542. KPR, image 7.

543. KPR, image 18. She was buried near the church.

544. "Extrait des registres."

545. KPR, image 21. The name was possibly Thérèse.

546. 1779 marriage contract, SGA, #50 names his parents. In Ste. Genevieve records, the name is often written "Delinel."

547. KM 24-9-10-1, signed by both Pottiers, the younger and the older.

548. Baptism at http://www.ancestry.com, Québec, Vital and Church Records (Drouin Collection), 1621–1968, L, Lachine, Sts-Anges-Gardiens, image 50 of 362, his parents were Jean-Baptiste, a notaire, and Marie-Etienne Beauvais. Also, Jetté, 937.

549. KM 28-11-11-1, estate division.

550. "Palucouasoua, Marie" is the name that appears in Jetté's compendium, (937), no source given. Marie Apechic8rata's name does not appear in records after the death of her husband, who alleged (before 1728) that the child she would bear was not his. The Superior Council in New Orleans rejected Guillaume Pottier's will, which attempted to disinherit the as yet unborn child, and decreed that the child must be treated as legitimate. See text. Marie's death date is uncertain, but KM 41-2-25-2 refers to the deceased parents (plural) of Charles Pottier.

551. KM 48-3-5-1, a half-sister, Marie-Louise Quesnel, was identified as an heir to the estate of Guillaume Pottier, the brother of Charles. Marie-Louise became the second wife of Estienne Govreau, who later moved to Ste. Genevieve. KM 51-1-7-1, SGA, Estates, #110. They had a son, Remond Quesnel.

552. KPR, image 11, baptism of Marie-Marguerite. The godmother was Marguerite 8assecam 8c8e.

553. KM 28-11-11-1, Guillaume, Charles, and the widow were Guillaume Pottier's heirs in the estate division.

554. KPR, image 14. Godfather Nicolas-Michel Chassin, clerk of the Company of the West (*d'Occident*) godmother Marguerite 8assecam8c8e. Noted as eighteen years old in 1739, KM 39-4-16-1.

555. KM 48-3-5-1, inventory of effects of Guillaume Pottier.

556. "Extrait des registres." Noted in the margin of the baptism record as deceased.

557. KM 41-2-25-2, Charles Pottier was fourteen or fifteen years old in February 1741.

558. KM 28-11-11-1, estate division; KM 41-3-19-1, lease of land and slave Auipie (Awiipie). Auipie had a daughter, Marianne, who figures in Carl J. Ekberg, *Stealing Indian Women: Native Slavery in the Illinois Country* (Urbana: University of Illinois Press, 2007), 97ff.

559. KM 25-12-1-1, La Renaudière was a witness at the marriage of Françoise Rabut and Pierre Melet (Census, no. 87) in May 1724, KPR, image 22. Renaudière left France with his wife on the *Comte de Toulouse* in 1718, Conrad, *First Families*, 1: 22. See Liberge, Census no. 99 below, with whom Pivert had an illegitimate child. The child, christened Antoine, was buried at the age of eight weeks on January 4, 1726, noted as a "natural" child rather than illegitimate. KPR,

image 21. The name of the father was omitted in the sacramental entry but recorded in notarial records.

560. KPR, image 16.

561. "Extrait des registres."

562. The census seems to read "Melet." There are several men with similar names, but this couple fits the profile best.

563. KM 26-5-28-1, estate inventory. He was killed at *trois cheneaux audessous des Tonicas*, south of Fort Natchez. A detailed account of Rabut is presented by Moreau-DesHarnais "The Other Bienvenu Family of Kaskaskia in present-day Illinois: Philippe Bienvenu and Françoise Allaire Part 5A Françoise Rabut, wife of (1) Pierre Durand; (2) Pierre Desené dit Melet" *Michigan's Habitant Heritage* 36, no. 3 (July 2015): 143–49.

564. KM 24-4-22-1, marriage contract. Sacramental marriage May 8?, 1724, KPR, image 22.

565. One of the *Baleine* women, age twenty-five on arrival. Moreau-DesHarnais, "Baleine Women," 3, 40.

566. De Ville, *New Orleans French*, 40. Pierre Durand, resident of Illinois, born Poitou, France.

567. KM 26-5-29-1, marriage contract. Françoise's birthplace given as the parish of St. Hypolite, diocese of Paris. The marriage contract with Bienvenu mentions a daughter, Françoise Melet. Sacramental marriage record, KPR, image 24. Marie-Claire Catoire was a witness at their marriage.

568. *VC*, 10, perhaps the unnamed daughter baptized January 1726. Marriage record for Françoise Mellet, daughter of Mellet and Rabut, KPR, image 7 of 118. A child named Jean-Baptiste by Pierre Durand, Rabut's first husband, was born November 3, 1723, and was interred November 12. "Extrait des registres."

569. Sometimes Quadrain or Quadrin in the KM.

570. Baptism at http://www.ancestry.com Québec, Canada, Vital and Church Records (Drouin Collection), 1621–1968, I, Ile d'Orléans, Ste. Famille, 1687–1695, image 11 of 49, son of Nicolas and Françoise Delaunay.

571. KPR, image 21, burial of Nicolas Cadrin.

572. KM 24-1-8-1, note of the marriage contract. English translation of marriage contract of Becquet and Marie "Jeanne" Fafar, widow of Nicolas Quadrain, in *VC*, 920-23. The bride's father donated his property rights to Becquet in case the daughter died first and without issue from the marriage.

573. Baptismal record, KPR, image 7. Her mother's name reads Accica Pat8kic8e. Fafard must not have been Cadrin's first wife, for there is a burial in 1724 of a 6-year-old son of Cadrin, "Extrait des registres." The extract record of the marriage on January 11, 1724, of Marianne and Michel-François-Marie Quadrin, son of Nicolas and Françoise Delaunay of Canada, gives Marianne's mother's name as Thérèse Axiga.

574. KPR, image 26, marriage May 4 of Becquet and Marie Fafart de "Bojoly."

575. KM 41-3-3-2, petition against Du Couadie regarding the loss of a slave referred to him as the third husband of Marianne Fafard.

576. F-B 2:206, left this name uninterpreted. There is no "Beaujoly" in the KM sacramental or notarial records. Given that the census contains associations in sequential entries, and that the spelling "Bojoly" appeared in the sacramental record for Marianne's marriage to Becquet, the father of Cadrin's wife is a reasonable interpretation here.

577. Jetté, 410, Pierre Fafard dit Boisjoly, son of François & Marie Richard, birth date estimated from 1681 census. Boisjoly owned land next to a grant made by Boisbriant and des Ursins to Jacques Lalande in 1722, KM 22-5-10-4 and wrote a will, KM 22-8-27-1. *VC*, 813, (KM 23-6-2-1) in 1723 he brought suit against his Native wife, Marguerite Anskekae, for adultery, and she is not enumerated here. Named as captain of a militia company in KM 23-9-16-1. KM 38-5-2-1, Boisjoly divided the marital estate with his (unnamed) wife, giving to his daughter Marianne, a *pièce d'Inde* slave named Sansregret and a Native slave woman named Fanchon. Possibly they are enumerated with Cadrin above.

578. See also nos. 28 and 67.

579. KM 22-1-30-1, note of debt of Lalande the younger to Bellegarde.

580. Baptism of Jean-Baptiste Guillemot at http://www.ancestry.com Québec, Canada, Vital and Church Records (Drouin Collection), 1621–1968, M, Montréal, Basilique Notre-Dame, image 202 of 229, son of François and Madeleine du Pont.

581. KM 21-12-11-1, note of marriage contract of Jean-Baptiste Lalande and Catherine "8abana Ki8oi."

582. For the meaning of her name, see note 10 above.

583. KPR, image 18, noted his death at Natchez in June 1721.

584. KPR, image 7, a daughter Symphorosa was baptized on February 11, 1717.

585. A translation of the marriage contract appeared in the *New York Times* in 1876. St. Ange died at the hands of Chickasaw warriors in 1736. Ekberg and Person, *St. Louis Rising*, 28–31.

586. KM 41-11-18-1, note of marriage contract.

587. KPR, image 7. Godfather Jean Olivier, godmother Magdelaine Quesnel.

588. KM 44-1-29-1, Marie-Rose attempted unsuccessfully to claim three-quarters of the estate of her deceased brother Paul. Judge Louis Auguste de La Loëre Flaucour based his denial on Article 340 of the Coutume, and divided the estate equally between Rose-Marie and Marc-Antoine Lalande, her half-brother. Paul's death first noted in KM 41-8-16-1.

589. KM 23-10-7-1, born at Ouiatenon. "Extrait des registres." born October 7, baptized October 20, 1723.

590. *VC*, 9-10, and SAPR, image 7. A Jean-Baptiste Lalande, age two, was buried April 17, 1724, "Extrait des registres." Charlotte Marchand signed the marriage record of her daughter Charlotte to Pierre Aubuchon (son of Pierre Aubuchon and Marie Brunet, Census, no.80) in 1763 in Ste. Geneviève, http://www.familysearch.org, Ste. Geneviève Church Records, 1759–1993, roll#008119539, image 541.

591. Marriage at http://www.ancestry.com Québec, Canada, Vital and Church Records (Drouin Collection), 1621–1968, M, Montréal, Basilique Notre-Dame, 1734–1740, image 13 of 204. His age was thirty-eight; hers was twenty-four.

592. KPR, image 34. Burial of Charlotte Marchand, widow of Lalande.

593. KPR, image 8. He was eight days old.

594. KM 49-2-1-1, marriage contract. Sacramental marriage, KPR, image 14 of 118. She re-married Pierre Aubuchon. See note above.

595. Belting, *Kaskaskia Under the French Regime*, 113.

596. Belting, *Kaskaskia Under the French Regime*, 113.

597. KM 21-9-13-1. Estate of Paul Texier, son of Louis Tessier, KM 44-1-29-1.

598. An unnamed slave of Franchomme was interred in September 1727, KPR, image 21.

599. No mention of a wife found in documents in Kaskaskia or in New Orleans. A Native slave of La Rigueur was interred in August 1727. The grammar indicates the slave was male, KPR, image 21.

600. KM 22-9-23-1, purchaser in an auction; land grant in May 1722 mentioned in KM 39-12-1-1.

601. A series of succession papers in New Orleans, for example, LSM 1740-01-22-01, stated that he died on his way to New Orleans.

602. KM 39-12-11-1, will. KM 48-5-12-1, marriage of Dorothée Olivier, mentioned the bequest also. He bequeathed a Fox slave woman named Catherine to the Ursuline nuns in New Orleans, and a Black male slave named Jupiter to the Jesuits. LSM 1740-01-22-04.

603. KM 41-11-22-2.

604. This is a reasonable interpretation of the calligraphy of the census. F-B 2:206, transcribed this as "Biennant" but no such name appears in records. Antoine Bienvenu would have been called "the younger" in relation to his father Philippe Bienvenu. Father and son had been hired by Pierre Melique (Census, no. 64) in France to come to Louisiana. Gail Moreau-DesHarnais, "The Other Bienvenu Family of Kaskaskia in present-day Illinois: Philippe Bienvenu and Françoise Allaire Part 2 : Lorient, Morbihan, and La Rochelle, Charente-Maritime, France," *Michigan's Habitant Heritage* 35, no.2, (April 2014): 87. Philippe Bienvenu, widower and joiner, married Marie Forret, widow of Pierre Verrier June 6, 1723, "Extrait des registres." Jeanne, daughter of Philippe and his first wife Françoise Allaire, married Charles Gossiaux in September the same year.

605. Gail Moreau-DesHarnais, "The Other Bienvenu Family of Kaskaskia in present-day Illinois: Philippe Bienvenu and Françoise Allaire, Part 1: Ploemeur and Lorient, Morbihan, France." *Michigan's Habitant Heritage* 35, no.1 (January 2014): 44. It includes an image of Bienvenu's original baptismal record.

606. Antoine Bienvenu became one of the wealthiest and most important residents of Kaskaskia in the mid-eighteenth century. After relocating to New Orleans, Bienvenu still had ties to the Illinois country, especially through his brother-in-law, Valentin Devin. Sharon Person, "St. Louis Trade and Traders in Indian Country 1766–-1774: Valentin Devin and Jean-Baptiste Papillon" *Nebraska History* 99, no.4 (Winter 2018): 252–65. See also LSM 1775-09-18-01, claim of Marie Marthe Devins, widow of Antoine Bienvenu.

607. Marriage at Kaskaskia June 3, 1726, KPR, image 24.

608. Joseph Adam has a more frequent presence in records; Estienne appears in KM 24-12-14-1. Joseph was a godfather to a slave in March 1726, *VC*, 17. Jetté, 2, a Joseph Adam was born in Beaumont in 1699 and signed a contract in 1720 to go to the west, image at http://www .familysearch.org, Catalog, Author, David, Jacques, 1719–1726, film#008272724, image 1231. He was the son of Jean Adame and Marie Mezeray.

609. This Adam witnessed two records related to Melique's lease to Gardon in January 1725, KM 25-1-12-1 and 25-1-13-1, meaning he cannot be ruled out for this census. Jetté, 1054, Solingue married at Nouvelle Holland. His wife Marie Deslique died at Kaskaskia November 10, 1725, at the age of thirty-nine. KPR, image 21 of 82.

610. See Part I on Noyon. KM 26-10-30-1, François's brother Ignace assumed care for the livestock belonging to François, who was either in Canada fulfilling Bourdon's requests, or in Cannes Brulées, where he relocated.

611. Baptism at http://www.ancestry.com Québec, Canada, Vital and Church Records (Drouin Collection), 1621–1968, B, Boucherville, 1669–1695, image 15 of 99, son of Jean Noyon and Marie Chauvin. Jacque Bourdon's mother was his godmother. LSM 1747-11-13-01 will of François Noyon. Noyon was a business partner with Jean Huet dit Dulude, see below.

612. The handwriting on this name is unclear, appearing to read Gautier, but the Gautier family seems not to be in records after the children's baptisms. Charles *Gossiaux*, sometimes, but rarely, is spelled Gaussiau.

613. Contract to travel from Montreal to the Ottawas, August 21, 1692, image at http://www .familysearch.org, Catalog, Author, Adhémar, Antoine, 1668–1714, film #008274298, images 2348–49.

614. Spelling of her name is inconsistent in the KPR, image 6.

615. KPR, image 6.

616. KPR, image 6.

617. KPR, image 6.

618. Extract of marriage record in "Extrait des registres." Their birthplaces above are as they appear in the extract, read the same by Belting, *Kaskaskia Under the French Regime*, 80. The image of Jeanne's baptism at Lorient on November 11, 1706, is in Gail Moreau-DesHarnais, "The Other Bienvenu Family of Kaskaskia in present-day Illinois: Philippe Bienvenu (and Françoise Allaire) Part 1: Ploemeur and Lorient, Morbihan, France." *Michigan's Habitant Heritage* 35, no.1 (January 2014): 44. Two children of the couple died in 1724, and the birthdates of later children could not be found. The guardianship documents after Jeanne's death in 1729 mention children, and Belting, *Kaskaskia Under the French Regime*, 116, identified a son Jacques in addition to daughter Jeanne, see KM 39-12-14-1. Perhaps at the crucial time of information gathering for this census, the couple had no living children. After Jeanne died, Gossiau married the widow Villeneuve, Census, no.110.

619. Jetté, 120, birth year calculated from 1681 census. Purchased a deerskin in an auction September 1722, KM 22-9-23-1. His full name is in KM 25-8-16-1, inventory of estate of Marie 8canic8e Rouensa.

620. SGA, Estates # 36, for death date. Her husband "abandoned" her small estate to her heirs.

621. KM 27-2-16-1, marriage contract. The bride was sixteen years old, and the groom forty. KPR, image 25, sacramental marriage. In both documents Thérèse is identified only as "of this parish," parents are not named.

622. KM 40-1-30-3, note of marriage contract of LaCroix and Boisseau.

623. A Guillaume Liberge is identified in Québec sacramental records, baptism at http://www.ancestry.com Québec, Canada, Vital and Church Records (Drouin Collection), 1621–1968, Q, Québec, Notre-Dame 1691–1703, baptized May 1, 1700, image 213 of 287, son of Jacques and Angélique Simon. KM 25-12-1-1. Identified as the father of the illegitimate child of Mme. Renaudière. Death of Guillaume Liberge, voyageur in the Illinois, LSM 1740-06-07-03.

624. A Brosse/St. Cernay appears in several documents in New Orleans in 1723, giving his age as about thirty-six, LSM 1723-07-15-01. Brosse/St. Cernay served as witness at the marriage of Villeneuve (Census, no.110). *VC* 17-18, Raimond Brosse was godfather in April 1726 to a daughter of Antoine Sorel and Lucie Rollet (Census, no. 53).

625. A La Bonté was a worker in a contract to dig trenches and place posts for Fort de Chartres, KM 25-3-12-2.

626. KPR, image 19. He was an unmarried man, age fifty.

627. KM 24-5-6-1, Cailloux owed the estate of Pierre Etevenard five *plats cotes*; KM 24-6-18-1, he bought a house at Kaskaskia. KM 1723-25-4, agreement with Pottier the younger. KM 1723-25-8, several men agree to build a well; KM 26-5-4-2, Cailloux's task was to quarry the stone. No wife or children identified in records. In 1750, a François Caillou appears as a voyageur, but his documents do not help identify him as a son of Pierre, KM 50-8-24-1.

628. This entry may be a repetition of the other Pottiers in the census, but there was this possibility.

629. KPR, image 23. Pottier's parents' names are in the sacramental record, Étienne and Louise Sulret. KM 24-5-20-3, marriage contract contains names of the children. Marc Clement was a sergeant in the brigade of miners who came with Renaudière from France in 1718. Conrad, *First Families* 1:22. We can assume Clement's wife and daughter accompanied him, though unnamed on the manifest "four wives of miners three children of miners." Agnès Anard and Marc Clement married October 1710 in Condé sur l'Escaut, Département du Nord, on the present-day border of France and Belgium, http://www.ancestry.com. Oise, France, Marriages 1600–1907.

630. KM 29-7-2-1, marriage contract.

631. KM 37-1-15-5, marriage to La Brière. KM 47-12-12-1, La Brière was married to a new wife, the daughter of Pierre Hullin.

632. The other men known as St. Jean, one Arteau and Jean Poture, could not be identified by name earlier than 1749 (Arteau) and 1737 (Poture). We are likely looking at the same St. Jean that was enumerated above, Census, no. 25. KM 31-10-30-1 and KM 35-8-20-1, St. Jean and his wife Jeanne Bailly had no children of their own.

633. Yves Pinet is identified as an *armurier* (gunsmith) in a 1706 contract to travel to Détroit and work there for three years, Moreau-DesHarnais and Wolford Sheppard, *Le Détroit*, 2:315. A name chosen by others working with this census was St. Roch Pinguenet/Pinguenet dit St. Roch, which appears in records appropriately dated, but he was never identified as a gunsmith. Yves Pinet was present as early as 1722, and his name appears in several Bourdon-related documents (as well as Marie 8canic8e Rouensa's will). Yves Pinet, *armurier*, and his brother appear on a 1727 census of New Orleans, Maduell, Jr., *Census Tables*, 92. Jetté, 922, Yves Pinet travelled from La Rochelle to New France in 1698, and was twenty-two years old in 1700. A Hubert *Finet* appears first in notarial records in August 1726, KM 26-8-18-1.

634. There are signatures of Lavigne beginning in 1723, KM 23-1-30-1. Jean-Baptiste Texier dit Lavigne is consistently distinguished from Louis Texier, who died in 1721, and whom Jetté considered to be the brother of Pierre Tessier, Census, no. 58. Jean-Baptiste Texier dit Lavigne married Marianne Milleret (daughter of Pierre Milleret and Suzanne Kerami) in 1726, KM 26-5-18-1 (see Census, no. 81).

635. KM 23-9-12-1, Dulude the younger. Baptism at http://www.ancestry.com Québec, Canada, Vital and Church Records (Drouin Collection), 1621–1968, B, Boucherville, 1669–1783, image 128 of 199, son of Joseph and Catherine Sicot. Also Jetté, 578. Marriage contract, KM 35-5-23-1, is torn where the groom's parents' names should appear. Dulude married Marie Ma8e8ensic8e, the widow of Du Long Pré, Census no. 68 above. Charles Huet dit Dulude was a farmer and middleman who supplied flour (*farine*) to his brother Jean, a *voyageur* who operated between the Illinois Country and New Orleans, Census no. 109.

636. Jean-Baptiste Poudret received a land grant in 1723, KM 23-9-27-1. He was a trader and became involved in the western Indian slave trade. See Carl J. Ekberg, *Stealing Indian Women*, 18–21. Jetté, 937, Vincent Poudret, born and baptized October 11, 1694, in Montreal, son of Antoine and Catherine Gendron, at http://www.ancestry.com Québec, Canada, Vital and Church Records, M, Montréal, Basilique Notre-Dame, 1681–1694, image 212 of 229. The name Vincent appears just once in the KM, in 1725(KM 25-3-27-1), and it is not a signature. A 1736 testimony in the Fafard-Turpin case by Father Mercier mentioned Poudret, fils (the son). No first name was given. Testimony online at LSM 1741-10-17-10. In 1721, Jean-Baptiste Poudret was a witness at the marriage of Dorothée Mercier and Nicolas Thuilliers Devegnois, LSM 1745-02-16-01.

637. KM 24-9-21-1 signed by Dulude the elder. LSM 1738-10-20-01, will of Jean Dulude, habitant at Cannes Brulées, mentioned his relatives in Canada and his brother Charles in Kaskaskia, to whom he sent merchandise in exchange for flour. Jean Dulude was a business partner with François Noyon. KM 30-6-13-1, Dulude acted for Noyon, selling his real estate in the Illinois Country. The two men made a donation of 3,000 livres (in flour) to Jeanette, the daughter of a female Fox slave owned, and freed, by Dulude, LSM 1744-12-26-02.

638. Baptism at http://www.ancestry.com Québec, Canada, Vital and Church Records (Drouin Collection), 1621–1968, B, Boucherville, 1669-1695, image 45 of 99. François de Noyon's sister Marguerite was his godmother.

639. LSM 1735-07-13-01, will of Jean Dulude. The slaves at Cannes Brulées, where Dulude had land adjoining the land of his partner, François Noyon, were Marie, a Fox woman, and

Black slaves La Chicane, Jassmin, Mory, and Soileau. Dulude wrote the will on the eve of his departure to the Illinois Country. Dulude did not die, and the only slaves mentioned in his final will in 1738 were Marie, a Fox woman, and Jeannette, her daughter.

640. De Ville, *New Orleans French*, 69, He was the son of Jean and Catherine Chapin, and she was the daughter of Pierre and Marie-Rose. DesHarnais, "Baleine Women," Sister Gertrude, who had made the voyage from France with the girls as their chaperone, was one of the witnesses of the marriage, as were Guillaume Pothier/Pottier, C.C. du Tisne, and Raimond Brosse. Conrad, *First Families*, 1: 80, Claude Marechal, sergeant, from Moulons in Bourbonnais, age thirty-nine, departed France on the *Profond* in June, 1720. Illinois Country records, KM 23-2-23-1 and KM 23-2-23-3, purchase of a house in Kaskaskia. Death estimate from the remarriage of his widow, see below.

641. Moreau-DesHarnais "Baleine Women," 28.

642. KM 29-9-14-3, note of marriage contract. He was the widower of Jeanne Bienvenu. KM 29-9-12-1, election of Gossiaux as guardian of the children with Bienvenu. Eventually Goneau and Gossiaux filed for a legal separation of property, KM 43-1-30-2.

643. Named in KM 40-7-11-1 as the son of Villeneuve and Marie-Roze Goneau.

ESSENTIAL ILLINOIS COUNTRY READING

Alvord, Clarence W. *The Illinois Country, 1673-1818*. The Centennial History of Illinois, vol. 1. Springfield: Illinois Centennial Commission, 1920. A classic, one hundred years old, remains a fundamental introduction to and overview of the Illinois Country.

Arnold, Morris S. *Unequal Laws unto a Savage Race: European Legal Traditions in Arkansas, 1686-1836*. Fayetteville: University of Arkansas Press, 1985. The first of Judge Arnold's foundational books on Arkansas Post, all presented in graceful prose.

Arnold, Morris S. *The Rumble of a Distant Drum: The Quapaws and Old World Newcomers, 1673-1804*. Fayetteville: University of Arkansas Press, 2000. Shunning stereotypes and clichés, this study lays bare the complexity of Indian-White relationships at Arkansas Post.

Baade, Hans W. "Marriage Contracts in French and Spanish Louisiana: A Study in 'Notarial' Jurisprudence." *Tulane Law Review* 53 (December 1978): 1-92. Seminal scholarship on an overwhelmingly important topic.

Belting, Natalia Maree. *Kaskaskia Under the French Regime*. Urbana: University of Illinois press, 1948. Reprint edition, Carbondale: Southern Illinois University Press, 2003. Remains the most readable, vibrant, and accessible introduction to the French Illinois Country.

Brown, Margaret Kimball. *Reconstructing an Eighteen-Century Village: Chartres in Illinois*. Belleville, IL: Village Publishers, 2020. The irreplaceable result of a half century of archaeological and historical research.

Edmunds, R. David and Peyser, Joseph L. *The Fox Wars: The Mesquakie Challenge to New France*. Norman: University of Oklahoma Press, 1993. The best volume on the bloody, interminable Fox-French conflict, largely from a Canadian perspective.

Ekberg, Carl J. *Colonial Ste. Genevieve: An Adventure on the Mississippi Frontier*. Gerald, MO: Patrice Press, 1985. A comprehensive overview of Ste. Genevieve from its origins (ca. 1750) as a satellite of Kaskaskia to the time of the Louisiana Purchase.

———. *French Roots in the Illinois Country: The Mississippi Frontier in Colonial Times*. Urbana: University of Illinois Press, 1998. An award-winning book, essential for understanding settlement patterns and agriculture in the region.

———. *Stealing Indian Women: Native Slavery in the Illinois Country*. Urbana: University of Illinois Press, 2007. Focusing on Native American women, analyzes how Indian slavery was intertwined with Illinois-Country society throughout the colonial era.

Ekberg, Carl J. and Person, Sharon K. *St. Louis Rising: The French Regime of Louis St. Ange de Bellerive*. Urbana: University of Illinois Press, 2015. A detailed examination of how St. Louis emerged during the 1760s as the last major French settlement to coalesce in the Illinois Country.

Havard, Gilles. *Histoire des coureurs de bois: Amérique du Nord 1600-1840*. Paris: Les Indes Savants, 2016. Sweeping and captivating, from the French master of French North America, regrettable that is not available in English.

———. "'Protection' and 'Unequal Alliance': The French Conception of Sovereignty over Indians in New France." In *French and Indians in the Heart of North America 1630-1815*, edited by Robert Englebert and Guillaume Teasdale, 113–37. East Lansing: Michigan State University Press, 2013. Raises fundamental issues about the complexity of French-Indian relations.

Jones, Linda Carol. *The Shattered Cross: French Catholic Missionaries on the Mississippi Frontier, 1698–1725*. Baton Rouge: Louisiana State University Press, 2020. Based on deep, dogged archival research, this study shines as honest and admirable scholarship, evincing sympathy for Native Americans and Catholic missionary priests alike.

Lawn, Katherine E., and Claudio R. Salvucci. *Women in New France: Extracts from The Jesuit Relations*. Bristol, PA: Evolution Publishing, 2005. A useful and compact volume, collecting Jesuit impressions of Native American women from the voluminous published *Jesuit Relations*.

Leavelle, Tracy Neal. *The Catholic Calumet: Colonial Conversions in French and Indian North America*. Philadelphia: University of Pennsylvania Press, 2012. A balanced and nuanced overview of Jesuit missionaries and their long-time relationships with Native Americans, including the Illinois.

Lee, Jacob E. *Masters of the Middle Waters: Indian Nations and Colonial Ambitions along the Mississippi*. Cambridge, MA: Harvard University Press, 2019. Focusing on the middle Mississippi River Valley, this study strives to place Native Americans on center stage, always.

MacDonald, David. *Lives of Fort de Chartres: Commandants, Soldiers, and Civilians, 1720–1770*. Carbondale: University of Southern Illinois University Press, 2016. Indispensable reference book on the many colorful personalities that enlivened Illinois Country society.

Masthay, Carl, ed. *Kaskaskia Illinois to French Dictionary*. Privately published. St. Louis, 2002. Intriguing and unique reference book, unexpected pleasures on every page.

McCafferty, Michael. "Jacques Largillier: French trader, Jesuit brother, and Jesuit scribe *par excellence*." *Journal of the Illinois State Historical Society*. Vol. 104, No. 3 (Fall, 2011), 188–98. Deftly explains how Jesuits during the early eighteenth century went about compiling an astonishing Illinois Indian-French dictionary.

———. "The Latest Miami-Illinois Dictionary and Its Author." *Papers of the Thirty-Sixth Algonquian Conference*. Winnipeg: University of Manitoba Press (2005): 1-16.

McDermott, John Francis, comp. *A Glossary of Mississippi Valley French, 1673–1850*. Washington University Studies, New Series, no. 12. St. Louis, MO: Washington University, 1941. A must to keep close at hand as a reference book.

Morrissey, Robert Michael. "The Power of the Ecotone: Bison, Slavery, and the Rise and Fall of the Grand Village of the Kaskaskia." *Journal of American History* 102 (December 2015): 667-692. Useful portrayal of the brutality of Kaskaskia Indian society at the end of the seventeenth century.

Palm, Mary Borgias. *The Jesuit Missions of the Illinois Country 1673–1763*. Cleveland: n.p., 1931. A foundational book based on extensive archival research, modest in its pretentions, fundamental in its results.

Person, Sharon K. "'The Forlorn Hope of France in the Heart of the Continent': Belle Famille and the Founding of St. Louis." *Missouri Historical Review* 114, No.1 (October 2019): 1–15. The crushing defeat of Illinois Country forces, including Illinois Indians, at Belle Famille (outside of Fort Niagara), provokes a migration of French villagers to the west bank of the Mississippi.

Peterson, Charles E. "Early Ste. Genevieve and Its Architecture." *Missouri Historical Review* 35 (1941): 207-32. Ground-breaking study by the early discoverer of French Illinois Country architecture.

Thurman, Melburn D. *Building a House in 18th Century Ste. Genevieve*. Ste. Genevieve, MO: Pendragon's Press, 1984. A detailed, hands-on study and the best book ever done on the subject.

Walczynski, Mark. *Inquietus: La Salle in the Illinois Country*. Plano, TX: Center for French Colonial Studies, William L. Potter Publication Series, no.12, 2019. An accessible, engaging account of LaSalle and his legacy in the Illinois River Valley.

White, Sophie. *Wild Frenchmen and Frenchified Indians: Material Culture and Race in Colonial Louisiana*. Philadelphia: University of Pennsylvania Press, 2012. A probing and useful (though problematic) attempt to uncover racism in the French Illinois Country.

INDEX

Page numbers in italics refer to illustrations

Carl J. Ekberg is emeritus professor of history at Illinois State University. He has published many books and articles, including *French Roots in the Illinois Country* and *Stealing Indian Women: Native Slavery in the Illinois Country*.

Sharon K. Person, emerita professor of English at St. Louis Community College, Missouri, is the author of *Standing Up for Indians: Baptism Registers as an Untapped Source for Multicultural Relations in St. Louis, 1766–1821*. Together, they are the authors of *St. Louis Rising: The French Regime of Louis St. Ange de Bellerive*.

A Shawnee Book

Also available in this series . . .

The Next New Madrid Earthquake: A Survival Guide for the Midwest
WILLIAM ATKINSON

Forgetting and the Forgotten: A Thousand Years of Contested Histories in the Heartland
MICHAEL C. BATINSKI

Reckoning at Eagle Creek: The Secret Legacy of Coal in the Heartland
JEFF BIGGERS

History as They Lived It: A Social History of Prairie du Rocher, Illinois
MARGARET KIMBALL BROWN

Foothold on a Hillside: Memories of a Southern Illinoisan
CHARLESS CARAWAY

Growing Up in a Land Called Egypt: A Southern Illinois Family Biography
CLEO CARAWAY

Colonial Ste. Genevieve: An Adventure on the Mississippi Frontier
CARL J. EKBERG

A Nickel's Worth of Skim Milk: A Boy's View of the Great Depression
ROBERT J. HASTINGS

A Penny's Worth of Minced Ham: Another Look at the Great Depression
ROBERT J. HASTINGS

Southern Illinois Coal: A Portfolio
C. WILLIAM HORRELL

Always of Home: A Southern Illinois Childhood
EDGAR ALLEN IMHOFF

*Lives of Fort de Chartres: Commandants, Soldiers, and Civilians in French Illinois,
1720–1770*
DAVID MACDONALD

Kaskaskia: The Lost Capital of Illinois
DAVID MACDONALD AND RAINE WATERS

20 Day Trips in and around the Shawnee National Forest
LARRY P. AND DONNA J. MAHAN

Land of Big Rivers: French and Indian Illinois, 1699–1778
M. J. MORGAN

America's Deadliest Twister: The Tri-State Tornado of 1925
GEOFF PARTLOW

Escape Betwixt Two Suns: A True Tale of the Underground Railroad in Illinois
CAROL PIRTLE

Fishing Southern Illinois
ART REID

All Anybody Ever Wanted of Me Was to Work: The Memoirs of Edith Bradley Rendleman
EDITH BRADLEY RENDLEMAN
EDITED BY JANE ADAMS

The Civilian Conservation Corps in Southern Illinois, 1933–1942
KAY RIPPELMEYER

*Giant City State Park and the Civilian Conservation Corps: A History in Words and
Pictures*
KAY RIPPELMEYER

Fluorspar Mining: Photos from Illinois and Kentucky, 1905–1995
HERBERT K. RUSSELL

A Southern Illinois Album: Farm Security Administration Photographs, 1936–1943
HERBERT K. RUSSELL

The State of Southern Illinois: An Illustrated History
HERBERT K. RUSSELL

Snake Road: A Field Guide to the Snakes of LaRue–Pine Hills
JOSHUA J. VOSSLER